Praise for Diana Nyad's

Find a Way

"What makes Nyad's story so remarkable, beyond the harrowing trials she faced at sea—unpredictable currents and weather, deadly sea animals—is the strength of a resolve that would not admit defeat and knew no boundaries. 'Whatever your Other Shore is,' she writes, 'whatever you must do . . . you will find a way.' Inspiring reading for anyone who has ever dared to dream the impossible."
—*Kirkus Reviews*

"Fascinating. . . . Nyad's writing is clear and direct, with her grit and determination finally finding a way." —*The Seattle Times*

"Astonishing. . . . Her message to readers is that anyone who has a dream and perseveres can also be successful."
—*Houston Chronicle*

"Exciting. . . . A life-affirming story."
—*Milwaukee Journal Sentinel*

"Nyad fiercely owns this story. . . . [She] also envelops those friends, family, and colleagues who helped her along the way, and any readers who would take heart from it."
—*Booklist* (starred review)

"A fascinating glimpse into her life as a talented and fiercely determined athlete. . . . [A] moving account." —*Library Journal*

DIANA NYAD

Find a Way

For her maverick open-water performance of the 1970s, Diana Nyad was known as the world's greatest long-distance swimmer. For the next thirty years, Nyad was a prominent sports broadcaster and journalist, filing compelling stories for National Public Radio, ABC's *Wide World of Sports*, and others. She is a national fitness icon, has written three other books, is a talented linguist, and is one of today's most powerful and engaging public speakers.

www.diananyad.com

ALSO BY DIANA NYAD

Boss of Me: The Keyshawn Johnson Story

Diana Nyad's Basic Training for Women

Other Shores

FIND A WAY

The Inspiring Story of One Woman's
Pursuit of a Lifelong Dream

DIANA NYAD

VINTAGE BOOKS

A DIVISION OF PENGUIN RANDOM HOUSE LLC

NEW YORK

FIRST VINTAGE BOOKS EDITION, JUNE 2016

Copyright © 2015 by Diana Nyad

All rights reserved. Published in the United States by Vintage Books, a division of
Penguin Random House LLC, New York, and distributed in Canada by Random House of Canada,
a division of Penguin Random House Canada Limited, Toronto. Originally published in hardcover in
the United States by Alfred A. Knopf, a division of Penguin Random House LLC, New York, in 2015.

Vintage and colophon are registered trademarks of Penguin Random House LLC.

The Library of Congress has cataloged the Knopf edition as follows:
Nyad, Diana.
Find a way / Diana Nyad.
pages cm
1. Nyad, Diana.   2. Swimmers—United States—Biography.   I. Title.
GV838.N9A3 2015   797.2'1092—DC23   [B]   201500932

Vintage Books Trade Paperback ISBN: 978-0-8041-7291-2
eBook ISBN: 978-0-385-35362-5

Book design by Maggie Hinders

www.vintagebooks.com

Printed in the United States of America
10   9   8   7   6   5   4   3   2   1

It's been said that each of us would thrill
to the good fortune of having one profound, loyal,
unconditional friendship in our lifetime.
Count me doubly lucky; I have two such
steadfast, lifelong friends.
Candace and Bonnie, every moment spent with each
of you is a treasure—then, now, forever.

Tell me, what is it you plan to do
with your one wild and precious life?

MARY OLIVER

"The Summer Day"

Contents

Find a Way

ONE

Crisis

The chanting begins in a gentle chorus and grows to an adrenaline-fueled frenzy. Our voices emanate from the dock at Marina Hemingway in a resounding boom, sweeping over the cobblestoned streets of Old Havana, wafting across the sea toward faraway U.S. shores.

The Xtreme Dream Team is thirty-five strong. We are huddled. Closest to me in the center is Bonnie. And Candace. And Mark. And John. They are my lifeline.

I yell. The cadence falls in:

"Where we swimming FROM?"

They answer:

"CUBA!!"

I pump it up a notch:

"Where we swimming TO?"

They escalate:

"FLORIDA!!!!!!!"

We are giddy with faith. Our secular version of a religious revival, the congregation chanting in a fever. We are as one. This will be Our Time. Our collective passion catapults us into an altered state of zeal. Our voices pump through the humid late afternoon of a sultry day in Havana, September 23, 2011. We are believers.

The crew scatters to their respective boats while I return to the hotel room. They need to be through customs and waiting for me to swim out of the mouth of Marina Hemingway Harbor in two hours.

I go back to the silent rituals. Hydrating. Yoga. Stretches. Deep breathing. A meditation of calm and focus. I am talking to myself, very slowly. I inhale with one syllable, exhale with the next, imbuing my brain with the mandates of this possibly impossible endeavor, this endeavor that drives my life force:

Take every minute, one at a time. Don't be fooled by a perfect sea at any given moment. Accept and rise to whatever circumstance presents itself. Be in it full tilt, your best self. Summon your courage, your true grit. When the body fades, don't let negative edges of despair creep in. Allowing flecks of negativity leads to a Pandora's box syndrome. You can't stop the doubts once you consent to let them seep into your tired, weakened brain. You must set your will. Set it now. Let nothing penetrate or cripple it.

I visualize pulling on a titanium helmet before the first stroke. This is my will. This strength of mind cannot be diminished. We think, after our two failures, that we know every possible roadblock that can emerge to thwart our journey, yet it is truly a vast, unfathomably powerful wilderness out there. This is a swimmer's Mount Everest, the great epic ocean endeavor of our blue planet. It's never been done. Strong swimmers have been questing across this ocean since 1950. No one has made it all the way across unaided.

You can do this. You will do this. The mantra takes on a rhythm with each breath, through the toe touches, the shoulder rotations. The body is warming, loosening. The mind is steeling. The spirit is reaching its necessary, indomitable plateau.

Bonnie and I, silent together in the austere, Communist Hotel Acuario room, go about our business. I have a blanket spread out on the floor. Neck circles, hamstring reaches, trunk twists. I drink a few ounces of water in between each exercise. My robe is ready, goggles in one pocket, cap in the other. Yet I still check to see they're there, neurotically, over and over. My suit is hanging on a hook next to the robe. The surreal feeling is coming on. I am ultra-aware of the molecules of oxygen traveling with each long sip of air to the bottom of the solar plexus, then the carbon dioxide inching back up toward my lips. The folds of the robe, revealing the words "Fearless Nyad" across the back, appear as a million puffs of fleece and cotton I've never noticed before. The cool water streams down my throat as if drop following individual drop. Bonnie's voice every few minutes is a steady, low-register, checking in. Monosyllables. We don't need to talk. It's all been said. We're ready.

Candace pays me a soulful last visit. I'm the lucky one. Two lifelong best friends. Candace's touch imparts a wave of calm as she lays her hands on my shoulders, my neck. She is breathing slowly, deeply and that makes me take on her rhythm. She settles my nerves. She heads off to her boat, assures me she'll be there every stroke of the way.

The golf cart shows up at four forty-five p.m., right on time to take us to the start. Bonnie and I sit close. Silent. We know our friendly driver, Jorge. He doesn't say a word. He understands. The significance of the moment is palpable. When we come around the corner and see the ocean, we share the surge of hope simultaneously and dare to exchange a knowing glance. It's flat as glass. The reflection of clouds stands still on the surface, all the way to the horizon. We know better than to imagine we will have sixty hours of this perfection. Or thirty. Or ten. Or two, for that matter. But for this moment, the vision of this calm washes over us like fairy-dust magic, perhaps an omen for many hours of smooth swimming ahead.

My "big bear," my dear friend El Comodoro José Miguel Escrich of Havana, and my cherished friend from Mexico, Kathy Loretta, our Xtreme Dream Cuba Ops Chief,[*] are waiting for me at the rocks. The start will be a plunge off the boulders that line the mouth of famous Marina Hemingway, where Ernest Hemingway himself fished, drank, and told bon vivant tales, where the Kennedy clan and Sinatra's Rat Pack and Mafia dons partied many nights away on luxury yachts before the Revolution of 1959. The place shimmers with textured fables, which is of course a big part of the allure of this crossing. The natural rock wall, first buttressed to protect this island country from pirates and

---

[*] The terms for Teammates' positions within the working expedition are capitalized throughout the book. This is my way of honoring my colleagues, who dedicated themselves to the Dream.

invasion, has by now kept Cubans in as much as it has kept others out. To swim all the way from one nation to another, from this particular forbidden land to my home country, to fully comprehend the lives of so many Cubans who left this very shore, in makeshift rafts in the middle of the night, speaks a compelling drama. Apolitical as I am, it's a drama written by impactful events that has always gripped me.

This passage, considering the powerful Gulf Stream, with its attendant eddies and countercurrents, the particular dangerous animals lurking beneath, is unlike any other hundred-mile ocean crossing on Earth. Were you to spread out the nautical charts of all the globe's equatorial waters, those warm enough for a swim of this length, you simply couldn't find a more challenging hundred miles for a swimmer. This stretch, Cuba to Florida, is where Mother Nature rages. We all, the Cubans and our Team alike, grasp the gravitas of the occasion. History extends across the sea before us.

The Cuban press corps is lined up in full force, their cameras set up in a sweep along the rocks. The beautiful royal-blue stripes of an oversized Cuban flag stretch strong and proud across the start area. Our five boats stand sentry off the rocks, along with a number of Cuban boats that will escort us out to international waters, twelve miles off the coast.

As I step down onto the flat rock area, the Team roars: "Onward! Onward! Onward!" Bonnie and I pump our fists toward them.

Bonnie begins the smearing of grease as I get the cap and goggles ready. I answer a few polite questions from the press, the lengthy questions having been handled at the press conference earlier. These are simply a few of the "How do you feel?" "Are you heartened, to see the calm sea in front of you?" "Will this be the last time?"

Fair enough. This is my third attempt. Will this be the last time? Of course this is the last time. But I did say that twice before.

The overwhelming scope of the quest tugs me away from all this immediate activity for a minute. I am sixty-two years old now, no longer the cocky twenty-eight-year-old who stood here all those years ago, not so evolved. I know only too well what monumental Nature lies out there.

The big picture, the Dream still alive after all these years, takes over as I look toward that elusive horizon. The enormity of it all wells within: the outrageously extreme training sessions, all the knowledge-able, dedicated people who have stuck with me. The epic crossing carries profound meaning for them, too; it's not just me. We shared heartache on the first two failures, the first thirty-three years ago and the second only six weeks back, both times very difficult to accept on the heels of such mammoth efforts. Yet pride swelled in our chests from the bravery we showed, the professionalism of the expeditions we put together. It's all huge for me right now. The panoramic perspective stuns me, takes me up and away from these solid rocks. It's in my soul, this Cuba Swim, far and away more than a mark of athletic endurance. This crossing has come to emblemize all I believe in, my worldview. Reaching stroke after stroke toward this particular horizon is my version of Browning's reach-ing for heaven. The vision of it, the planning, the training, the unwaver-ing belief in the face of overwhelming odds—this swim demands and defines the person I want to be. The person I can admire. But the depth of it all—it's too much for this moment. There will be plenty of time, on the other side at long last, for soulful contemplation. Right now I need to take that first stroke, to get a rhythm, to start the work.

We hear of football players pausing in the tunnel before running onto the field for the Super Bowl, tennis players waiting for their names to be announced before walking onto the grass for the Wimbledon Championship, track stars crouching for the start of the their Olympic sprint final. They all talk about their various tricks for calming their screaming nerves, their virtual blinders turning their attention inward and away from the outside distractions, the thirst to hit that first ball and get to the work they know so well, the wisdom to push the grand perspective to the back of their minds. I snap back to reality now. I'm back on the rocks. Bonnie is real again. I need that first stroke.

I salute the Team. No bugle this time. Low-key is our MO. Bonnie and I hug and say "Onward" quietly to each other. She gives me the nod, and I take the leap. The real leap. The metaphoric leap. In the air I say out loud, to myself, in the French pronunciation: *"Courage!"* After the punishing weeks, months, years of hard work, after the maddening wait for weather in Key West, now the first stroke is under way. It's an indescribable relief.

I make my way toward *Voyager*'s right (starboard) side. *Voyager* is my escort boat, my navigation boat, my Key West training boat, my beacon for the nearly twenty-nine hours of the last attempt. I feel tremendous fondness for this thirty-seven-foot catamaran at this point. My guide. My protector. She is more than a boat to me, *Voyager*. She has a spirit. She's got my back. My sturdy seafaring vessel, with her surface-level transom where Bonnie and my Handlers take such tender care of me. Her steering wheel has been reconfigured from center to far starboard now, so that Dee Brady and her crew of Drivers can keep an accurate course, dictated by our genius Navigator, John Bartlett. They need both to set the perfect course, constantly reconfiguring in small increments per John's directions, and to keep the perfect speed, one that neither leaves me behind *Voyager* nor puts *Voyager* behind me. The Drivers need to concentrate every single minute, to position the boat so that I am directly out from Bonnie's station. Nobody talks to the Drivers except Bartlett and Bonnie and Mark. Once I am away from *Voyager,* danger becomes more likely. And once I am away from *Voyager,* the shortest route from Havana to Florida is lost. Added yards escalate into added miles, and the possibly impossible becomes truly impossible.

John's navigation space is at the stern, a cabin right above the Handler's low station. I can see John, head buried in his charts, reading his various instruments, when I breathe to the left, toward the low Handler's transom. We occasionally catch each other's eyes. We exchange looks of solidarity, sometimes while I'm stroking, sometimes while I tread water during the feeding and hydration stops. John can talk to Bonnie and her crew right out the navigation cabin window. He can jump up onto the deck to talk to Mark Sollinger, our Ops Chief, and the Drivers and all other crew on board.

The Shark Divers take their sentry positions way up top, on the roof. The visibility of dark shadows below in the daytime Gulf Stream from up on that roof is as far as half a mile, with deep ocean views, so they feel confident they can handle any shark well in advance of it poking around close to me. Nighttime is a different story. We use no lights of any kind at night. Lights attract jellyfish, and bait fish, and then sharks. With no moonlight, the situation we are facing tonight, you literally cannot see your own outstretched hand. The Handlers know I'm still there, twenty-one feet to the right of Voyager, solely by the slapping of my hands on the surface. The only people who actually see me in the pitch-black night are the two Kayakers on duty, the electronic Shark Shields tethered to the bottoms of their boats. The paddler to my right needs to keep that Shield very close to me, within three feet, in order for it to cast its elliptical field wide enough underwater to be effective. Another paddler, with another Shield underneath, is right behind me, alert to stop quickly if I stop quickly. These first two are in formation out by *Voyager*. The other four paddlers are back on their mother ship, resting and ready to take their next shifts, two by two.

Bonnie has been transported from the start to *Voyager* and has snuggled into her transom perch by the time I get there. I am warning myself over and over not to let this glassy sea seduce me into any fantasies of it lasting very long. I'm just trying to cruise, not push, as the early-going excitement is making me feel like a million bucks. The temptation is to click off some fast miles, use this dead calm to push forward while we've got it. Push the stroke rate up a bit. But a pro knows better. One must settle into the pace that is viable for the long haul. Draining the body a bit now, to cover more ground while it's flat, will not serve us well later, when every ounce of reserve energy will be called upon.

Bonnie signals me to calm down, slow down the stroke rate a bit. Back in the old days, in my twenties, I always swam at sixty strokes per minute. Like literal clockwork. I would count six hours of sixty-stroke blocks: an hour of 60×60 in English, an hour in German, an hour in Spanish, an hour in French, then an hour of half English, half German, and an hour of half Spanish, half French. I'd look up after those six hours of 60×60 stroke counts and we would be at precisely six hours. Not five hours, fifty-eight minutes or six hours, one minute. Precisely six hours. But now, mostly due to the new freestyle stroke I've learned to lessen the burden on the torn biceps tendon in my shoulder, I am averaging fifty-two to fifty-four strokes per minute. Bonnie is signaling that I'm up around fifty-eight and she wants me to bring that down slightly.

It's just about dusk and, trying hard to not project into the night and imagine how long this delicious calm is going to last, I am nonetheless very happy. I'm starting to sing my songs. Sunset spreads like melted butter across half the horizon to the left, the direction toward which I breathe, golden-yellow cellophane with orange trim. The skyline of

Havana is slowly fading behind us. I can see the *Voyager* crew is settled, everybody at their posts. The Kayakers, the tails of their electronic
Shark Shields trailing under their boats, are swinging into formation
next to me. We are in sync and, gliding toward the horizon, I let our
chant well up in my ears and sing it in my head one hundred times.

Left arm, right arm: Where we swimming from?

Left arm, right arm: CUBA!

Left arm, right arm: Where we swimming to?

Left arm, right arm: FLORIDA!!

The night is coming. Every few minutes, the sky grows darker. I'm
prepping my counting progressions and song-list goals for the night.
While it's true that it's best to take each minute unto itself, or at least
each ninety-minute session between feedings, my strategy also includes
working on a bigger series of goals, and that's nighttime, daytime,
nighttime, daytime. And now it's time to get into a groove until first
light tomorrow. I'm going to start with Bob Dylan tonight. Dylan and
a counting pattern between each song of two thousand strokes in each
of the four languages. Here we go.

> It ain't no use to wonder why, babe
> If you don't know by now

I'm content. The water is warm. I'm high up on the surface, the
stroke strong, goggles and cap comfortable. Let's get through this first
night. That's all that's in front of us, this first night. I can't wait to look
back and no longer see the lights of Havana. We're only two hours in,
but Mark and Bonnie and John and Dee have been elated with the ideal
conditions so far. All the way around, we're doing what we came to do.
We're in a groove. The groove is in rhythm.

"Woaaaooohhwww! Wawoooh! Ouoooohhhh! It's intense! One, two,
three, four, five, six. I'm on fire, I'm on fire. I'm on FIRE!! Help me . . .
Bonnie, HELP ME!"

I know the sharp sting of the Portuguese man-of-war. Penetrating
pain, often followed by pulmonary distress. Maybe nausea. But this is
not the Portuguese. This is otherworldly. The stuff of science fiction.
My entire body as if dipped in hot burning oil. I AM ON FIRE!! I'm
close to the boat now, struggling.

I sputter syllables in choking breaths, trying to tell Bonnie that I am feeling paralysis. My mid-back, lungs area, is seizing up. Now I can't get my arms to come up above the surface. My spinal cord seems in seizure. I can't breathe. I struggle to blurt out, "What is it? How long is this going to last?"

Jon Rose, our EMT diver, gets in the water with me now. He's our solo Med Team for the moment. He's primarily part of our Shark Diver Team, experienced in the water with all kinds of animals, but this is new territory for him. Jon wipes my arms with a dry sponge. He sees jellyfish all around, with the lamp on his headgear. He pops his head up, reports that there are thousands of them swarming. They're small, the size of a sugar cube, a clear dark blue. He's never seen this type before.

And now, diving without full wet suit, as the water is very warm, Jon is stung himself. Hit with the same symptoms I'm dealing with—extreme breathing constriction and sensation of spinal paralysis—he struggles to pull himself up onto *Voyager* and tells Bonnie he's in trouble. Jon is six foot three, 205 pounds, so less likely to feel full effects of the venom, compared to me at five-six, 142 pounds, yet he's writhing on the deck in distress. He gasps that his breath rate has gone down to three per minute and he's worried about surviving. Bonnie tells him to take care of himself somehow; she's got to focus on the swimmer. Jon gives himself two injections of epinephrine but, without knowing the exact species of jellyfish, he is reluctant to give me the same shots. The full Med Team won't be with us until the international waters line, at least a few more hours.

The official observer, Steve Munatones, says he will okay a short break out on the boat, given the life-or-death nature of the stings. But I don't want out. This is my Dream. I'm not going to throw it away and potentially move this swim into a "Staged" category (by the rules of marathon swimming, this is when a swimmer gets out at a specific latitude/longitude, takes care of whatever crisis is at hand, and then gets back in at that same spot and continues). No one on this expedition wants a staged classification. We've worked too damn hard.

I stay in. Bonnie has me pull on a thin rash guard, a non-neoprene shirt (neoprene is not allowed in the sport, due to its flotation properties). Not so easy to swim in but Bonnie hopes at least protective from further stings on the arms and shoulders. The feeling of the hot-wax burn wanes as I swim on into the night, but the sensation of paralysis and the compromised breathing continues all through the night and even into the next day's morning hours.

On the deck next to Bonnie, Jon's recovery takes several hours (although at a press conference three days later, he will report that he is still feeling pressure at the throat and is not able to breathe normally). Now he says to Bonnie: "She's unreal. I almost died. And she's still swimming. Unreal."

By early morning, the sun still not up, the University of Miami Med Team has joined the flotilla. They interview Jon Rose and get his description of the particular jellyfish and the symptoms we both experienced. They also interview most of the expedition members and those who heard the scene from their respective mother ships say my bloodcurdling screams across the night, magnified by water transporting sound, were chilling. They were truly afraid for my life.

The Med Team is ready for every emergency imaginable. Everything but this. They have never heard of this particular description of jellyfish. They are a combination of ER and sports medicine docs; they don't work in the jellyfish universe. Common sense tells them to open my airway the best they can. Once they are on the scene, they start with inhalers, injections of epinephrine, oxygen-mask treatments, injections of prednisone, puffs from a nebulizer. And these protocols are administered more often than my usual food and hydration breaks, which normally come every ninety minutes and consist of my treading water for four to eleven minutes while taking in nutrients. A swimmer is not allowed to touch or hold on to the escort boat, a kayak, a surfboard, or any object out at sea. She must support herself on her own power for the entire crossing. But people can tend to you, hand you food, inject you with a needle, without aiding you with flotation. From the predawn hour of the Med Team's arrival, around two or three a.m., until maybe two or three the next afternoon, I am laboring to catch my breath and struggling to find power in my stroke. Bonnie calls me in to the feeding station of *Voyager* more like every half an hour during that long post-sting recovery period. I am doing the best I possibly can, but Bonnie, Mark, and John are painfully aware that I am only making forward progress, and slow progress at that, about 60 percent of every hour. The northward push necessary to get across this easterly flowing Gulf Stream is both weak and not enough minutes per hour. We are, unbeknownst to me, heading east, for the Bahamas.

After midafternoon, I'm not stopping quite so often for oxygen and treatments. Yet I'm not swimming at normal full strength, either. My body feels at half-mast. The press of the hands underwater is not the normal lock onto resistance and surge forward. I am instead feebly going through the motions. The energy that comes from my normally superior lung capacity is flat. It's by this time a double whammy: debilitation from the jellyfish venom itself, coupled with body shock from the long list of meds administered in constant repetition. I am limping along. Yet the goal of getting through the first night is now a fait accompli. And getting through the next daytime session is progressing.

I am aware that I'm weak. But I don't waste any time or energy on anger or self-pity. These ultra-endurance epics often serve as a microcosm for life itself. As they say, life happens when we're making plans for Scenario A, with backup plans for Scenario B, while even being smart enough to prepare for unlikely Scenario C. When Scenario Z smacks us in the gut, we gather our wits about us and dip into every resource within and without.

After a speech in Texas a couple of years ago, I was hanging with the group for a nice outdoor deck lunch. I happened to grab a seat at a table where a young couple told me their story. Their first child, a boy, suffered oxygen loss, and hence brain damage, from umbilical cord strangulation in the womb. He made it to age fourteen. Their second child had no major health issues. But their third baby, a girl, on a billion-to-one bad-luck chance of two in one family, was born with brain damage, again due to umbilical cord strangulation. So what do you feel when a bright-eyed, smiling couple tell you they've lost a child, are struggling as they raise an intellectually challenged child, and are trying to give their "normal" child the best life possible? I felt the tears welling up, but the husband told me they're okay. They turn to all they have, instead of what they've lost, and are grateful for every day of health and joy.

So I'm thinking of that couple out in the wide blue expanse of the ocean. I can see their brave faces, full of resolve. A good team, standing strong in the face of unspeakable tragedy. Living their best lives. Now here I am, scrapping, floundering. But neither I nor the Team has allowed even a wink of negative desperation to infiltrate the expedition. We are marching onward. The chi is wounded, but the words still drive every lift of the left arm, then the right.

"Where we swimming to? FLORIDA."

Back on automatic pilot, the titanium will wrapped tight around my brain, although weary and impaired, I have now fully embraced Scenario Z. We won't get to Florida as fast as we forecast. The suffering has already been even greater than imagined. But we're on our way. We are approaching twenty-four hours. The worst is behind us.

Stroking atop a translucent, glazed surface, the sun yet again fading down and away to the west, my mind is happy again, for the first time in more than twenty hours. I am singing. Gentle James Taylor. Just right for nurturing the wounded body. "Rock-a-bye sweet baby James." The crisis is truly over. I survived. No. I more than survived. I prevailed. I am beginning to relax back into my rhythm. The focus demands of the last twenty hours, talking my body into steeling through it, it was all-consuming. Coaxing the arms to continue lifting and pushing, begging the lungs to calm—it was exhausting. Not a single moment of escape from it. Those twenty hours took everything we had. From all of us. Now we are regaining our composure.

With the luxury of now letting my mind roam, able to take in the clarity of the stunning blue Gulf Stream, tracking the sun's downward movement every fifty or so strokes, I am taken back to a childhood moment, one I hadn't recalled for a long, long time. I always talk about the Cuba Swim Dream first flickering in my imagination in 1978, at age twenty-eight, when I first put an expedition together to attempt it. But in truth the initial spark harkened way back to a day I stood on a beach in Fort Lauderdale, Florida, when I was nine years old. The Cuban Revolution had just happened and thousands of Cubans were flocking in exile overnight into my hometown. I was making Cuban friends, hearing the stories of their beautiful country, dancing salsa in their living rooms, eating Cuban food. Like millions of Americans—I daresay millions of people worldwide—I was (and have continued to be so all my life) captured by the mystique of Cuba. The photos were enchanting: the mustards and pale greens and sponged blues of the colonial buildings, their tall European windows flung open to reveal men playing saxophones and dominoes, couples dancing salsa in the cobblestoned alley outside the fabled Hemingway bar El Floridita, the iconic and stylish American cars of the 1950s streaming down the wide Malecón esplanade of Havana. I was enthralled with Cuba—its art, its architecture, its music, its athletes. At this semi-delirious, semi-calm moment, somewhere between these two lands, somewhere between consciousness and unconsciousness, I remember standing on that Fort Lauderdale beach at age nine with my mother.

"Where is Cuba, Mom? I can't see it. Exactly where is it out there?"

And she pulled me close to her and raised her arm to point toward the horizon. "There. It's right over there. You can't see it but it's so close, you could almost swim there."

TWO

The Deadly Box

Last light is evaporating. Darkness envelops the sea in every direction. One corner of my brain is filtering through the night's playlist, but I can't get settled enough to think which tunes will engage me all night long. There is a nagging obsession. Whatever that was that attacked at dusk last night, will they hit again? I truthfully would not wish that assault on my worst enemy.

Last night was a thunderbolt. It came with alarming confusion. We were in the grip of the unknown. And yet Bonnie and I remained hard-core. The Team fell in. Silent. Loyal. We pressed toward control. We never let the mission crumble. Our backbone, our grit, was intact.

At daybreak today, more than twelve hours after the siege, we had discussed how those creatures must have come up from the shallow ocean shelves off the Cuba shore, figuring that we'd be okay this second night, way out in deep waters. The University of Miami docs had used the sat phone to call their marine biology department with a description of the jellies from Jon Rose. The experts' answer was they were perplexed. Sounded an awful lot like the deadly box jellyfish, but until they could examine my sting marks up close, they couldn't be sure. But they did report the box usually delivers a fatal sting. More people have died from the box than from shark bites. Each tentacle carries hundreds of thousands of harpoons. As the tentacle whips around the jellyfish's prey, the harpoons penetrate the skin and fire their venom, with explosive speed, into both the cardiovascular and the central nervous systems. They had no effective counsel of how to protect my body from these animals. This was all new territory. For all of us.

About an hour ago, at dusk, Bonnie suggested I put the rash guard back on. I had taken it off at first light this morning. It's loose and blousy. The drag makes lifting the arms considerably more strenuous. But it seems most of the stings occurred around my neck, biceps, forearms, and armpits, so the drag of the rash guard is not a hardship, in comparison to enduring that experience again. The marine biologists had also told us an individual becomes sensitized to these stings. In other words, you build an immunity to some venoms as you're stung or bitten over and over. People who work with certain species of snakes expose themselves to bites to build up their immune defenses. To other venoms, you become sensitized—you tolerate the venom less and less. Such is the case with the box.

As a general rule, once we begin the expedition, whether it be sharks or navigation or weather issues, anything except how I'm doing physically and mentally, it's the various Teammates who confer and attend to any and all problems, without my cognizance. Best that I'm not aware. My job is to keep myself together and proceed *onward.* Before we start, I am the CEO, so to speak. I organize everything, and every detail goes through me. Once we start, I am the swimmer. Bonnie, Mark, and John, as a matter of fact, refer to me as "the swimmer."

But today, because I was stopping frequently, treading, and doing breaststroke with my head above water, as opposed to the normal, oblivious freestyle routine, I was apprised of what the Team had learned vis-à-vis the box jellyfish. After the ship-to-shore conference with the marine biologists, it's not that we now know for sure what hit me and Jon; nor do we have any clue as to the behaviors of these animals or what to do to protect me. But we certainly know, through our own experience with many other species of jellyfish, that dusk is the time for them to rise and sting. Yet surely, in this vast expanse of ocean, that was just sheer bad luck last night, running into those particular jellies. We should be okay.

Even so, envisioning again plowing through an army of small blue deadly sugar-cube shapes en masse, a commanding paranoia buzzes through my brain, which is never the case with sharks. When it comes to sharks, I am rarely aware if the Team has sighted an animal. They do their business quietly. Being apprised of what they're seeing does me no good whatsoever. Sharks are never on my mind. What would I do? I am helpless out there. The goggles are somewhat fogged, and I'm turning my head some fifty-two times a minute to breathe. I basically don't see anything. After every long training swim, in St. Maarten, Mexico, Key West, I overhear the crew joyously recounting the pods of dolphins that played along with us for hours, the big sea turtles that surfaced and dived all around me, the gorgeous French sailboat that cut a few circles around us. Me? I see Bonnie or Mark and the starboard side of *Voyager.* My hearing is also impaired. The cap is tight over the ears, in an attempt to keep core body temperature as normal as possible. This immersion is as close to a full-on state of sensory deprivation as exists in the world of sports. While other issues, such as altitude, challenge an extreme alpine climber, and yet other factors press an ultra-endurance runner or cyclist or Antarctic trekker, no adventurer is as alone with her own thoughts, or more incapable of being alert and in touch with the environment for safety reasons, as a sensory-deprived extreme endurance swimmer.

I can't be on the lookout for sharks. Absurd. Every cloud that casts a shadow on the surface, every dark underside of a wave crest—to the tired eye, they all begin to look like shark fins. I need to let go and trust my Shark Diver Team. And I do. The world-renowned shark diver Aussie Luke Tipple captains the Shark Team. Luke swims with these animals on a daily basis. He understands them. I asked him point-blank in front of the entire Team at the Havana Team meeting yesterday, if I am 100 percent safe from sharks on this crossing. He looked at me point-blank and said there is no such thing as a guarantee. This is their ocean. We're just asking them to allow us a peaceful passage through their world.

Luke also didn't blink when he assured me that he and his five Divers will position themselves in between any curious animal and myself. He added that, like all predators, sharks don't want to risk their own lives by getting mixed up in something unfamiliar, such as our flotilla of boats, the kayaks, the electric field we're emitting under me. Luke is a shark conservationist, meaning he will never kill a shark. This is their natural habitat and he works year-round to protect them. Humans are killing 170 million sharks a year these days, largely in a horribly inhumane way of slicing off their fins and letting the live animal sink, helpless, to the ocean floor. With the radical eradication of the big predator of the seas, other species in the ecosystem are proliferating at an alarming rate, which is the case with the box jellyfish. Luke will not kill any shark, but his Team will be brave enough to put themselves in harm's way, with probing sticks to bother the sharks' sensitive snouts. He can't swear that a rogue, starving animal won't swoop up to take a bite, yet he assures me he and his Team are very familiar with their behaviors and have the skills to dissuade a shark from rushing in. We have total confidence we are in good hands.

Four of the Divers work from *Voyager* and in the water near me, while the other two rest on their respective mother ship off to the side of *Voyager,* getting ready for their next shift. When they see sharks, they don't alert the rest of the flotilla. As Ops Chief, Mark is the only one who needs to know if Divers are deployed. He is always on count as to how many people are in the water, where they are, when they're back up on board. We don't want to leave a Diver out there as we motor on. They work together, with soft murmurs. The last thing I need to know is that a large animal is following below. And I don't know, not as a general rule.

But now the second night has come, and I perhaps know too much about the jellyfish. Or, better put, I know nothing yet fear everything. None of us experienced ocean types, not even the Shark Divers, have felt or previously witnessed what hit us last night. I'm not in normal swim mode. I'm not focused. That pain is too recent. The post-traumatic stress is too fresh. My mind is not prepping for a long series of numbers and songs to get through the night. It's as though I can't think. I'm scattered.

We're twenty-six hours in now, twenty-four hours since the attack. Now it's pitch-black. And sure enough, like clockwork . . .

"Whoa! . . . Whoa, Whoa, Whoa, Whoa!!"

The ravaging pain is unmistakable this second time.

The seizure of the spinal cord. The fire! The immediate attack on the lungs. Maybe I'm weaker this second night, both from the first night's stings and from even greater than normal duress in swimming twenty-four hours after those rips—not to mention a body racked with chaos from the long laundry list of meds administered repeatedly over so many hours. The rash guard has not protected me. Steve Munatones again okays a life-or-death interruption of the event, but this time I am not conscious enough to protest. Bonnie and Mark pull me onto *Voyager.*

My memories of the next two hours are of course disturbed. I have watched the scene in the documentary film *The Other Shore.* My Med Team quickly jumps into triage protocol. Bonnie holds my head, emphatic but not panicked: "Breathe, Diana, breathe!" I see glimpses of Mark, Candace, the docs. In and out of consciousness, I'm incoherent and unaware most of those two hours.

Because we are in crisis mode, out of the water more than a few minutes, being officially categorized as a Staged Event is now inevitable. So be it. We have come too far, given too much, to just pack it up. None of us likes Scenario Z. But we're living it.

John Bartlett is confused when Mark asks him to get back to the exact GPS point where I had been hauled out. Bartlett goes to the lead doctor, Cliff Page, and says he has just witnessed a serious medical event. My life truly in the balance. Surely we won't be continuing. Dr. Page says he has never seen anything like it, yet I am asking Bonnie to help get me back in the water.

Some ten of us are working to get the boat, the crew, and me ready. Voices are low. There is an unspoken gravity in the air. How could one swim for twenty-four hours after these crippling stings? How could one enter the water again, after a second bout with these potentially fatal animals? No answers. Only resolve. Bonnie and Candace, having literally just witnessed their friend almost die, nevertheless show no doubts. Their jaws are clenched, their eye contact with me sure and steady. Common sense dictates to the rest of the Team that we are done. The Med Team knows full well these are dire circumstances and we need to get to shore and a hospital, but the standard has been set, from the beginning, and the human will is far and away stronger than fear and common sense combined. I cannot be deterred. Bonnie is shoulder to shoulder with me. The *onward* code of conviction we live by is mighty.

The Shark Team has been busy fashioning a mask out of one of their cotton hoodies. It's not going to be ideal: just cotton cloth with holes for my eyes and mouth, cut out for my goggles and ability to breathe. Bonnie is gingerly pulling on my Lycra booties and gloves, the rash guard. All this added clothing is going to cause considerable drag. The shoulders are going to be burdened exponentially. But none of this makeshift protection is against the rules, and all of it is necessary for survival, although it's spur-of-the-moment grasping at straws. We already know the rash guard did nothing to keep those tentacles from finding my skin.

John announces we have arrived at the precise latitude and longitude where I was hauled out. The flotilla swings into position to carry on. Hearty cheers from every boat echo across the black corner of the globe that is uniquely ours tonight. We're together again. I slip into the inky sea and the rousing chorus of boat horns and shouts of encouragement help me more than my friends can imagine. Staged category now upon us, Scenario Z is deeply disappointing, even shocking, to me. But I will not quit.

My stroke is slow. The breath is at half capacity. The body weak but the will strong, now the chant in my brain, left arm, right arm, turns to Churchill:

"Never give in. . . . Never, never, never, never . . ."

That second night, from the triage scene on *Voyager's* trampoline deck to the slither back again into the dark ocean toward a distant dawn, is sketchy in my mind. I never do gain a firm grip on reality during those long hours of darkness. That second night is far and away more desperate survival than swimming. I resort to a slow breaststroke, to catch my breath, after every hundred or so freestyle strokes. Then, when my muscles are drained from lack of sufficient oxygen, I go over onto my back to gasp, holding my lungs with my hands as if to coax them toward composure, to get my pulse back down to 130 or so in order to continue. It's slow-going, Scenario Z, but agonizing hour by hour, we make it through the night. I recall clearly, back in the '70s, I loved to swim at night. It seemed so stealthily exciting, to glide under the stars, happy to escape the glare that stuns the mind under the blazing summer sun. But in these more modern times, staggered by these new jellyfish blitzkriegs, the night has become a living nightmare. Bonnie encourages me to hang in for the sunrise.

It comes slowly. It's no longer summer, and late September means longer nights, less daylight. I am looking virtually every stroke for the black to lighten, telling myself it won't be long until I can take all this heavy clothing off. My hands are aching. The Lycra gloves are not skintight, by any means. Each pull meets with so much resistance that pressing through the stroke requires every fiber of my concentration. The good news is that I haven't been stung again, since reentering. Is this combat outfit effective? Or do these animals only surface and sting in the early evening?

I have to take long breaths, raise the head higher than usual, to see if the stars really are fading. Yes, the sky has gone from ebony to a deep midnight blue. I stop for a couple of seconds to ask Bonnie if she thinks it safe to take the floppy shirt and headgear off yet. She asks me to hang in another hour or so, until true daylight. Sure enough, an hour later, I'm singing for the first time since those first minutes off Havana. The Beatles. "Here Comes the Sun": "Little darling, it's been a long cold lonely winter . . ."

All those hellishly long training hours, of course to get the body ready, but also to calibrate the mind to cope with the depths of the numbing solitude, and yet it's taken me by utter surprise that those number progressions and the specific songs for specific moods, which I've purposefully and painstakingly developed, have basically not come into play on this swim. We are some thirty-six hours in now. Except for the first two hours, right out of Marina Hemingway, we have been in crisis all the way.

John Bartlett, at the navigation station, has had to get creative with the math, squeezing a bit of difficult swimming northwest, into the muscle of the easterly screaming Gulf Stream. Evidently, he's neither happy nor hopeful about our position thirty-six hours in.

I'm not apprised of the navigation progress. The cardinal rule, which Bonnie issues to the Team on the docks before we sail out, is that *nobody ever* tells me where we are. Somebody might take a look at a GPS setting and see that we're, let's say, fifty-five miles out from Havana. So they get excited, thinking we're halfway. But we have no idea if we're halfway at that point. So many variables are in play, from fickle and sudden weather to swirling eddies to animals (we're learning the hard way) to my own frailties. Just because I might have been covering miles over the bottom at a certain speed the first half of the journey doesn't mean I'm going to replicate that progress from fifty-five miles on. I never look up and forward, anxious to catch a glimpse of a palm tree by day, a flicker of land lights by night. All I'd see is vast, depressing horizon. Better I should engage in the moment, just keep working, turning my head like a programmed robot, fifty-two times a minute, toward *Voyager.* I never ask where we are, how we're doing. They never tell me. The cardinal rule.

The plan is that John, Mark, and Bonnie will come to me when they believe we're approximately ten hours from the Florida shore. Up to that point, no matter how heartened they may be about our headway, or how concerned they are about our lack of headway, I have no idea where we are until I get the word we're about ten hours from U.S. sands. And on this day, September 25, 2011, totally unbeknownst to me, they are terribly concerned.

For me in the water, glorious sunshine and glassy seas sparkle with positive spirit and seem to warmly embrace me from every point on the compass. I remove all the heavy material. I'm free. I have not lost hope, not for a nanosecond, of that Florida shore.

I know I'm not making terrific progress. I'm still resorting to a slow breaststroke, to catch my breath, after every hundred or so freestyle strokes. Normally, many thousands of strokes ensue without any kind of break or change of stroke or pace. Just as I don't allow myself to start kvetching and complaining, because then the cascade of grousing flows out of control, I also don't allow myself, under normal circumstances, to stop for a minute or two just because I'm fed up with the demands on both mind and body. You start to take a minute here to stretch your legs, a minute there to float and trip out on the cloud formations, and pretty soon you're stopping for five here and five there. It all snowballs and you're no longer in it, the way you need to be in it, relentless, to the end. Usually, the only stops are the feeds, called for by Bonnie. But we are clearly under the duress of abnormal conditions.

On each gasping stop, through the spells of breaststroke, as lovingly but as urgently as she can do it, Bonnie is prodding and pleading with me to try to swim more freestyle minutes per hour. I guess, subliminally, I am hearing her say that we're not going to make it if I don't make more steady northerly speed. I try. But with my lungs pressed to the limit, muscles underfed with oxygen, I once again revert to breast-stroke, and then flop onto my back, in dire need of air. (I will discover later that the log of the serious meds I've taken over two days covers four single-spaced pages. In retrospect, I was probably weaker and loopier from the onslaught of medications than from the jellyfish venom itself.) Long about midday, the sun high above, I notice Bonnie and Mark and John huddling just above the Handler's station. Something's going on.

I will also find out later that this is the last of their many conferences since day broke that twenty-fifth of September. Bartlett has been poring over his charts, crunching his numbers. It's over. I am simply wounded too badly, since hour number two, to push as need be to the north.

Bonnie signals me. Mark, John, Candace, and Jon Rose are all kneel-ing on the Handler's platform. Other Teammates hover just above. Bartlett says it out loud. We are forty-four hours, thirty minutes in. At this rate, it would take a minimum of another seventy hours, and that would not be to reach Florida; that would be to hit one of the islands of the Bahamas.

We all cry. Bartlett tells me these are the toughest moments of his life, having to bear the bad news. He says all of them know how incred-ibly hard I've worked for this, how badly I've wanted to achieve it, how much I've suffered over these forty-four hours. His tears flow when he tells me it's been an honor to witness this herculean effort. They reach to hold my hands, touch my head. But I'm not ready for tears. I push away from *Voyager* and erupt in a tirade: "This isn't what I trained for, surviv-ing these damn jellyfish! This isn't the noble quest this Cuba Swim is supposed to be. This isn't the sport of ocean swimming! These fucking jellyfish are the bane of my existence!"

That's right. Life is not what we expect.

I swim over to the center of the flotilla and wave up to all the crew on the four other boats. I've been weakened too much by the stings. We can no longer hope to make Florida. Steve Munatones tells our Team that in his long history of observing ocean swims, he's never seen a swimmer continue—much less continue for forty-two hours—after a life-threatening box sting.

The continuation of Churchill's "Never give in" quote, by the way, goes: "Never give in, except to convictions of honour and good sense." Good sense has now taken over. The Dream is dashed.

The spirit, I suppose, just can't go from full-tilt on to flat-out off in a heartbeat. I tell Bonnie and Mark I want to swim until nightfall, just because I can, out of high regard to our beautiful Xtreme Dream. We crank it up again, but all that time swimming hurt has cost me, and the dark and the deadly stings of a third night loom only a few hours away.

Here's where the strength of will becomes apparent. With the end goal firmly in mind, anything is possible, even surviving and continuing after two potentially fatal box-sting episodes. But without the destination brimming in the imagination, the will collapses. I take only twenty strokes, stop, and signal Bonnie and Mark that we are done.

I am dragged onto the little inflatable and transported to one of the larger fleet boats. For the first time, I can now see the rips of sting lines, wrapped all around the biceps, forearms, neck, thighs; I am told my back shows long red zips as well. The Med Team starts an IV. Sure, the body is whipped, but this is nothing compared to the crushed spirit. You don't leave room for imagining defeat. Every cell of your being rousingly believes you're going to make it. An endeavor of this magnitude couldn't be achieved any other way. So to lie wounded and defeated on the deck, still far from land (we covered 81.7 miles in 44 hours, 30 minutes), is just plain crushing. 81.7 miles seems awfully close to the finish line, if the closest straight vector from Havana to Key West is 103 miles, but our 81.7 miles were largely to the east, toward the Bahamas. We are a long way from Florida.

The spirit needs time to heal, no different from the body. Motoring these interminable hours back to Key West, in acute exhaustion, I am daunted to consider another year of training and organizing. Yet by the time we arrive, I know this Dream of mine is still alive.

THREE

Aris

It all started, really, on my fifth birthday, when my father called me into the den. Aris was dramatic. Theatrical. Larger than life. He stood at the desk, his hands stretched across one page of a large, opened unabridged dictionary. I thought he was on the verge of tears. But that was nothing unusual. Every day was an emotional exaltation for Aristotle Zanith Nyad.

He would wake up the whole family at three in the morning and, in his thick, charming accent, buzzing z's and rolling r's, implore us: "Come on. Hurrry. Getting drressed. I have just been to ze ocean. Ze moon is shining like Rembrrandt painting coming to life, just forr us. You will neverr seeing such beauty again in yourr lives. Hurrry!"

"Dad, we can't go to the beach in the middle of the night. We have school. We need our sleep."

"I am telling you, sleep is overrated! Trust me, you will never forget it. Come on, get dressed!"

Twenty minutes later, the whole family stands awestruck at the ocean's edge, not far from our home in Fort Lauderdale. The moon casts a sweeping path of glory gold from our feet in the shallows all the way to the horizon, seemingly beyond. He's right. It's a Rembrandt come to life. I never forgot it. That was the vital, exciting Aris who sometimes enchanted us.

Dashing in a white dinner jacket, Aris resembled Omar Sharif in his prime. Only better-looking. I remember walking to our table in restaurants when I was little, noting that women were tracking my father, jaws agape, forks hanging limp. He was a beauty.

Aris made his living as a con artist. He was superlative at lying and stealing and, from what our family could surmise later, even more egregious criminal activities. He was a magnetic storyteller. He used his constantly miming hands and animated facial expressions to great effect. He held people captive for hours. He claimed to speak seventeen languages. I do remember hearing him chat fluidly with people in Arabic, Greek, French, Spanish, Italian, Portuguese—just about everything but the Asian languages. He was born in Greece, to a French mother and a Greek father, but evidently moved to Alexandria, Egypt, when he was a boy and went to tony French schools. Mind you, in the end, we never could believe anything he said, so even that background is suspect. Con artists are inherently elusive and, true to form, Aris wasn't around much. He was out playing cards, scheming people into emptying their bank accounts for some fictional project, dressing to the nines for some flashy yacht outing. Sounds perhaps like an amusing home to grow up in—you never worried about banal dinner conversation with Aris. But when it came to our father, the three of us kids were always somewhere between delight and distrust.

On this day, when I turned five, his sense of urgency was so fervent, I was all ears. He said, his emotions running high, his accent thicker than ever: "Darrling, you arre coming here. I have been waiting so very long for zis day. Now you arre five. Today iz the day you are rready to underrstand ze most significant zing I will ever tell you, darrling. Coming here. Look in zis imporrtant book, ze dictionarry, darrling. Look, printed in bold black and white, here iz yourr name, ze name of my family. My people."

He cast his eyes up to the heavens as if in rapture.

"And let me tell you somezing, darrling. Tomorrow you will go to yourr little preschool and you will ask your little frriends iz hiz name in ze dictionarry? Zey will tell you no. You arre ze only one, darrling. You arre ze special one. Coming herre, darrling. Look. Arre you listening to me, darrling? Yourr name: Nyad [naiad]. Firrst definition, from Grreek mythology."

He pauses and clutches his chest and looks to the skies again, his voice now trembling.

"My people, darrling. Naiad: in Grreek mythology, the nymphs zat swam in the lakes, oceans, rrivers, and fountains to prrotect ze waters forr ze gods. Listening to me, darrling, because now iz coming ze most imporrtant parrt. Next says 'naiad: in modern colloquial terrms . . .' "

A natural actor, he pauses a long time, squares me to him, and delivers each syllable with meaning:

"A girrl or woman champion swimmerr. Oh my God, darrling, zis is yourr destiny!"

I didn't latch onto the words "girl or woman," or "swimmer." I was, after all, only five. What I heard was the word "champion." From that day, I started walking around with my shoulders held just a little higher.

My father was alive with a life-affirming sparkle. He was a showman extraordinaire, the ultimate charmer. He was also an angry tyrant and, worse, a man without conscience. Everyone in our home was afraid of him.

A short fuse sent him off on Greek and Arabic swearing tantrums, his hands flailing toward the skies, and not far behind was a quick trigger to the belt or hairbrush for beatings. He struck my mother many times, leaving Bill, Liza, and me upset and in tears, helpless. The time in the forefront of my memory, Mom went to the kitchen floor. We thought her cheekbone was broken. She had a large bruise for a while and she fabricated some story about it for friends. Turned out she was okay, but it was yet another outburst hard to witness. Touched our souls—Bill's, Liza's, mine.

There was a road trip. My sister was probably only three. Liza is five years younger than I, my brother in between us. Liza kept saying she didn't feel well. She was carsick. Aris was in one of his despotic moods. He told her to shut up: We weren't going to stop; we needed to make wherever we were headed by nightfall. Mom knew Liza was going to vomit in the car but, per usual, was too afraid to push him. When Liza threw up, his rage blew like a powder keg. He screeched to the side of the highway, ran around the back of the station wagon, dragged little Liza out, and spanked her viciously. I remember it vividly. I was in tears. My brother hid his head in shame. Mom was upset but never opened her car door, did not come to my sister's defense.

Bill and I knew the welts from his belt only too well. Aris came home from "business" trips with foreign money for us kids. Bill and I hid our paper bills in the upstairs freestanding heater. The heater was turned on one day, and a fire ensued. Fire trucks rushed to the house; firemen entered the upstairs windows with their hose. It was pretty serious, rugs and some furniture burned. Aris sat us three kids down and gave the false speech we had heard many times before: "Don't worry. I'm not mad. You not going to be punished. But zis verry, verry serrious. I need to know how zis is happening. Tell me ze truth—we need ze truth, making surre neverr happening again."

Bill and I hemmed and hawed and finally confessed that we had been keeping our foreign bills in the heater. Whoosh! The belt came off, we were bent over, and the lashes came whipping across the backs of our legs. When Aris was angry, there was never an iota of restraint.

The roller coaster between adventure and fury was the modus operandi of our home life. To add insult to injury, Aris also acted out his sexual deviance with me. One glaring incident happened on a fun family day at the beach. Mom and my brother went to get the car. Aris, Liza, and I went to rinse off at the showers adjacent to the parking lot. I was probably about ten years old, Liza only five. Kids would strip their suits off, take a quick rinse, and wrap up in a towel. I was naked under the shower, as I'd been hundreds of times before, but this day when I reached to Dad for my towel, he instead grabbed me, hard, between the legs. The automatic systemic reaction was familiar to my body, from other such shocking moments that happened earlier with him. I froze. Couldn't move. Couldn't speak. Couldn't breathe. He stared into my eyes, a gargoylish grin on his face as he pinned me there, petrified and ashamed. I'll never forget little Liza's face, looking to me. Helpless. Terrified.

Many years later, when my mother was out visiting me in Los Angeles, Mom told me she was sorry for not believing me back then and sorry for not rushing to help me. Maybe she carried the burden of always feeling it was all her fault and she just couldn't live with that. But that morning she said she finally wanted to share something with me, something that might help me in the work I was doing with a therapist at the time.

I had always remembered the trauma of being grabbed at the beach and similar incidents in the shower, but the story she told me that morning I didn't remember. She said I was five, so I guess it was, ironically, the same year Aris bestowed me with that empowerment moment from reading my name in the dictionary, the year the concept of champion seeped into my little spirit. Aris came home one night drunk as a skunk. He told my mom he was going to sleep with me. I had my own room with a little single bed. Mom said, "No, you're not. Come to bed," meaning their room. He slapped her. He was boss. He went into my room, and Mom cowered into their room and shut the door. In the morning she opened my door, and I wasn't there. Aris was still sleeping it off, his pants off with a huge erection. And my mom ended the story there. "But," I said, "Mom, what happened then? Where was I? Was I trembling under the house with fear? Was I down the street, torturing some younger kid to express my own anger?"

She simply said, "Well, I don't know. I have no idea where you were." So my mom thought I should be aware of this incident for my own good, and yet she didn't really glean from that story her part in it all.

Until I was around twelve, we moved just about every year. Dad needed to be on the run. Yet I have very few memories of any of those homes. I do remember the imperative to somehow get from the back door to my room, from my room to the kitchen, without him seeing me. But I can't picture my different bedrooms, beds, bathrooms, front doors, yards, trees, kitchens, living rooms, televisions, house layouts. Nothing concrete. This is evidently a common syndrome among children of abuse. A child can't escape, literally, so they escape mentally. They enter the scenes of the paintings on the walls. They go far away, to safety, in their imaginations. Anywhere But Here.

I *can* visualize a particular set of venetian blinds at the front of one of our homes. I heard Mom calling us kids to come kiss Daddy good-bye. He was going on one of his "business trips." I hid in the dark and peered through the slats of these blinds. My brother and sister were out front in the driveway, hugging Aris. Mom was calling for me, insistently. I stayed right there, motionless, silent. And I remember saying to myself, "I hope his plane crashes and he never comes back."

My parents got divorced when I was fourteen. That was one of the more jubilant days of my childhood. Aris would be out of the house. My days of living scared would be over. He came to the house to pick up some things and say his final farewell. He stared at my breasts, grinned that twisted gargoyle face, and said, "You're getting so big!" When he reached to fondle me, I ran to my room, locked the door, and lay pressed to the floor until I heard his car start. I ran to the front and watched the car round the far corner, full of hope and relief that he was forever out of my life.

Soon after he drove off that day, we got wind that he had to leave the country. People were looking for him. They came to our house, usually in the middle of the night. They were aggressive. He owed them money. He had done bad things to them. And we honestly didn't know where he was.

Years later I was in a Chicago bookstore when a man introduced himself and told me he and his wife had been down in the Honduras on vacation and his wife had stepped on a sea urchin walking along the shallow edge of the surf. Evidently, my father had sprinted out of his house and rushed down to them with a pair of dive booties. Aris told them that I wasn't going to be down there for a few days for my usual visit, so the wife could borrow my dive booties until then. I stayed quiet to learn as much as I could about Aris Nyad's secret life in the Honduras.

This man told me they went to dinner at Aris's house a few nights later. He was living with a beautiful young Latina. No surprise there. There were press clippings and photos of me all over the walls, from my marathon swimming days in the 1970s, and Aris was proud in telling them I visited him there all the time. I hadn't talked to him or received as much as a postcard since I was fourteen.

A few years after that bookstore incident, when I was thirty-four and living in Manhattan with my then partner Nina, we decided to throw a dinner party one night, even though neither of us had ever cooked anything. Nina took the day off work. We were going to sleep late, go out shopping for the dinner, get flowers, and spruce up our Upper West Side apartment for this fabulous soiree. We had about twelve close friends coming over.

That morning, before dawn, the buzzer rang. It had been twenty years since I had heard that accent, but it was unmistakable. It was Aris. He said, with those familiar rolling r's, "Darrling, it's your fazer. I am missing you so much." I pressed the button. The curls were now salt-and-pepper, the teeth still such a dazzling white you almost had to avert your eyes from the gleam. He of course came in bearing an exceptional bottle of champagne, extravagant flowers, fresh-baked croissants. He was in great shape, tanned and trim. When I told him that Nina was still sleeping, he was inappropriately excited by the fact that I was with a woman and bragged that one of the best times of his life had been living with two lesbians.

A leopard doesn't change his spots. This is my father. Entertaining, as always. Shady, as always.

Nina got up, and the three of us went out to shop for all the groceries. Aris cooked the meal, salmon with caper butter-lemon sauce. He went back to his hotel and returned, wearing the iconic Aris white dinner jacket. He was the life of the party, as he'd been the life of every party. He danced with all the women and chatted up a storm, in an array of languages, with every guest. Whereas a normal successful evening of this sort would wind down around midnight, he kept us up till dawn, regaling us with his fictitious stories. The next day as our guests called to thank us for the evening, every single one of them used the phrase I had heard all through my childhood: "Your father is the most charismatic person I've ever met in my life." One said his work as a translator for the UN is fascinating—how impressive to be so facile with all those languages. The next said she realized Aris couldn't talk much about his work with the FBI but the hints he'd dropped revealed some of the things he was investigating, and he was obviously leading a devastatingly interesting life.

The only one not hoodwinked by Aris that night was my friend Candace, who reads palms as a hobby and by that time had perused hundreds. She read Aris's palm: the only one she had ever seen that had no indication of a conscience. Not even a faint trace.

That was the last time I saw or heard from Aris. On his way back to the Honduras, or wherever he was hiding out at that time, he saw my mother in Fort Lauderdale, and she put him up for the night in the back bedroom. She said they had a nice dinner and a nice chat, speaking in French, *comme toujours*. In the morning, Aris was to take a cab to the airport. My mother left the house a bit before he did for some appointment. She told Aris to just close the door—it would lock automatically—and wished him well, saying it was nice to see him. When she came home all her silver and all her jewelry were gone.

Even though I was often disappointed at my mother's weakness in not protecting me when I was young—not protecting all three of us, not even protecting herself—the truth is, she was very much in love with Aris. There was a lot of passion there and when she finally divorced him, it wasn't for her. It was for us. She may not have come to my aid, even when she suspected he was being inappropriate with me, and I was very troubled and deeply angry about that for decades. But in the end she did what was right for her children, even though it left her lonely.

People who haven't lived abuse can't fathom why wives don't simply leave abusive husbands, how children can speak lovingly of an abusive parent. But love and attachment are complex, nonlinear emotions. No day is black or white.

I'm now in my mid-sixties and one of the reasons I consider this the prime of my life is that I have come to positive perspectives on just about everything I've experienced, Aris included. Oh, I've always been envious of my friends with warm, loving, protective, decent human beings for fathers. Seeing Bonnie's father, Herbert, tall and strong and yet gentle and sensitive, envelop Bonnie in the warmest bear hug and tell her he loves her, I was mystified as to what that must feel like—that trust, that unconditional affection from a father. Same with Candace's father, Floyd. His blue eyes sparkled as they tracked Candace crossing a room. What would that be, to experience that kind of abiding devotion from a father?

I'll never know, but through the years I've evolved and dropped my survival suit of steel and now, weeding out the good from the bad, I choose to look back on that conscienceless bastard for his outlandish and engaging spirit as well. That's part of our growth, isn't it? Our opportunity to rework our old stories and somehow find the worthwhile in what at one point rendered our days distressed and traumatic.

No matter what other inner journeys I've traveled, my perception of myself as champion, as read to me from the bold black and white of the dictionary at such an impressionable age, has superseded all the rest. And for that, along with considering sleep overrated, I can thank Aris.

FOUR

Lucy

My mom Lucy would stand at the door to say good night when I was a child. I wanted her to come in and cuddle with me, read to me. But she stood her distance, exactly as she stood in an old photograph of herself as a child, peering around a corner, shy. She called to me each night, in her soft melodic voice: *"Dors bien, chérie."* (Sleep well, darling.) And I would call back to her: *"Dors bien, Maman."*

Today, my mom gone since 2007, I have nothing but tender feelings. A delicate little personal urn of her ashes sits on my desk and the inscription on the brass rim reads *"Dors bien, Maman."* The regrets of her not being bolder, more engaged, coming right to my bed and plopping up against the pillows, are gone. Now all the memories are gentle and make me sigh, her voice wafting back to me as tenderhearted French poetry, not cold, timid fear. And there were, after all, snuggling times. She would wrap me in a fluffy towel and hold me to her chest on a lounge chair at our beach club. She read me the tales of Babar the elephant, in French, and to this day I melt when I see an illustration of that magical Babar in his green suit. In our youth we want our parents to be more, or different, and later, with the wisdom of age, we come to appreciate who they were and what they did for us. In my maturity, I've found myself awash with Lucy's sweetness. And the more I've understood her own journey, I've come to forgive her shortcomings as a mother, especially and glaringly her inability to protect me from childhood sexual abuse.

Lucy Winslow Curtis was born in New York City in 1925, daughter of a wealthy, erudite man of society: businessman, artist, and college professor George Warrington Curtis, age seventy-one. Her mother was a young show dancer and gold digger, Jeanette, age twenty-one. The Curtis family had come from a century-old successful clan of New Yorkers, starting back in the early 1800s with the first Lucy Winslow, one of the first female physicians in Manhattan. (My mother was named after her and I, in turn, also have the middle name Winslow.) This forebear Lucy evidently invented a soothing syrup for babies, long before such products were regulated. The syrup was laced with a pacifying ingredient, and it was the consumer product, the rage, of its time, catching lightning in a bottle when Dr. Winslow's husband, Jeremiah Curtis, threw his marketing skills into it.

Broadway playbills carried ads for Mrs. Winslow's Soothing Syrup. Mark Twain at the time even put his dry wit to wink at adults taking swigs of the stuff. Blowup posters for the product were pasted onto horse carriage stops.

I was to learn most of this eccentric family history later in my life. Even my mother knew only the bare bones of it, but Candace has found for me on eBay one of those posters, as well as a beautiful, slender, azure-blue bottle of the syrup that was dug up in a New Orleans excavation in 1862. The bottle catches my eye on my desk every day, right next to Lucy's elegant urn.

It's quite the American business story, that this brilliant nineteenth-century marketing campaign catapulted this product into a megahit that made the Curtis family wildly well-to-do. "Is your baby keeping you up all night? Mrs. Winslow's Soothing Syrup will guarantee you a night out dancing with your husband!"

By the turn of the twentieth century, they had a four-story home on the corner of Fifth Avenue and Fifty-second Street in Manhattan, with stables across the street, on the west side of Fifth. Today, these would be properties of staggering value. If I ever decide to pursue the genealogy of the Curtis tree, the first thing I'd want to know is what idiot ever sold those parcels!

They also had a stunning mansion out in tony Southampton, near the Jackie Bouvier Kennedy family's fabled manor, Grey Gardens. I've seen pictures of that Curtis home. Oh my.

The lore of Mom's parents is sketchy, but the story goes that this young dancer had a baby in 1925. She had this older gentleman of a husband and all of Manhattan at her fingertips. Scuttlebutt has it that George was ill with pneumonia in the winter and his windows were suspiciously left wide open. However it transpired, Lucy's father George died when she was still just a baby.

The ink on Jeanette's inheritance papers had barely dried when little Lucy was packed up and sent to live in France with George's younger brother Atherton, sixty-eight.

Atherton was an expat in Paris, having moved there as a young man, and married to a Danish woman named Ingeborg. It was arranged. They would adopt little Lucy.

I have a diary of Atherton's from those days. He was an art collector, mainly of Egyptian artifacts. As a matter of fact, his collection was eventually donated to the Louvre. I have seen his name under glass there many times, always wishing I could have known him. Atherton and Ingeborg were patrons of the arts, lived next door to Gertrude Stein and Alice Toklas on Rue Notre Dame des Champs, and had soirees where the likes of Gauguin, Matisse, F. Scott Fitzgerald, and Zelda dropped by for cultured conversation.

Atherton's diary is mostly impersonal, but one entry does allow insight into the delight these two older parents, who had never had their own children, enjoyed in raising Lucy: "I came around the corner and there was little Lucy, holding the bars of her crib, taking her first steps! What joy!"

Mom talked often of Atherton and Ingeborg in loving tones. She was grateful for the French immersion, too—the language, the literature, the culture. But she missed having her own mother. Though too young when first sent to France to remember her mother, Lucy suffered deeply the sting from being abandoned by her. Stoic as she and her entire generation were about loss and hardship, it nevertheless troubled her all her life.

Atherton's diary reports that, starting at about age five and through to age fifteen, Lucy would write her mother in New York once a month, like clockwork. At first, each carefully written missive came back from Jeanette unopened, with a note to Atherton telling him she had said good-bye to Lucy and did not want her letters. Later on, Mom's mother simply didn't respond at all.

The Nazi occupation stunned Paris when mom was fifteen. Atherton and Ingeborg were too old, then in their mid-eighties, to leave France, but they worried for Lucy and sent her back to America. Here she was, completely alone, without her parents, without a mother to telegraph in the States. She banded with a group of French, American, and Spanish adults and children who made their way down through France, across the Pyrenees, into Spain, then Portugal, and somehow onto a boat bound for New York.

She found a few distant relatives who were very kind to her. And she found her mother.

Jeanette's apartment was on the East Side of Manhattan somewhere. When Lucy knocked and announced herself, her mother never even opened the door, not a crack. My mother said she wasn't looking for money or even a place to live. She simply wanted some guidance in this new city, this new life. Her mother, through that cold closed door, told her she gave her up a long time ago, there was a reason she had never answered any of her letters all these years, and she didn't want to have anything to do with her.

Mom let go of her family roots after that bitter experience. We grew up knowing virtually nothing about her parents or grandparents. But when I went up to the Columbia University pool for a photo shoot after swimming around Manhattan in my mid-twenties, I was struck by a photograph on the wall above the century-old original mosaic-tiled pool. There before the photographer arrived, I was strolling around the pool, fountains spitting into the center from each corner, looking at images of the old-time swimmers of the university, back at the turn of the twentieth century. That's when men wore the full-body swim-suits, parted their hair in the middle, and stood with arms folded strong across their chests. I read about this one and that one, and then came to a handsome fellow named George Warrington Curtis. My heart stood still for a moment. That was my mother's father's name. Could it be? The caption said that George was captain of the Columbia swimming and track teams and he was the first person ever to swim across Long Island Sound. Mom's father, a maverick swimmer! For someone with zero ties to family roots, Thanksgiving dinners always just Mom and us three kids, no aunts or uncles or cousins, this was an eye-popping revelation. I could picture a grandfather. And I discovered there was distance swimming in my genes.

But when Mom first came over from France, so badly wanting to connect with her mother, she had scant knowledge of her birth family and later had very little to pass on to us. She was left to fend for herself. Only fifteen. No real skills. She took a job as an au pair girl to a family in Dobbs Ferry, just a few miles north of the city. They had three girls and wanted Mom to teach them all proper French. (I spoke in Dobbs Ferry, at the Masters prep school, decades later, and members of that family remembered Lucy joining their home, with her impeccable accent and her enchanting tales of Paris.)

Those first years in New York, never again to see the aunt and uncle who raised her, Lucy was desperate for security and attachment and pretty much married the first man she dated, William Lent Sneed, a no-good from Park Avenue who skipped town with the impending birth of her first child, me. Mom was alone in the hospital, alone back at the apartment with me for a few days, maybe a few weeks? When Bill dragged in, he evidently went over to my crib and exclaimed, "Shit, she has brown eyes?"

Three years later, just before the birth of my brother, Bill again went off on some morphine-and-alcohol binge, and his return this time was the endgame.

He sees his son, my brother, Bill, and has a worse reaction to his brown eyes than he did to mine. "A son with brown eyes? No, that's too much."

Apparently Sneed was a worthless wretch, useless as a husband, worse as a father, and she wanted him gone for good. Mom gave him thirty minutes to pack and made him promise he would never again contact us. Her first business was to change our names legally and we never knew he existed until into adulthood, when it no longer mattered.

Mom moved to Palm Beach, Florida, to make a new start. She was sitting on the beach with me and baby Bill one day when a movie-star specimen—black curls and dark olive skin—approached with a thick accent, which led to talk of foreign shores and soon they were speaking French.

Mom and this Aristotle Zanith Nyad character did have French in common. And dancing. And the high life. The next couple of years took us from Palm Beach back to New York City, with summers at a grand lakeside property in New Hampshire. And when I was five, Lucy and Aris brought my little sister Liza home to that summer getaway. Through those childhood years, until my early twenties, I never had reason to question that Aris was my birth father, nor that Liza was my full-blooded sister. People write stories about me, calling Aris my stepfather, but the truth is, I never had a "stepfather." Aris was my father.

I distinctly remember two major conversations with my mother when I was home on breaks during college.

First was my coming out. We went to a French restaurant, which was always fun for us, to carry on in French all night. I let the whole meal slide by before getting up my nerve. Finally, I told her: I was gay and had a girlfriend. Mom was unflappable. Totally cool. She prided herself on having grown up in sophisticated Paris, far from the bourgeois, puritanical attitudes of America. She jauntily regaled me with stories of hanging out with Gertrude Stein and Alice Toklas. We were like best friends that night. We rode home in such a good mood, the two of us.

A mere twenty-four hours later, my college girlfriend came over to pick me up. We were giddy with Mom's thorough acceptance, so she wanted to meet Lucy. I was in the bathroom brushing my teeth when I heard a high-pitched, high-volume ruckus out front. I ran out, horrified to find Mom at the front door screaming obscenities, followed by "You pervert! You're not turning my daughter into a lesbian!"

My girlfriend went sprinting down the street, without the rental car she had arrived in.

Apparently, my coming out to my mom hadn't gone down as smoothly as our first conversation had indicated. Slowly but surely, though, Mom found peace with the gay factor. Honestly, I think her Parisian side more hoped that I would dress beautifully and wear the right shade of lipstick than worried about my sexuality. When we traveled together,

Lucy dressed to the nines in haute couture suit, hat, and gloves, she was horrified to associate with me in jeans and sneakers.

As for me, being gay was never a struggle. Coming out at twenty-one, the relief of finally knowing why I wasn't interested in boys, set me free. It happened in one instant, literally. I went to a party, oblivious to even the possibility of a gay world. I had read George Sand novels and used to imitate those later Parisian women of the 1920s and lock my bedroom door in high school and dress like a sleek, dapper Frenchwoman, out about town in drag. I also rescued a blue-eyed doll my sister had thrown out. I'd stand her on my dresser, play Roy Orbison records and we'd slow dance for hours.

But all that was fantasy. This night, at this party when I was twenty-one, I was slow dancing with a real woman for the first time. And I never looked back.

I never thought I needed a big coming-out announcement. From that first dance, I was simply, entirely comfortable in my gay sexuality. Colleagues told me years later that my broadcasting career at ABC Sports would have gone much further had I been straight—or at least pretended to be. That never bothered me, either. I could never be happy, wildly successful or otherwise, being anything other than my true self.

The second college-era conversation we had was the reveal that she had had two husbands and that Aris was not my father by blood. Mom and I put on our pajamas, snuggled into our respective corners on the couch, and watched a *Perry Mason* episode we must have seen a dozen times over the years. Never mind—we both thrilled to the black-and-white scenes of Los Angeles, the sound of car tires on a gravel driveway, Paul Drake's houndstooth jackets, Perry's courtroom shenanigans. Then Mom told me the mystery she had kept from me.

I was born Diana Winslow Sneed. What? Can you imagine? Aris may have been a rogue, a liar, and a deviant. But at the very least I got from him the very cool name Nyad. (Today I'm listed in all those books where people live out the meaning of their names, a phenomenon referred to by the term "aptonym.")

Nyad—naiad, nymph of the sea, girl or woman champion swimmer—may not have been my birth name after all, but it had been my name all my life. And it was the perfect name.

Forget about me. Let's consider the last two times my mother saw her two ex-husbands: One packed and walked out the door in half an hour. The other robbed her of all her jewelry and silverware.

So it turns out that both of my fathers were neither husband nor parent prizewinners. But my mother actually was a rare treasure. Classy. Cultured. Genuine. A great listener. A quiet person of deep feelings. Ready for action and adventure at any given moment. Not a lazy bone in her body.

To understate it radically, it was heartbreaking later on to see her revert to childlike ways in the throes of Alzheimer's. But at the same time, those last eight years of her life, after Liza and I had moved her to California to be with us, Lucy and I found and lived out the deep tenderness we had always harbored for each other. All the defenses and unspoken anger sloughed away on both our sides. Now there was only love. And forgiveness. Again, on both sides.

Those last years of Lucy's, once she was slowed and confused with dementia, Mom would say to me every once in a while, "I was the worst mother in the world, wasn't I?" And I'd pooh-pooh that notion right away: "Mom, you were the best mother in the world." But we both knew just what she was talking about. In her innocent, incapable state, she was trying to apologize for not protecting me. And the more I learned about her life, and her own childhood abandonment issues, the easier it became to accept her apology.

FIVE

Thirst for Commitment

It wasn't too long after Aris showed me my name in the dictionary that my elementary school geography teacher, a former Olympic swimmer, promised that any kid who came out for the swim team would get an A in geography.

I was poolside the next day. He told us all to swim up and down for a few minutes, so he could get an idea of just what he had to work with. After several laps, I stopped and found him standing above my lane. "Hey, kid, what's your name again?"

"NYAD!" I proclaimed.

"Nyad, you're going to be the best swimmer in the world."

Well, this coach turned out to be very similar to Aris, in terms of hyperbole and fire. After Aris, he was likely the second most charismatic character you'd ever meet. It's not that he recognized some premier talent in me. But he did sense a kid who was thirsty for commitment. From those early childhood days—that first day in the pool at age ten, all the way through high school—I had a blowup poster on the back of my door that read "A diamond is a lump of coal that stuck with it." Perseverance was always what I valued most.

By age ten I also felt the pressure of the clock ticking. My teacher at the time had us all write an essay about what we wanted to do when we grew up. Years later, when I first gained some notoriety as a distance swimmer, in my twenties, Mrs. Farr sent me my little essay, which she had kept all those years. The thrust of it was that I had evidently discovered my grandparents had died in their early to mid-eighties, one in his early seventies, and I seemed to be very concerned that I then only had about seventy years to go, perhaps only sixty. While most ten-year-olds can't imagine being eleven, I was fixated on the alarming speed of the passing days. There was too much to do, too many things to become, not enough time.

I think that choking unease about the brevity of life was somewhat behind my being attracted to the predawn wake-up call for swimming. I thrived on the superior feeling of being awake when most of the world was still sleeping. The progression to fanatic was swift. Even as a ten-year-old, I was getting up at four-thirty every morning, 365 days a year, no alarm clock needed. A thousand sit-ups and fifty chin-ups every day. Never 999, never 49. It wasn't long before I was the best backstroker in the state of Florida and competing around the country in national championships. Truth be told, I was never a gifted, fast-twitch sprinter at an überelite level. It wouldn't be until my introduction to open-water swimming, in my twenties, that I'd light onto my true genetic talent. But the vision of standing on the Olympic podium, bowing my head to receive a medal for the United States of America, provided a high that gave me purpose through those somewhat dark, troubled childhood and teen years.

Along with the focus and the confidence that comes with discipline, I found refuge in the pool. I left the house before dawn. And practicing four hours a day—in the pool, in the weight room, before and after school hours—brought me home after dinner hour. Swimming connoted safety to me.

And there was the coach. I was now lucky to have what seemed to me a real father. Gregarious and likable, he was also caring and involved in my life. Each month when report cards were issued, coach would have me sit with him in the bleachers. We would review every grade; he would ask me about which classes I enjoyed most, which teachers inspired me. He told me I could be anything I chose in this world, that I was smart and funny and a leader. I trusted coach as I had never trusted an adult before.

Age twelve. One night I arrived home to find Aris pacing back and forth, agitated.

"Now you arre fanatic. Yourr mozher packs yourr eyes in ice at night. You don't know yourr brozher and sister anymorre. You don't go to churrch. You are not eating home. You lock yourr door for hours to do zese crazy exercises. Even Chrristmas morrning, you arre getting up four-zirty for ze swimming. Yourr muscles are like football player. Darrling, yourr HAIRR IS GRREEN!"

"That's right, Dad. I am a fanatic. That's what it takes to get ahead in life. Trust me, I am going to be a world champion, and being a fanatic is how I'm going to get there. And I'm glad we had this little talk, Dad. I don't think you understand me. When, for instance, I say I'm going to bed at eight-thirty, I mean the whole family needs to go to bed at eight-thirty! You get it, Dad?"

"Oh, I do. I get you. I rreally call you in to tell you your mozher and I . . . well, your mozher and I are verry . . . verry affraid of you. Today we want to give you ze key to ze house and wish you luck becauze we just cannot live like zis anymorre."

Imagine. The despot, the perpetrator who terrified me, he and my mother were afraid of me!

My mother was both proud of and mystified by my discipline. But she never was one of those proverbial Little League moms who park their cars facing the driving range at night so their kid can take a thousand swings with the beams from the car headlights. Swimming was my thing.

Age fourteen. The big state championships were at our school that summer. I went over to coach's house for an afternoon nap before the evening finals. We swimmers were all part of coach's family. We babysat his kids, played touch football on the beach on Sundays, held poker games over at his house on weekend afternoons.

It was violent. It was shocking. It was humiliating.

He came into the bedroom, pounced on top of me, and ripped my bathing suit down. His voice was husky; he was breathing heavily. He was drooling. He grabbed my breasts hard and molested them violently. He tried to enter me, but I was locked tight. My legs wouldn't spread, even though he begged me to let him in. My entire body was in a vise grip. My legs were flexed like steel, frozen tight together. My arms were locked likewise down by my sides. My breath was caught high up near my throat. I was in a physiological and mental state of shock. In just a few minutes, he ejaculated onto my belly area and left the room as quickly as he'd entered. I vomited on the floor and then, shaking, cleaned up and got dressed. I had to ride in the car alone with him back to school. Usually very chatty, a couple of magpies, on this ride, not a word was spoken. I stared through the windshield, numb. I don't think I blinked the whole way. All systems—emotions, thoughts, body—shut down.

I lost my race that night, unheard of at that point, at the state level. The kids on my team thought I was coming down with the flu. We won the team state trophy and at the end of the meet, my teammates were on the other side of the pool, slipping on their sweats and getting ready to go out for pizza and Cokes. Usually, I would have been in the middle of the action, the leader of the cheers. But so much changed in terms of my dynamics within the team that night. I swam to the bottom of the diving well, sobbed silent, bitter tears, and screamed at the top of my lungs, "This is NOT going to ruin my life!"

I do believe that moment, that night, sixteen feet underwater in my high school pool, was when I turned my back forever on the concept of destiny. Being molested wasn't my fate. This was the moment I decided being a champion wasn't my destiny, either. Hard work and focus and will would shape my future. Nothing was meant to be.

I didn't tell anybody. The shame was heavy indeed. I certainly couldn't tell my mom. She had already made it clear, in not coming to my rescue when I was touched inappropriately by my father, that she would not be there for me. The days of the coach reading my report card were over. My teenage inner world was in turmoil.

I was no longer a shining star. I was a pair of breasts and a vagina. The thrill of being the first one to swim practice, and the last to leave, was over, too. I was afraid to be caught alone with him. My workhorse ethic was stifled out of fear. I was paranoid that my teammates knew. I became more reserved around them, a repression of my usual outgoing personality. I became fixated on somehow slicing my breasts off. In retrospect, that trauma, at age fourteen, was when I became a tough little soldier. I hid my vulnerabilities. I steeled myself.

That first incident at coach's house was quick and violent. Then the covert molestation started. I have since, of course, learned that this pattern is common, and I now understand how even strong-minded, strong-bodied teenagers (even those who consider themselves champions) feel they have no other choice but to obey their fathers, stepfathers, coaches, teachers, or preachers who molest them. As much as I dreaded those days—and I would go so far as to say I felt terrorized—when he would tell me to meet him after practice, I also somehow felt I was the chosen one. He told me he loved me so very much, that he was an adult and had needs, that I would understand some day. He told me we shared something very rare, that nobody else would comprehend it, that nobody else could ever know about it. It was our special secret. He told me I would never be a champion if anybody found out. I would be expelled from school if anybody found out. Our special secret.

One spring day, the top swimmers on our team were getting ready to leave for the nationals, in Oklahoma. Our high school was geared toward elite swimming, and many on the team were national-caliber athletes. The afternoon workout was light. We were all tapering, backing off tiring workouts, resting to prep ourselves into top sprint mode for the big meet. Those of us traveling the next day were supposed to go into coach's office, one at a time every fifteen minutes or so, to review each game plan for the big meet. My turn came. I didn't expect a molesting session. Those always happened off campus. He would take me on a ride in his car or to the motel down the street. His office was adjacent to the pool and the locker rooms. I toweled off and headed in for my turn to talk about my nationals. I was feeling important. This was ego time. I was one of the elite of my school, of my team, going to talk to my coach about my taper, which events I'd swim in Oklahoma. I was going to get a B_{12} shot and talk about what I should eat for dinner that night. This was my meeting about my life, my young, important life.

I sat in the chair across from his desk and I started in about not feeling I was tapered enough and needing some rest, but I didn't get far. His voice got husky and my body tensed because I recognized that voice.

He leaped around the desk and positioned himself behind my chair. He forced his hands down my bathing suit and told me it was absurd, this talk about the nationals. All that mattered were these breasts of mine. He was breathing heavily in my ear, telling me I would never be a great swimmer because my breasts were too big for that. Once again, I was paralyzed, frozen with fear, my breath again caught high up in my chest. In a quick, deft move, he dragged me the few feet into the little bathroom of his office and into the shower stall. I had certainly noticed the single mattress in that stall before but had never imagined what he used it for. It was standing vertically in the stall, leaning against the back wall. He pushed me up against it, yanked down my suit, and tried to enter me. As was my automatic, terrified response, I went into that clenched, steely flex, legs tight together, arms pinned by my sides. He begged me to open up, to let him in. I didn't speak. I breathed in short, spurting gasps. I waited until he finished pumping outside me, his semen again on my stomach. It was probably two or three minutes and he was done. He went back into his office and called out the door for the next swimmer to come on in. I hurriedly pulled up my suit and sheepishly went out to the curb to wait for my mom to pick me up. I remember sitting on that curb, hating my life, hating myself. Being me, and certainly being female, was hell on Earth. I wasn't important. I was worthless.

It's only been very recently that I've come to peace—even pride—about my breasts. I spent some forty years bolting awake from nightmares in which my breasts were being knifed off. Worse, I considered having my breasts surgically removed. Thank goodness I didn't mutilate my beautiful body and allow that pig to forever harm me. Trust me, I have never wasted much time wallowing in sadness over the sexual abuse of my youth. I have always been keenly aware that literally millions suffer far worse than I ever did. Yet I can only live my own life. This is my personal saga and the facts speak their own volumes.

A kid on our team drowned holding his breath underwater in his apartment pool, trying to increase his lung capacity and improve his performance level. Our whole team went to the funeral. Coach wailed throughout the service, much louder and more dramatically than even the boy's mother. The entire synagogue was taken aback. I had gone to the service with a few of the girls on my team, but when we were outside, coach came to me in tears and said that he really needed me that day. My friends went off together. I remember looking at their backs as they walked their way, angry that being a normal teenager was no longer an option for me. There I was, alone, once again hostage. I went with him to an apartment of a friend of his. It was as it always was. I was paralyzed with fear. He couldn't penetrate my steel-stiff body. I was awash with shame. And, as always, I was silent in my shame.

I fought the tears throughout those teenage molestations. Tears of rage were just under the surface; I felt totally powerless to stop what was happening to me. Tears of sorrow also held back, for the innocence stolen from me.

The imprint of sexual abuse on a child's soul is indelible. It's complicated. How could I be at once this indomitable spirit, even a defiant nonconformist, and yet unable to defend myself against this predator? That question haunted me much of my life, until about my mid-fifties. Why didn't I throw him up against a wall and go tell my mother or the school principal? The little soldier tightened her blinders and marched on.

Looking back now, I also think I had a sense of embarrassment at being a privileged kid. I remember not wanting to own up to going to a private school, when I'd meet kids from public schools in town. I would see Chris Evert practicing for hours at the public tennis courts and the proletarian in me admired, even envied, her working-class roots. I had been impressed by the "Desiderata" poem, warning that it is dangerous to compare yourself, whether in terms of your joy or your pain, to others. I was aware of young people living in poverty and enduring much worse abuse than mine. I thought it would be ignoble of me to complain.

Junior year I contracted a heart disease called endocarditis, which required three months of strict bed rest. This was the time my sweet little sister Liza and I carved out a forever bond. To be immobile, to picture the other swimmers going through their paces, passing me by, made me temporarily insane. Liza, more than anybody, understood. She spent every waking minute she wasn't at school with me. I made a plan to study three subjects, one each month, while I was stuck in bed, and it was Liza who shuttled back and forth to the library to get me books. That was the start of my interest in the cosmos, and Liza helped me organize file cards to take notes on the wonders of the universe. And she made dinner fun. She'd bring our two plates to my room and we'd laugh and talk. Liza has been my teacher of empathy and compassion, then and now. Actually, I think Liza taught our mother quite a bit about nurturing as well. Those three months were the bedrock of sisterhood that has taken us now through fifty more years.

Throughout the rest of high school, the goal of the four-thirty a.m. daily routine was obscured by the routine itself. That focused discipline had saved me from home life when I was younger and Aris was still around, and it saved me from school social life as I got older. I didn't yet know I was gay and just assumed my noninterest in boys, dating, proms, stemmed from the coach trauma. And the discipline buoyed me from spiraling down due to the heinous acts by my coach. I might have been broken internally, but externally I was tough and strong. The Olympics were no longer reality for me. Not even a distant fantasy. It wasn't only the endocarditis. Realism comes into sharper focus as an athlete progresses. By ages sixteen and seventeen, it had become clear that I was a second-tier pool swimmer, not first-tier. The ocean, my domain of superiority, was still unknown to me. But I still grasped onto the regimen of a high-caliber athlete as if it were a life raft in a storm far out at sea.

As graduation and my sprint swimming career were coming to a close, looking back on it now, I suppose I was flat-out lost. My father, for all his magic and charisma, was a louse. My mother, who in later years became a beacon of gentle spirit to me, back then made me angry and frustrated me with her remote inability to engage and come to my defense. Then the coach, the one I'd turned to for primary parental guidance, betrayed me. I'd be heading off to college in the fall, but I didn't know why. There were no athletic scholarships for women, no elite athletic college programs for women. I acted bold and confident, cocky even, but inside I was a mess.

The Olympic Trials for the Mexico City Games came that August. I of course had no inkling that my glory days as an ocean swimmer lay in front of me. Even if the Olympics were by now a pipe dream, I didn't want my swimming career to be over. The perseverance I had drilled down for through those troubled years of my youth had given me both personal strength and solace. I wanted to make the trials.

It was my last 100-meter backstroke. The last hoorah, with an outside, desperate chance at the elite trials. Top three would go on to compete for a coveted spot on the Mexico City team. The other five would go on to the rest of our lives.

Walking down the pool deck toward that 100 meters I felt the weight of the world on my shoulders.

I'm in a daze, as if striding on slow automatic toward my execution. Is this the end of my days, my high, of commitment? What am I, if not a swimmer? I'm thinking about the four-thirty a.m. vaults out of bed, every single day for eight years. My brother's and sister's dreams swept aside because mine were so big. My parents. The coach. The sit-ups, the chin-ups. The unrelenting dedication. I hadn't even smoked pot in the high school parking lot. The sacrifices had been weighty.

I got an earful of ideology that night, a fable of sorts, told to me by a seventeen-year-old, a credo I have carried with me my entire life. I'm always curious about the seminal moments when people hear words of insight from a grandmother or some wise sage and they begin to build their value system. For me, perhaps ironically, the foundation of my life conviction came from a teenage girl, when I was still a teenager. Just at this crucial end of a chapter, when I urgently needed guidance and grounding, my teammate Suzanne shook me awake.

"Diana, you look like you're in a fog! The most important race of your life is in front of you and you're not razor-focused? What the heck's going on?"

I started in: the parents, the siblings, the practices, the sacrifices, et cetera, et cetera, et cetera.

"Stop it! Stop! Only a month ago, you had us all sit in the bleachers and you gave us that rousing speech about reaching for the untouchable star. You told us to envision that star and then to put that vision aside and get into the trenches and work. You're the one who told us how it works. You put discipline and drive into the minutes, the hours, the weeks, the months. Then one day you either touch your beautiful star or you come so darn close that you're up there playing in the heavens, in rarefied air. Diana! *You* have given us all that very speech time after time!

"Come on, now! This is no time for the grand perspective, for ruminating. Listen, we just saw that documentary on Billie Jean King, remember? When she gets to Wimbledon, she doesn't go over and look down the main draw board and say, 'Oh, yeah, if I meet her in the quarters, I've heard she's improved her second serve a lot.'

"No, when Billie Jean steps onto that grass, she's a cheetah on the hunt. She is oblivious as to who the chair umpire is or what the impending forecast is. Billie Jean doesn't play the match or the point or even the ball. She plays the fuzz on the ball. As the ball comes across the net, she sweeps her racquet back, and with all those thousands of practice strokes behind her she draws on her deep well of genetic talent and brushes a flawless backhand. If the ball happens to come back, there's Billie Jean at the net, cheetah on the hunt, pouncing on an overhead. Two weeks later, Billie Jean holds the Wimbledon trophy high, above her head. (In the end, Billie Jean King won that Wimbledon trophy an astounding twenty times!)

"Look. It's not as poetic as the fuzz of a tennis ball, but look at this half-moon sliver of your pinkie fingernail. And you know why I bring up this little sliver of nail? Because that's the distance this race of yours will be won and lost by tonight."

I need this girl at this moment. For this race. For my life at this fragile juncture. I am under her spell. The crowd fades away into virtual silence as the two of us stand on the deck, hands raised to eye level, and stare in a trance at our pinkie half-moons.

"Yeah, I see it."

"Okay. How long," she asks, "does it take you to swim the width of this sliver of a half-moon in the one-hundred-meter backstroke?"

I ponder that for a moment. "I don't know. I guess that would take a thousandth of a second."

"No it wouldn't!" Suzanne is adamant. "Do the math. It's going to take a lot less time than that!"

"Okay, okay. Let's say it will take one-thousandth of one-thousandth of a second."

"That's it! So why don't you march up to those blocks. Blast off with the powerful shoulders you've built over these eight years! Dig in with the heart that's unique to you! Swim the race that is your one-hundred-percent potential. And when you hit the wall, don't look up to see the results board. Close your eyes, close your fists, and say, 'I couldn't have done it a fingernail faster.' If you can say it, and mean it, I guarantee you it will be all right, no matter what happens. No regrets."

Two minutes later I'm at the blocks. I blast off with shoulders and heart and swim the most perfect race of my life. I hit the wall, close my eyes, close my fists, and I say it. Out loud, with passion. And I mean it. "I couldn't have done it a fingernail faster."

Eyes still closed, I take a deep breath, then look up to the board. I am sixth. I go over to shake hands with the three girls who are moving on. Then I head into the locker room, sure that a flood of tears will erupt—not because of that night's race, but from the abrupt end to eight years of pushing, eight years of believing. But instead, I stand tall in the shower, hot water cascading over my earned, carved shoulders.

It wasn't only that race I had thrown all my best self into. It was every sit-up. Every lap.

I never became an Olympian. I may have endured some adversity as a kid. But I had a clear life philosophy at a young age, still a teenager. I walked out of that locker room determined to tackle my future just that way, each day not a fingernail better. No regrets.

SIX

New York City

My first year of college was at Emory University, in Atlanta. A fine school, a fine city, but a low time in my life. Debutante belles were pledging sororities, and I was gay but didn't know it. My lifelong self-identity as an athlete was gone. I became a loner, which neither suited me nor made me happy. I parachuted out a fourth-story dormitory window in a desperate, immature attempt for attention. The aerodynamics research of the stunt ran thin and I can tell you that you need to go a lot higher than four stories for a chute to even flutter, much less open. I was asked to leave Emory the next day.

Talk about lost. The star student athlete is now wandering the streets of her hometown. I would leave the house at sunrise and walk all day long: to the beach, town to town along the beach, west to the edge of the Everglades, down toward Miami. My mom convinced me to get a job, save some money, and go to France for a study abroad program. I waitressed at Howard Johnson's, and it was so much fun at night when Mom and I would toss all my change onto the living room rug and make piles of quarters together. She would be excited if I had a big night.

On forays to my old high school pool, to get in a few laps with the new generation of superstars, when the coach could get me alone on the pool deck, his assault of filthy and misogynist words stunned me speechless. These are the words, and the ones equally heinous that he used to his utter glee in our former intimate settings, that have haunted my brain all my life. These are the hateful obscenities that I've lashed out at myself with at trigger moments throughout the years.

I was struck a couple of years ago by the confession of an esteemed MIT professor that many years post childhood he would scream at himself the vulgarities his father yelled at him when he locked him in a freezer as a boy. Even those of us strong and successful and together can be deeply wounded by the crimes committed against us in our youth.

Lake Forest College, outside Chicago, offered a terrific program in France, so I landed there next. It was perfect for me at the time, small and friendly. I kept very much to myself, but the professors were wonderfully engaging, and I was terribly excited about the six months I'd get to spend in France.

The school program was in Dijon, but I took the train up to Paris at every opportunity. I rode my bike through the forests and over the hills of the Monet-inspired countryside by day, read Jean-Paul Sartre and wrote in my journal by night.

Sartre actually guest-lectured at a class I sat in on at the Sorbonne. A thousand French students—most of them chain-smoking Gauloises throughout the lecture, and most on the French schedule of bathing once or twice a week—and we are hanging on every word. He strolls in, smoking himself, cigarette pinched between thumb and index finger, upside down. He doesn't speak for many minutes, just gazes up toward nowhere, deep in thought. We are enraptured. And finally he starts:

"Ah, oui, la vie, c'est étrange."

And he goes on for a couple of minutes about how he was almost hit by a bus that morning. But, he asks himself, was that some accidental occurrence or was it not part of his own set of life choices? Good stuff.

The day I drove into Manhattan in my lime-green Volkswagen bug for graduate school in comparative literature at New York University was the day my loner period abruptly ended.

I was home. I was born in New York City, spent early childhood there, and no matter how I fell in love with the ocean and the warm sun of Florida, I knew all along New York was in my blood. I belonged. The very first minute there I felt as if awakened from a long, drugged slumber. I barked out from a corner of Washington Square Park that I couldn't find a parking place and sold the VW for $500 cash. I found a postage-stamp-sized apartment in famous Greenwich Village, Bob Dylan and Joan Baez haunts at virtually every corner. Bette Midler would half–tap dance, half-walk her fluffy dogs in her super-high heels and call out to me as I jogged by: "Good morning, Muscles."

Reading Turgenev and Flaubert, comparing their writing and their times in late-nineteenth-century Russia and France, seemed a rich way to spend those days of my early twenties. To be young in Manhattan was a natural high.

It was during that time, my early twenties, that I flew to Detroit to go to a Laura Nyro concert with my old high school swimming buddy Suzanne, the "not a fingernail better" philosopher. We later became groupies, following her concert to concert, sometimes taking two-day LSD trips with her and her cronies.

What? An athlete and LSD? Yes, I upheld the banners of my generation. Vietnam War protests, Dylan mania, mind expansion. On one LSD trip we built a full-scale Volkswagen out of snow and ice. Interiors precise, odometer, stick shift, perfect contour of seats. Took us thirty hours. Performance art of sorts.

Back to the concert. We go for a drink beforehand and Suzanne is clearly intent on something. She reminds me that I used to tell her throughout high school, that I wanted desperately to share something with her but just couldn't. She has opened the floodgates now and I tell her every graphic detail. I weep. This is the first time I have ever told my wretched story.

She holds me. We cry long minutes together. Suzanne then says, "Well, hold on to your hat, because the same thing happened to me."

My brain swims for a second. What does she mean? She went through molestation during teenage years, too? I flashed on her father but rejected that image. Fred was the kindest man alive.

She takes a deep breath and starts in on her own saga of horror. The coach, our same coach, molested her, too. Same exact words. Pushed up against same standing mattress in same office bathroom. Same fear. Same humiliation. Same silence. We never make the concert. Wow.

Suzanne and I quickly ferreted out several other girl swimmers of our era who had been violated by this coach. (I am loath to use the honored word "coach" for this criminal. A good coach earns that title, by more than teaching the skill of the sport. A good coach is a mentor, duty-bound to sculpt a young person's character. I spit on this charlatan of a coach of mine and Suzanne's, and the others he violated.)

Mine is a long story, and it's the typical story of the epidemic. My coach was the patriarch of the town. As is often the case with these deviants, he was charismatic, a regular at good ol' boy poker games, friend of the town's prominent power citizens. Intermittently, Suzanne and I pursued justice against him for years, decades. He was fired from our high school after we returned to tell the principal what he'd done to us. With lawyers from all sides in the room, Suzanne's and my reports corroborated each other to the nth degree, in separate statements given in separate quarters, so the principal gave him half an hour to clear his office. The principal told us that school officials and parents had warned him of the coach's sexual deviance with students for years, and he had confronted him about it several times, but it was always denied and he had never been able to catch him firsthand.

My high school principal did fire the guy, but as again follows the standard course of the epidemic, he didn't want to sully his school's good name and thus didn't make the incidents public, even to the point of not sharing the reason for his firing with the university down the road that hired the coach next. That university fired him after several years of sexual abuse allegations. He became coach of the 1976 women's Olympic team and eventually was inducted into the International Swimming Hall of Fame. And through all these accolades, he continued, unscathed, generation after generation, to molest innocent young girls. I got a call from the Fort Lauderdale police in 2004, a good forty years after he had molested my group of girls, saying they had recent reports of accusations against him. The police tried to set up a sting call between Suzanne and him but that was a bust. When statutes of limitations came into play, it was clear that Suzanne and I and the others were never going to wield the power to formally prosecute him.

The coach died just last year, never having made an apology to any of us, never having suffered any formal punishment. In 2004, at a Hall of Fame evening where I was honored, a minimum of four hundred people approached me to ask when something was going to be done about this guy. After the '76 Games, the managing editor of *Sports Illustrated* remarked to me that everybody in the swimming world knew of this coach's sex crimes and would shake their heads that he got away with it for so long. But it was largely that same group from the swimming world who brushed his misconduct (and that of others) under the rug. Many of those cases are finally coming to justice now.

Sexual abuse of young people by supposed leaders they trust is indeed an epidemic and not just in the United States. It's going on in egregious numbers right now as I write this, in every suburban neighborhood, on every urban corner.

The statistic du jour is that one in every four girls in our country, and one in every six boys, is sexually molested by someone they know by the age of eighteen. What's the real number, then? Those are only the few brave enough to speak up.

During my twenties, the first step toward my own personal healing came with the birth of my beautiful nephew, Tim (now in his mid-thirties and the producer and director of the documentary of my Cuba journey, *The Other Shore*). I'll never forget the first day I held his chubby newborn body. My heart melted, and that was when I opened my eyes to the concept that the male of the species in general is not evil. It was Tim, with his exuberant playfulness, his wild joy when I would come for visits of nonstop wrestling, who taught me that boys, individual by individual, can be trusted. Our favorite game was Eat the Couch, which goes like this: We chase each other, roughhouse with unbridled ferocity, and then I get his face square to the couch cushion and press him there for a few bounces, in rhythm with the chant "Eat the Couch! Eat the Couch!" Of course, when puberty hit and he had a chance to win and make me eat the couch, game over. Tim is deep in my heart forever, a son of sorts, our closeness forged at first by gleeful wrestling, sealed all these years later by his becoming a man of both strength and compassion, a virile man with a profound respect for women.

My second step toward healing, though I didn't recognize it as such at the time, came when swimming popped back into my life.

It took me by surprise, but I was once again immersed, this time not in a pool but in open water. I hadn't swum since high school. I didn't miss all those mind-numbing laps, and I had taken up running, the perfect combination of fitness and exploration. I ran daily, sometimes over the George Washington Bridge and up the historic Hudson River, or through the ghost town of Wall Street on a Sunday morning, or over the Brooklyn Bridge and out to the Coney Island Ferris wheel.

But a friend started telling me about the organized sport of marathon swimming, and my curiosity was piqued. The Earth is almost three-quarters water, and these people stood barefoot on many of those shores, sprinted into the water at the sound of the gun, and raced each other to the other side. My friend had enticed me by saying, "These swims mean long hours, often cold waters, usually also quite rough seas. There's a touch of masochism required and that's why, Diana, I believe the sport is going to appeal to you."

I found myself standing on the shore of a very cold Canadian lake, having just been greased down with ten pounds of wool fat, lanolin, a unique experience unto itself. The substance would provide a not very effective layer of insulation from the cold for the first hour or so, until it wore off. I'd known the sport was the rare sort in which men and women compete directly against each other, but to now see the muscular Egyptians greasing down to my left, the lanky yet also muscular Argentines greasing to my right, it hit me for the first time that those first strokes were going to be a slugfest. The best woman open-water swimmer of the time, Judith de Nijs, a Dutchwoman who stood at six feet tall and weighed 185 pounds—appearing to me more of a tight end than a swimmer—took this moment about a minute before the start of the race to introduce herself. She came swaggering over. Of course, the beach didn't tremble with each of her heavy strides. It just seemed that way. She poked her index finger into the grease on my chest with every syllable. I was so intimidated, I just stood there and took it; I had a bruise the size of a quarter for a month. "I hear you're very good svimmer," she said. "Vell, you're not going to beat me!" And when she swaggered off, I will tell you that the beach actually did tremble with each thud of her legs.

I reached around to my trainer and said, "These people are animals. I'm not going in." Then the gun sounded, and I ran down to the water, swearing in Arabic with all the Egyptians—and thus my marathon swimming career began.

There was little prize money, but expenses were paid, and I loved swimming in a wide variety of our planet's beautiful lakes, rivers, and oceans. The swims ranged from ten to twenty-five miles. This colorful cast of burly marathoners and skinny me stroked from the Isle of Capri across the Bay of Naples in Italian springtime, down the warm-water coast of Mar del Plata in Argentina during their February summers, across the chilly lakes of Quebec in July. Solo swims also have long been part of the history of the sport, and my first was frigid Lake Ontario, 1974. Eighteen hours, twenty minutes. I didn't like it. But I did it.

Training for Lake Ontario at a swim camp four hours north of Toronto, I had the chance to swim a few weeks for the renowned University of Indiana swim coach Jim Counsilman, Mark Spitz's coach. Coach Counsilman told me I was born for open-water swimming; he said I had the perfect stroke for gliding long distances. This was my element. I actually loved traveling by freestyle. A friend would paddle a canoe next to me and we'd go ten miles through the network of lakes to a little town, stop for a drink, get back in, and swim the idyllic lakes back to camp. I also loved the interior dialogue during those hours of solitude. With the world shut out—except for glimpses of the shimmering aspen leaves and reflections of boathouses on the lake's pristine surface—the rhythmic slapping of my hands, the distorted sound of my breath every second, put me into a state of self-hypnosis. I liked observing the mind's workings, the intellectual left brain watching the right creative brain, thoughts of the world at large and my own life's circumstances crisscrossing each other in rich visual tapestries.

Actually, the only time I came desperately close to drowning was training in Lake Ontario. I had put in a few hours one day but hadn't realized the wind had blown hard off shore all night. The next morning a short swim was slated, no need for an escort boat, to just loosen up a bit before a long flight that day to Europe for some races. I took a leap off a high bluff and went into shock the instant I hit the water. By the time I surfaced from the deep plunge, my body was fully numb. I turned to face the shore and wasn't far, maybe only forty meters. But panic set in when I couldn't move my arms. I was trying to kick but that action stopped as well. I was going under. My mouth was at the surface and I saw a man yelling frantically from up on the bluff. He was signaling a fishing boat to go rescue me. When the man reached over the gunnels to grab me under the arms and haul me up onto their deck, the heat of his hands on my frozen skin literally burned the flesh. The long scars at the front of my shoulders took more than twenty years to fade. I remember the helpless distress, only a few breaths from going under.

Years later, on the swim all the way across Lake Ontario, from Toronto to Niagara-on-the-Lake, cold was again the issue. At the end of those frigid eighteen hours, my core body temperature was too low. I was taken to a Toronto hospital, wrapped in a Mylar blanket, and put in a corner of the emergency room while my friends went to sign me in. Just then a young man was wheeled in on a gurney. He was in pain. Grimacing and calling out in agony, he was parked right next to me while his people went to get him help, our faces just a foot apart. Perhaps to keep his mind off his pain, he asked why I was there. Shivering uncontrollably, I told him I had just spent about twenty hours swimming across Lake Ontario. This news seemed to shock him out of his misery for a moment: "Why the hell did you do that?"

So we got to chatting. It turned out he'd been injured in a boat race on the lake that day. We stayed in touch, and I discovered he had broken his pelvis, his collarbone, his jaw, and suffered multiple internal injuries. I had every reason to turn the same question back on him. But it was interesting, our short exchange in the ER, in that it was the first time I voiced and comprehended what it was that drew me to the seemingly masochistic sport of long-distance swimming.

First, he told me that he thrilled to the adrenaline rush of holding the wheel, a fraction of an inch error at those speeds meaning serious consequences. He felt wide awake, alert to a state of giddiness, and wished he could re-create those sensations beyond his sport.

I told him the tremendous duress my sport thrust onto both body and mind presented a microcosm of the peaks and valleys of life itself. The swings up and down, during a long day at sea, brought into view all the physical and emotional terrain we travel on life's journey. One hour you're strong and moving effortlessly across the surface. The next you're in crisis and digging deep to stay in it. You're low. You're on empty. If you can somehow tap down to the depth of your drive, take one baby step, then another, you are soon climbing back up the next slope of the next mountain. You're responsible for yourself in the water—on your own, independent, never allowed out onto your escort boat, or even allowed to touch the boat—but your team is there to assist you when you're in trouble and lose your way. Again, just like life. And when you reach the other shore, the pride of not giving up is fuel for your life out of the water.

There were races where other swimmers would throw in the towel. And when I'd glance up and see them motoring by me, wrapped in a comfy blanket, on their way to a hot bath, I would first think, "Ooh, that blanket looks good." But I'd grit my teeth with a resolution not to quit. I admit I threw in the towel myself a couple of times. That down feeling, quitting, was far worse than suffering it out to the end, because that decision to quit haunts you and bleeds over into your outlook on everything else, just as not quitting buoys you for all else.

The young man was prepped for surgery. I was slid into a body-warming oven. And we took our separate paths toward bringing what we each valued from our sports into our daily lives. He was looking for adrenaline, every way, every day. I was looking to be a person who never, ever gives up.

SEVEN

Manhattan Island Swim: Game Changer

I had spent half of 1975, as I had the previous five years, on the competitive marathon swimming circuit.

When I came back to New York City that fall, still working on the degree in comparative literature, a friend asked why I was gallivanting all over the globe to these somewhat remote waters when the most famous island in the world was right here: Manhattan.

A little research told the stories of a handful of men who had swum all the way around, in the early 1900s, but it hadn't been done since 1927, except in stages of getting out of the water and back in. I got excited about it. The Coast Guard helped me analyze the tide charts. Their advice was to start in the East River, at the mayor's mansion, at slack tide, and swim north into the Harlem River, west over to the wide and spectacular Hudson River, all the way south toward the Statue of Liberty, around the corner of Wall Street, and back up the East River to the starting point. Twenty-eight miles.

I needed a boat to accompany me, so one sunny Sunday afternoon in late September I went down to the West Seventy-ninth Street Boat Basin. Swank yachts were lined up, slip by slip. Swank yacht types were sipping their dry martinis in their seersucker slacks. A brash twenty-six-year-old, I squared myself at the stern of each boat and announced myself: "Hi! My name's Diana Nyad and I'm going to swim around Manhattan Island next Wednesday. It's going to be the adventure of a lifetime. Want to guide me around with your boat?" One by one, they called the dock captain and ordered this lunatic be removed from their private haven. The last boat, at the end of the dock, was broken down, its floorboards cracked, with a guy named Ed on deck. His khakis were stained with oil and bait grease, his dog too thin around the ribs. Ed, in his thick New York accent: "Yeah, well, that sounds kinda interesting. Wednesday, you say? What time you think we'll be done? Got a vet appointment for my dog here at five p.m."

I had no concept of when we'd be done, but promised Ed he'd make the vet appointment. The next day we pored over the tide charts, got a couple of my handlers to meet with Ed, and they went provision shopping, throwing in a few treats for Ed's dog. The adventure was set.

September 24 was a bit windy, but the real issue was a series of storms that had just passed across the Gulf of Mexico, below Louisiana. This sport teaches you how small our planet is. We are subject to the effects of weather and water conditions from thousands of miles away. Sure enough, the entire eastern seaboard had surging tides higher than normal for those few days after the Gulf storm had subsided. We got in and through the East River in the morning from Gracie Mansion just fine. I do remember the gang on my boat cringing and covering their eyes in disgust as we plowed through the Harlem River. I didn't want to know and never asked what they were observing. The Hudson was choppy, but we made progress all the way down.

Somewhere down the Hudson, about halfway around, I noticed helicopters starting to swirl above. And boats started hooking up to ours, passengers climbing on and off board. On one feeding, taking in some hot drink and refueling some lost calories, I asked Ed if he was worried about the time and his vet appointment. He was wild-eyed: "Forget about the vet! I'm having the time of my life! *Sports Illustrated* just interviewed *me*! I don't care how long you take. Take days. This is the greatest day of my life!"

At the Battery, however, the outgoing tide was way off the tide chart readings and they figured on board that it wouldn't slow and start to turn north again for another several hours. No swimmer beats those tidal speeds. I treaded for a bit, and we all decided it was silly to spend hours standing still. Better we should come back another day.

That day was October 6. Fall weather was creeping in, meaning the water temperature had dropped from comfortable summer warmth. Gracie Mansion was again our start point. The Harlem wasn't quite as nasty this time. And I will never forget making that turn into the glorious wide expanse of the Hudson. The George Washington Bridge spans this legendary river, and the sunshine of a perfect fall day glistened all the way south to the Atlantic Ocean at the other end.

Part of the allure of these long swims is the significance of the particular geography. That was the initial draw to the English Channel, the first swimmer making it across way back in 1875. The legendary crossings throughout all that storied history between the European continent and the British Isles made the Channel the stuff of folklore. And such is the magic of swimming around Manhattan. Coming down the mighty Hudson, as tugboats honked their cartoonish baritone notes to wish us good luck, I flashed all the way back to the original settlers of this big slab of bedrock, the Native Americans, paddling their canoes down this very stretch. The gripping arrival of the boats into the docks of Ellis Island, carrying the Jews and others escaping the horrors of the Holocaust, their hopes uplifted by the raised arm of Lady Liberty. The *Queen Mary* coming up past the Statue of Liberty to midtown Manhattan with European passengers excited to visit arguably the greatest city of the modern world.

And there was my own personal history. My mother's family and their deep New York roots. Although the Bay of Naples and all those other swims I had done in other corners of the globe were each one exploits to capture the imagination, each one with long and interesting histories, this was the first time I had an emotional attachment to the waters I was gliding over. I breathe to the left only, and as we circled the island counterclockwise, all I saw all day long was magnificent Manhattan. Every glance brought a tender feeling for this unique place millions of us have called home.

Actually, all these years later, whenever I fly into New York and the pilot dips a wing down the Hudson on the way to landing at LaGuardia or Kennedy, the emotions of that chilly but thrilling October 6 day waft back through my memory bank.

Before we'd started the first attempt, we'd had no indication that this swim would be a big deal to the public. This was a personal mission. But the buzz again grew as we made our way around, this time the tides behaving according to the charts. Starting on the West Side, through midtown, and all the way around the Battery, a chorus emanated from people lined up along the seawall. They yelled out good-luck wishes, gesturing frantically. There was a little crowd of press reps and New Yorkers at the end. I was the first woman to swim around Manhattan and had set a new record, for both men and women. Seven hours, fifty-seven minutes.

The Manhattan Island swim was a kick in the pants. I wound up on the front page of *The New York Times* next day, plus a booking to talk to Johnny Carson on *The Tonight Show*. It was fun, to be sure, the public and media interest. But I was grounded enough even at that young age to realize that it's the fundamental challenge that motivates an athlete, not what we might get from success. Even the highest-profile athletes who make multiples of millions, they ensure their contracts protect their futures, but they practice and compete for pride; they play with character. Those are the values that drive them to be winners, most of them.

My motivations in doing the Manhattan swim were high-minded, but afterward I had a ball, enjoying mover-and-shaker status in the City That Never Sleeps. I swam with Jackie Onassis, romped around Central Park with Andy Warhol, had some dinners with Woody Allen. Mayor Abe Beame gave me a key to the city (and asked if I could swim around the island again next to a mega-yacht for a fund-raiser, akin to a trained seal for their entertainment—an offer I declined). This was perhaps what they call living a charmed life. I'd come to the city alone and a loner, but now I was known by every New Yorker. Cabdrivers greeted me out their windows as I walked down the street.

Also of great pride to me was that I was included in the great pantheon of women athletes who achieved maverick marks in that same era. Activist Billie Jean King led the fight to equalize prize money for women in tennis. Janet Guthrie became the first woman ever to drive the fabled Brickyard of the Indianapolis 500. Kathrine Switzer pulled her hair up under a cap and crashed the then-all-male Boston Marathon. I was doing things in open water that even men hadn't done. It was an historic time for women in sports, and I was honored to be part of that history.

The public life was scintillating for me, but I also at that time met someone to share this charmed life with. We were both twenty-six, and it was love at first sight.

Billie Jean King's magazine *womenSports* had done an article on me, and the staff invited me to a tennis match between Chris Evert and Evonne Goolagong in Madison Square Garden. It was a sparkling late Friday afternoon in spring, with thousands of happy faces scrambling to subways and buses. I was across the street from the magazine's offices when my heart skipped a beat. Waiting to cross at the light was a young Elizabeth Taylor. Stunning. I elbowed through the crowd, introduced myself, and invited her to join me for the match. She introduced herself as Candace Lyle Hogan, stated that she was an editor at the magazine that had profiled me, that it was in fact they who had invited me to the match, and we all went down to the Garden together.

Ours was a puppy love, but it was my first love and thus special. And we shared New York City in a constant state of high adventure.

We were playing volleyball in Central Park on a beaming summer day when a guy went chasing another guy across the Great Lawn just below our field. The guy giving chase was yelling for help, screaming that this other guy had stolen all his money.

I said to Candace, "Come on!" She retorted, "Come where?"

We sprinted after the two until the robber exited the park and headed up Central Park West.

His pursuer was gassed. I was the only one giving chase now. I told Candace to find the police and went running alongside the park after this guy.

He kept looking back at me, perplexed. I was gaining ground and beginning to wonder myself just what I would do when I caught him. He threw something shiny over the park wall at one point. I noted the street.

Maybe three or four minutes into this thrilling pursuit, I hear the siren. Yes! Sure enough, a cop car screams past me and jumps the curb right in front of the thief. Two policemen, plus Candace, jump out and throw this guy up against the stone wall. Now I'm with them. Everything the cops yell, Candace and I yell louder: "Spread your legs. Hands wide up on the wall."

Our chorus: "Yeah! Spread your legs. Hands up on the wall!"

It turned out the guy had been robbing people all over the park that day. Candace and I next day wound up on Page Six of the *New York Post,* making headlines: SHERLOCK AND WATSON CATCH THIEF. Life in New York was heady.

I appeared on *Saturday Night Live* at one point, and Candace and I were invited to the show's Christmas party. Talk about heady: chatting all night with Gilda Radner, Chevy Chase, John Belushi. Frank Zappa was the musical guest that night. He put his face within inches of mine and said slowly, "Muscles and tits. What a dazzling combination." Candace was sure I was going to deck him, but instead the three of us slid into a booth and talked evolution and theology until four in the morning.

The Manhattan swim was a game changer for me. People have come up to me all my life to tell me they took the afternoon off work that October 6 to stand down at the river and cheer me on. I remember them. And I remember the Hudson, the connection to history, the swell of emotion.

Suddenly, after the Manhattan swim, a PhD in comparative literature seemed irrelevant. Some television-announcing offers were coming in, including from ABC's *Wide World of Sports.* It was my generation who grew up with *Wide World,* and I'd always wanted to say on the air, "The thrill of victory, and the agony of defeat." I planned to retire from my sport by age thirty and take my purported gift for gab into the broadcasting arena. But before I hung up my bathing suits a second time, this time for good, I decided to attempt an outrageous, possibly impossible world record of one hundred nonstop miles in the open. Nobody at that time had gone even half that. I hadn't yet been inspired as to just where that swim would be, but while researching it, I kept in shape.

Ocean training while living in New York as a general rule went like this: Candace and I would take a random train from Manhattan out to a random spot in Queens for the weekend. We'd get off the train in, say, Far Rockaway and have the gall to walk up the stairs of a seaside brownstone and knock on the door. "My name is Diana Nyad. I'm the one who swam around Manhattan. I'm training for my next swim. This is my handler, Candace. Would you possibly be kind enough to take us in for the weekend so that I can train in the ocean right out here?" Every time, some nice family would open their doors and let us bunk in with them for a few days of training. Simpler times.

It was time to get focused. Candace and I gathered the charts of the Earth's oceans on the floor of our Upper West Side apartment. We had lived among boxes there for a year when to our delight, we discovered a half bath off the kitchen we never knew about. We culled through the unlikely spots, such as the Arctic Circle. A swim of this distance, two or more nonstop days, would dictate warm waters. We started scouring the equatorial belt. Hundred-mile choices are virtually endless throughout our oceans. But in those days the rules of the sport called for both starting and finishing on land, unlike these modern times, when accurate GPS markings allow a swimmer legitimate swims from and to latitude/longitude points, no land involved. To this day, though, I'm old-school. Nothing speaks to a classic journey, reaching back to the Greeks, more than walking off one shore and up onto another.

I remember it as if it were yesterday. My eyes swept the charts and, zowie, there it was. Cuba. My heart pounded. Cuba, the land of mystique of my childhood, the island of enchantment to millions around the world. We Americans have long been beguiled by the beautiful colonial architecture of Old Havana, the colorful vintage American cars, the intoxicating rhythms of the Buena Vista Social Club, the advanced medicine and education in general, the myriad world champion athletes coming out of this tiny, poor island. My parents had gone, before the revolution, to dance salsa at the oh-so-fabulous Hotel Nacional, playground to JFK and Jackie, Sinatra and Ava Gardner, Hemingway and his Scotch.

And, of course, by now we had lived through the Bay of Pigs and the Cuban Missile Crisis. The United States was nearly twenty years into the embargo. Fidel was touted in our history books as part hero—swooping on horseback into Havana to change the corrupt dichotomy between the vastly rich and the desperately poor—and part dangerous Communist, in bed with the Soviets to threaten our safety.

For many reasons, not the least of which was the epic journey from one country to another, walking up onto the shores of my homeland, the obsession with swimming from Cuba to Florida was in serious play. These particular hundred miles, along with a swimmer's long list of natural obstacles, meant something to me personally. The swim would establish a new endurance standard and the geography itself teemed with history. It was starting to live in my innards, this crossing. I was inspired. I would make the attempt the summer of 1978.

EIGHT

The First Expedition

All those marathon swims before Cuba were distinct life experiences. It's a tough sport, period. Anybody who swims around Manhattan Island or to Catalina Island or across the English Channel has my respect. But as I began to research Cuba in 1977, I quickly understood this was to be an entirely different mountain to climb. And I use that alpine climb analogy specifically, because this was to be a full-fledged, major expedition. This is the Mount Everest of ocean swimming.

It seems others had tried, going back to 1950. And springing forward to today, a few more have given it a go. It's an intoxicating venture, to swim from nation to nation, and especially between these two countries, steeped in their particular dance of both friendship and estrangement. But whereas thousands swim ocean stretches around the world, year by year, only a handful of individuals have been brazen enough to try this stretch. It's not only the mammoth, unlikely distance for a human being to traverse. It turns out that a swimmer would be hard put to find a more challenging hundred miles on the planet. It's a vast, dangerous, unknown wilderness out there, from a swimmer's vantage point. It's Mother Nature on steroids. I wouldn't find out the extent of those obstacles until all these years later, in my sixties. Back then, 1978, age twenty-eight, it simply seemed a long, long way.

On paper, I figured fifty-five to sixty hours. The first question everybody asks is: When do you sleep? You have to sleep, right? Wrong. The rules of the sport are such that you may not receive any aid at any time, in either moving forward or in staying afloat. Now, you can stop anytime you want, to receive nourishment from your Handlers, to stretch out your back, which becomes stiff from constantly arching and flexing in the freestyle stroke position, to switch out your goggles, to vomit from saltwater intake, to poop and pee, even to float on your back and trip out at the dazzling universe above, which seems to expand before your hallucinating eyes. But I find that you need to take care of business. You're not really resting and regenerating while treading water. All you're doing is using valuable calories and precious time, calories and time you'll never get back, that you will need in later, desperate hours. Pressing forward is an imperative.

Back then, a sleep-study lab in New Jersey asked to do some research on me. They were interested in brain function levels when the will pushes the body to stay awake to continue rigorous physical activity. The first thing I learned is that you cannot store sleep. I was considering trying to sleep some very long hours before the swim, maybe a week of twelve-hour sleeps, to create a bank to call on when asking my body to perform for fifty-five or sixty hours. There is no such thing as a bank of sleep. They had me float in one of their sensory-deprivation tanks for twenty-four hours, to see how the brain would begin to behave after being awake that long. But we found out that floating, even though you're awake a full twenty-four hours, does not replicate the brain fatigue that occurs when you're pushing nonstop in the ocean. And the factor that supersedes brain fatigue is the extreme stages of sensory deprivation that a swimmer working hard in the open sea for more than two days experiences like no other athlete. The folks at the lab were astonished to find a person who found floating in their tank for twenty-four hours a delightful way to pass the time.

They discovered that my left brain and right brain were actually fully functioning, together, while I was out there in the ocean for long hours. I told them I had the sensation that I was asleep and dreaming but also awake and observing my dreams. They confirmed scientifically that this was the case.

Your ears—sealed by a tight cap, to keep your head as warm as possible—are rendered virtually deaf. Your eyes—the goggles fogged, the head turning some sixty times per minute, unable to focus on anything but a flash image of the escort boat—do not function well after the first twelve or so hours.

To maintain focus and some modicum of reality out there, I developed a playlist in the 1970s, which didn't change all that much in my sixties. The great tunes of my hippie generation. Dylan, Joplin, Neil Young, the Beatles. It takes a certain mind-set to withstand the monotony and the isolation of singing the Beatles' "Ticket to Ride" 210 times, starting note to finishing note. That's 210 times, hearing nothing, seeing nothing from the outside world. In my head, singing "Ticket to Ride" to myself. At the last note of the 210th version, I will hit seven hours on the nose. And I never lose count. It takes a certain mind-set.

The extreme nature of the event can be quickly understood by stating that both hyperthermia and hypothermia are probably going to be issues over the time frame. Summertime, the Florida Straits between Cuba and Florida, considered tropical waters, measure about 84 degrees near both coastlines and higher, 85 to 87, in the middle of the Gulf Stream, the huge band of powerful current that runs east across the north direction that you need to swim between Havana and the closest U.S. point, Key West, Florida.

At the start, fresh and juiced on adrenaline, 85 is going to seem warm. My Handlers are going to have to be diligent those first six to eight hours, to hydrate me properly and keep ahead of hyperthermia. But we choose summer, when the waters are warmest, because to do a swim of this distance and number of hours, the water temperatures need to be warm enough to survive once you start losing weight and the body depletion of electrolytes and other crucial basics reaches critical levels. That's when hypothermia sets in.

So, you ask, how could anybody possibly feel cold in bathwater as warm as 85 degrees? Well, it's not technically bath temperature. Imagine. You draw a bath. You're not exhausted. You're not working hard, not under duress. You just want to laze in a soothing, warm bath while you do the crossword puzzle. You probably set the tub to about 102 degrees, typical Jacuzzi temperature. You loll around, luxuriating with some bath salts, tackling your puzzle, and some ten minutes later, as the water dips below your 98.6-degree body temperature, you don't like it. A slight chill skims over your skin. If you just don't feel like reaching up to add more hot water and the bath goes down below 90, you're no longer warm. Now you reach for the hot faucet until the water bumps back up above 99, above body temperature.

So now imagine swimming nonstop for two-plus days. Your brain isn't functioning well after some thirty hours. Your body is expending more than you can replace. Believe me, 85 can give you a chill. But I find that, when trained to a superlative level, and when carrying more fat than normal walkabout weight, I can maintain a metabolic rate that keeps me from hypothermia while actually stroking. It's those feeding stops and emergency stops that bring on the chills. Hence, our Team tends to make those necessary stops as short as possible.

Keeping warm through continuous movement, shortest possible stops, was one of the first lessons on our learning curve of 1978. We prepared a hot chocolate electrolyte drink for the nights. Warming from the innards brings at least temporary relief from the cold, though keeping the body moving is the answer to fending off hypothermia.

You're immersed, virtually naked, in a liquid colder than your body temperature. And the sport's rules do not allow for wearing warming materials such as neoprene, because neoprene is an aid in flotation. Your body is working in the supine position, not conducive to normal vertical digestion, and your desperately needed nutrients don't all go into your bloodstream to directly feed your muscles for their contractions. The food winds up in what they call "empty spaces," literally outside the digestive system, unusable. We learned to prepare feedings of seven hundred calories per hour, knowing that I would only get the benefit of about half that amount. We consulted NASA nutritionists and got some of their high-calorie compressed foods. But this was decades before the current knowledge of sports nutrition. We stuck to commonsense basics, such as peanut butter, yogurt, bananas, and honey. And lots of liquids. Fruit drinks made me ill, but fortified chocolate milk seemed to calm the stomach. And water. Water. Water.

You're going to ingest a certain amount of salt water, a nasty proposition. Wave action means even more salt water down the hatch. Plus, you simply don't feel well from the drag and surge of the tides, the dips and rolls of the waves.

The longest swim I had done before attempting Cuba was the crossing of Lake Ontario in 1974: eighteen hours, twenty minutes. That was not nothing, but this? This would be more than triple that, and not in a freshwater lake, free of life-threatening animals. A large lake can whip up nasty waves and chop, but surface action is benign compared to the powerful swells and tugging currents of the ocean.

I got to work in 1977, a year before the attempt, starting with eight hours a day in New York pools and New York–area ocean swims. Then I spent a few months with an elite group of pool swimmers in Southern California, working my ass off to stay up with them. Come winter 1978, I moved down to Miami to train in the very waters I'd be facing. I got to work on engaging the mind and steeling the body for long hours. A hotel in Miami Beach generously gave me and my Handler Margie Carroll a couple of penthouse rooms as our training camp. By this time, Candace and I were no longer a couple but we were very tight. She would come down from New York when she could, but basically, it was me and Margie. I considered myself in good shape, after eight years as a sprinter, followed by eight years of pretty tough marathon swimming. But it was abundantly clear that this swim was to command a deeper commitment.

Margie had been one of my student swimmers during my only coaching stint. The spring before swimming around Manhattan I had been doing a few laps in the Columbia University pool when the men's team coach stopped me. "Hey, Nyad, you want to make a thousand dollars?" Heck, yes. But when I found out it was to coach the Barnard College women's swim team the following year, I hesitated. I know how many hours go into swim practices and meets for an entire school year. But the coach said, "No, it's not like that over at Barnard. They're really low-key. Not athletes, really. They'll want to practice a couple of times a week. That's it. Easy gig."

Well, in the meantime I had swum around Manhattan and the turnout for the Barnard team was huge. The bleachers were jammed, the deck crowded with young college women, never before interested in joining the swim team, now excited to have this somewhat famous character as their coach. One stood out. She was wearing one of those old-fashioned caps with a strap that snaps under the chin. And she was smoking! Smoking on the pool deck! "Hey, what the heck! There's no smoking on the pool deck. Put that out right now! And, all of you, get in the pool and start circle-swimming for the next twenty minutes. I want to see what I have here."

The smoker, a tough kid from the Bronx, yelled out, "Twenty minutes! What, is this broad high or something?" She was right out of central casting for *West Side Story*.

That was Margie Carroll: yes, a tough kid from the Bronx, but also a brilliant student and the most motivated swimmer on the team. After two years of coaching at Barnard (the team got motivated for two-a-day practices and spring-break training in Florida, the most labor-intensive $2,000 I've ever earned), Margie was my most improved swimmer, a team leader, and my devoted friend. When the Cuba Swim crystallized, I asked Margie to join Candace as co-heads of my Handler Team, and we settled down in Miami to make it happen.

Back-timing the prep, both training for me, the athlete, and organizing the entire expedition, we were shooting to be fully ready by early July. It seems odd to the lay public that those few of us who try the Cuba Swim choose summer, hurricane season, when the storms are highly unpredictable and calm sea days are few and far between. But the waters don't hit peak temperatures until about Fourth of July and then start cooling down end of September. Just as Everest has its climbing season—usually May, before the monsoons sweep across those glaciers and couloirs—the best chance to survive the long hours from Cuba to Florida is the heart of summer.

My views on training have changed in these modern times. Back then, I rarely took a day off. Margie would drag our inflatable boat and motor and our supplies down to the water's edge, and every day we'd go eight, nine, ten hours. And usually once a week I'd swim all the way from Miami to Fort Lauderdale. Depending on the tides and currents, we'd average eleven hours for that swim, thirty-one miles. (As a reference, although cold water, the English Channel is a twenty-one-mile swim.) My mom would meet us, we'd deflate the boat, throw it in Mom's trunk, and she'd drive us back to Miami.

So we got to work, Margie and I, each month escalating the hours. I love that aspect of sports where you can see what kind of work, how much work, an athlete's been doing by how her body is carved. By May, my shoulders, back, biceps, and triceps were built, undeniable evidence of all the hours spent powering in the ocean.

As the training progressed through winter and spring, I started to put together the rest of the expedition. First on the agenda was finding a competent and motivated Navigator.

The navigational complications can't be overstated. The mighty Gulf Stream comes catapulting east, from its squeeze through the Yucatán Channel, between Mexico and the west end of Cuba, and its first loop trajectory shoots up into the Gulf of Mexico. One of Earth's major ocean currents, the Gulf Stream sweeps up the entire Atlantic seaboard of the United States, travels east across the northern Atlantic Ocean and splits: Some of it moves north, to Britain, some sweeps down the western side of Europe to Portugal, and then full circle west, back to Florida. Ships use the Stream to boost their speed and save fuel. Wildlife teems along its edges. It's one of Earth's glories, this river in the ocean, and it's not to be denied its power, its roadblock status, for a swimmer trying to cross its current.

Take a look at a map or a globe. You can see the goal, Havana to Key West, is close to due north. Now picture a wide "river," so to speak, across that passage. Some days its parameters are so wide, maybe eighty miles, that it takes up almost the entire space between the two countries. At the point between Havana and Key West, this river is pushing just about due east at speeds varying from 3.5 to 5.5 miles per hour. For an extreme distance such as this, I average a speed of about 1.7 miles per hour. My actual forward swimming speed over a long haul of more than two nonstop days is 2 miles per hour, but factoring in the short feeding stops and the occasional and reliable crises, the hourly progress averages more like 1.7. There are faster swimmers, to be sure, but none can make headway against the Gulf Stream for even a short time. The axis of the current flowing faster east than your speed north means it's up to the Navigator to plot your course, and to change that plotting literally every fifteen minutes or so, as the Stream varies with eddies and countercurrents, to somehow get you "northing."

Some days the Stream's axis gives a swimmer a break and has a northern component, meaning it still flows east but it's pointing more northeast, and you have half a chance. On very rare occasions, impossible to predict, you could get lucky and defy historical records by finding the axis tugging just about straight north. But those days are a freak of nature. Mainly, the Stream is going east, faster than you are, while you are wanting to go north.

The further quandary is the geography of the Keys. Those islands stretch somewhat east from Key West, but they also track to the north, hopping one after the other up toward the mainland of Florida. So if you can't make Key West—and chances are heavy against that, because you're just going to have to travel at least somewhat east with the Stream—you're now shooting for another of the Keys. The shortest measurement point to point, Havana to Key West, is 103 miles.

(By the way, it irks the heck out of me that for many years and to this day there is a big buoy in Key West at the GPS southernmost tip of the United States where millions of people from all over the world have posed for snapshots. On this buoy there is an arrow, pointing toward Havana, with 90 MILES painted in bold black. Well, that 90 is a nautical-miles measurement, used only for large ships. None of the rest of us measures distance across the planet in nautical miles. We use statute miles or kilometers. And the accurate measurement from that southernmost point in Key West to the closest point in Havana is 103 miles. I have made a friendly yet sincere proclamation to the City Commission of Key West that, if they don't officially change that buoy, I'm going to go stealth in the middle of the night, commit a misdemeanor, and paint it over myself. They tell me the change is under official consideration.)

The farther east you are carried by the Stream, your potential landing point shifts north, to perhaps Big Pine Key, Marathon Key, or Key Largo. Now your total swimming distance grows longer and longer. And if you're carried too far east while out in the middle, with mainland Florida curving north and away, the tangent distance to land becomes untenable. The Bahamas are now your only realistic landing site.

Aside from the drag of the large Gulf Stream itself, navigating the tricky countercurrents and counterclockwise eddies is much more specific to a swimmer than I realized back in '78. We had a skilled America's Cup navigator who had sailed all over the world, but he was lacking in two fundamental areas. One, his ocean experience was wide, but none of it was spent right here in the Florida Straits and he was unfamiliar with its myriad currents. No map or view via space telemetry is going to inform you of the countercurrents at the edges of the Stream, or of the powerful swirling eddies throughout, unpredictable and calamitous for a swimmer swept into their vortexes. Beyond that, he hadn't gone out with me on scores of training swims, and both of those errors were on me. You can find dozens of sailors and fishermen from both Cuba and the Keys, people who know these waters like the back of their hand. But if they haven't spent considerable time with the very swimmer in question, factoring in the speed, the ability of that swimmer to handle wind and waves from every direction, the types of issues that tend to come up for her, that might require crisis management, hence, treading time, well, you're just plain lost.

But all that's hindsight now. At the time, I didn't think I could do any better than a pedigreed America's Cup navigator. So that was my choice.

My Handler Team fleshed out with three of my squash buddies from New York: Jon Hennessey, Wendy Lawrence, and Steve Germansky. All good friends, all up for the adventure.

The Handlers are your lifeline, keyed into both your physical and mental well-being. You might picture them as we do the cornermen in a boxing ring. Before the bout, these guys get the fighter ready. During the bout, they live and breathe every punch to his gut, his jaw. They know, better than the athlete himself, when he's given and taken too much and continuing might be catastrophic to his future health. That's why it's usually the cornerman who literally throws in the white towel, not the fighter. Conversely, he knows just what simple word will summon this guy's last drop of courage and send him back in at the bell.

My Handlers were in charge of my safety, my comfort, my nutrition, my physical ability to continue, my mental clarity. It was largely Candace and Margie who knew me best and spent the lion's share of time with me training off Miami. The others came down now and then through the spring, to familiarize themselves with the pace, the needs, but they were mainly at the ready for the long Cuba haul itself, as they would need to work in shifts, making sure to be fresh, with sharp eyes and ears, when on duty next to me.

This ocean is a veritable shark playground. Even the great white visits from time to time. The array of species commands our respect, from the quick and fearless oceanic whitetip to the aggressive bull shark to the lemons and tigers. I lined up seven shark experts, in Florida and the Bahamas, and interviewed them all about shark behaviors, asking them to help us design an effective protocol. First cardinal rule for our Team: We kill no animals on our crossing. We are passersby, wanting to peacefully travel through their universe for a short time. No animal will die on our watch. The Divers, experienced with hundreds of hours and all kinds of sharks, will use sonar on board to spot dark shadows lurking near me. Their plan was to dive all around me with sticks for prodding a shark's snout, a plan that made sense to me for daytime. But I was very nervous about the nights.

All seven of the experts, no matter their varying opinions about olfactory deterrents or comforting statistics indicating sharks don't attack because they know we are not their normal food, they each one had as their last statement to me on my way out the door: "But keep in mind, they are highly unpredictable creatures. The truth is, we know very little about what they might do to a swimmer splashing around fifty miles off shore. You're in their territory, and while you have no idea where they are, they know exactly where you are."

A swimmer splashing by and making enticing low-frequency sounds on the surface sends signals to sharks as far away as two miles. What if an oceanic whitetip hasn't eaten in a couple of weeks, out there where there are no reefs and not much food? The vibrations of the surface swimmer indicate a wounded fish—or as one shark expert at the time put it to me: "You are a slow-moving, very attractive dinner bell." Especially in the pitch black of night—and we would have to go through a minimum of two full nights—we feared the risk was high. We planned to use no lights at all at night, as lights attract baitfish, such as tuna and mackerel, and the sharks come snooping in right behind them.

We learned sharks don't behave as you see them in movies (*Jaws 2* was released that very year). They don't politely make figure-eight warning circles, dorsal fins in plain view. They attack from the deep to the surface. Their jaws hinge only from the bottom, so they can't lift the upper jaw and hence need to bite from underneath. It didn't take many of these interviews before we started engineering a cage.

I was aware that a cage would categorize our swim differently, meaning we would have forward-speed aid from the cage. Asterisk next to our 1978 expedition notwithstanding, we had a cage built.

The cage started with two big pontoons of a catamaran, secured parallel to each other, about twenty feet apart. Thin-gauge chicken wire was built below the pontoons, four vertical walls and a floor, so that when I swam in between the pontoons, nothing could get me. I wouldn't be immune to jellyfish slithering through the wire holes, but sharks would be kept at bay. It's cumbersome, but nothing protects you from sharks like a steel cage.

The public misunderstands why a swim "without a shark cage" is meaningful. The interpretation seems to be that a swimmer without one is some combination of brave, reckless, and foolish. But what swimming without a cage means to the long-distance-swimming world is that you are not receiving a forward-motion push from the cage. As the big structure moves forward, even at a slow pace of under two miles per hour, small swirling eddies form on the sides of the pontoons. Those little eddies travel to the back of the "boat" and thrust forward, giving the cage a push. In a cage, you're swimming as much as twice, at certain points three times, your normal speed. In 1997, a terrific Australian swimmer named Susie Maroney did go from Cuba to Florida in a cage. I don't for a moment denigrate Susie's achievement. I know firsthand the security of a cage and made that choice myself in '78. Back then, going without a cage seemed an alarmingly imprudent course of action.

We were also aware of the danger of an abundant and potent jellyfish in these waters, the Portuguese man-o'-war. Actually, the man-o'-war has two very different aspects. Above the surface is a gas-filled blue-violet bubble that is not venomous. You might have seen the bluebottles washed up on the beach. But below the surface, dozens of elaborate tentacles rhythmically relax and contract, "fishing" down sometimes as far as one hundred feet. Despite their beauty, Caribbean and Atlantic men-o'-war grow very large and their stings can kill a child.

The animal can deliver a massive sting that not only rips pain at the skin area where the tentacle has wrapped itself but often causes both nausea and pulmonary distress. A Shark Diver or Handler or Driver might be alert enough to spot a bluebottle at the surface and guide me to swim far around it. But what about the dead of night? And the insult to injury about the man-o'-war is that its tentacles are potent for some seventy-two hours after they're severed. A propeller or a mass of seaweed might break one of those fragile, gelatinous tentacles, and those fragments retain their sting properties for as long as three days. Now you're down to a close to zero chance of seeing danger ahead of time.

The learning curve on jellyfish has been steep since the 1970s. Although it is still de rigueur on most beaches around the world to pee or splash ammonia on the sting site, those are ineffective solutions while still in the water. But we had an equally amateurish protocol on board back in '78. The Handlers would reach out to me to pack the area with Adolph's Meat Tenderizer, to draw the protein of the tentacle up and out of the skin. Our doc also had injections of epinephrine ready, to open the airways at the onset of anaphylaxis.

We never encountered the deadly box jellyfish in the 1970s. But we were to learn three decades later, when attacked by the box, that they in fact had been sighted in those waters going back all the way to the 1800s.

In addition to developing procedures to protect against dangerous animals, there was also the lengthy and tiresome application process of getting the expedition officially into Cuba. Sailing in on a flotilla of boats with sophisticated electronics on board—appearing more like an armada, from Havana's viewpoint—required a securing of several government permissions.

On the U.S. side, the embargo was in full force. We needed an OFAC (Office of Foreign Assets Control) license from the Treasury Department, as well as a license from the Department of Commerce. There are literally only a handful of days through the summer when continuous optimum conditions—three or four days of under 10 knot winds, with no north component and not from due east—present themselves for a possible crossing. We couldn't afford to miss one of those precious weather windows while waiting on edge for these licenses. But by mid-May, having applied for all government issues in January, we were still nervously waiting.

On the Cuban end, the problem wasn't the applications. It was communication. You couldn't just pick up the phone and call the minister of sport. Contacting any government official led us through a tricky labyrinth. We would send notes over with fishermen who had friends of friends of friends. We would ask friends in Washington to take coffee with delegates at D.C.'s Cuban Interest Section. Especially given the media interest in our expedition, the Cubans were well aware that we were trying to contact them and secure their permissions. They made it clear that they would respond on their terms, at their own sweet pace.

The pressure of not knowing if we would even be allowed entry to Cuba was some days worse than the long hours of training. Very few days were free from pleading phone calls and cajoling favors from anybody who knew anybody. Finally, in late May, the Cuban minister of sport sent word through Washington that we were cleared, and in early June the U.S. government followed suit with our OFAC and Commerce licenses.

I will say that fund-raising for the event came through in a ten-minute meeting. I had read an article in *The New York Times Magazine* about Rocky Aoki, the CEO of Benihana, and learned that he was a huge fan of all things ocean. I called and was quickly given an appointment to see him. There was a lot of bowing, and then Mr. Aoki used an interpreter to hear my opening statement: "Mr. Aoki, this swim from Cuba to Florida is going to be seen by millions of people as one of the grand, epic ocean adventures in all of history." He stopped me right there and asked how much it was going to cost. I told him $300,000. He pressed a button, and one of his accountants soon entered with a checkbook. A brief Japanese dialogue ensued, and I left Mr. Aoki's office with a check for the full amount. Margie and I also started eating all our dinners in Miami at Benihana.

By early July, the Team was organized and on weather alert. I was in the best shape of my life. We were ready.

NINE

Havana

'm standing on Ortegosa Beach, a few miles west of Old Havana's famous Malecón. It's August 13, 1978, and my six Handlers are with me, staring out in disbelief at a sea of raging whitecaps. All the rest of our crew is out on the fleet boats, standing by for me to swim out to the cage.

We've been in Cuba four days, waiting for our Navigator to observe the winds and call for the go.

The crew has enjoyed some sightseeing. I've been sequestered in my hotel room, putting on a few pounds now that training is over, to carry some fat protection from hypothermia. I've been preparing mentally, envisioning every crisis, steeling my mind to endure even the worst. Envisioning also the hours, day and night, day and night again, until those Florida palm trees come into view. President Castro has sent a personal note with good-luck wishes.

The Navigator has done all his Gulf Stream studies and is focused on nothing but wind and weather. We have agreed that apart from a short-lived summer squall, we need a forecast of a minimum of three days with winds under 10 knots. Ideal would be wind from the south or southwest. Southeast would be tolerable, if under 10 knots. North unacceptable. West not good. East out of the question. With the Gulf Stream moving toward the east, an east wind moving toward the west collides with the current and jacks up nasty waves. The predominant trade winds through the Florida Straits come from the east, and we waited patiently in Florida for a change in the pattern. There are forecasts of a potential window, light winds from the south-southeast. That's why we are in Havana, believing our window will materialize.

While I was holed up, beefing up to get ahead of the extreme calorie output to come, and the Team was exploring Havana, the Navigator kept in touch with the National Hurricane Center, in Miami, pried whatever forecast data he could from the Cubans, and went out himself a few times a day to observe firsthand how the winds were behaving; his limit was twelve miles off the Havana shores, the international waters line. None of us can wander out beyond the twelve-mile line or we'll need a new set of OFAC and Commerce licenses to enter Cuban territory again.

After the excruciating long months of excruciatingly long training swims, after the intense push of research and Team development and government permissions, after the on-edge wait for an unlikely weather opening, our time has come. Now the seven of us are on that beach. But we're not excited; we're concerned. I get on the walkie-talkie to the navigation boat. "Hey, what's going on here?! We're not going to start this thing in this rough sea! I won't stand a chance. If unexpected winds pick up on our way across, that's one thing, but we're not going to start in whitecaps! Come on!"

We hear the scratchy voice respond over the hand radio. This is strictly a coastal wind, typical in summer, that blows from the east for about three to four miles out. Once we get away from shore that distance, the wind switches from the east to the southeast, maybe south-southeast, and it's fairly calm. The Navigator assures me he's been out checking the pattern every day. He asks us to get ready and not to worry. I just need to buck up to withstand the whipping wind these first few miles. A series of conversations, more akin to arguments, ensues. We stall for a few hours, me wanting some definitive weather word from Miami, the Navigator insisting the early-morning forecast is as he states it. Early morning lapses to morning. We continue to discuss back and forth.

Finally, we look at each other on the beach, the Handlers and I in a line facing the sea, the seven of us obviously in a serious state of doubt, our shoulders slumped, concern on our brows.

We suspect an additional factor is that Fidel's birthday is nigh and we are being pressured to leave the country before the festivities begin. Literally all government officials will be involved, and it is out of the question that a bunch of Americans, with their boats and equipment, would be allowed free rein to wander around Cuban marinas and beaches on their own or leave the country with no official escort. We need to go.

Candace and Margie grease me with wool fat lanolin under the arms, across the back of the neck, down the insides of the arms to postpone chafing. Chafing is the bane of all endurance athletes. Runners and hikers and climbers work hard to get the right socks and shoes or boots. They smear a lubricant where the upper thighs rub, especially once sweating produces salt to add to the friction. I remember seeing the great boxer Floyd Patterson finish the New York City Marathon with his white singlet soaked down the front in a deep red. That was blood that came from his nipples, rubbing with salt friction against that material those twenty-six miles.

Ocean swimmers can chafe to a severity of third-degree burns. I've seen men start out a long swim clean-shaven and wind up at the end of nine hours with a bloody gash on their breathing-side shoulder, chin rubbing that spot all day long, the salt grinding the stubble into the shoulder. My grease back in '78 wore to a thin layer pretty quickly, so the Handlers had to constantly reapply from the boat, which wasn't easy. Once the skin is wet, that goo won't stick. The Handlers are not allowed to prop me up or even grab a wrist to hold my arm above water so they can get the lanolin down under the armpit. I have to tread water and pump my legs hard enough and long enough for them to be able to dry the area and apply the grease in one motion. We worked literally hours on that move in practice sessions. I had perpetual bloody grooves along the bathing suit's shoulder and underarm touch points in those days.

I was brash and generally cocky as an athlete at that time, but that moment, taking those first few uneasy steps through the shallow surf, looking out at the rough chop, sucked all the bravado out of me. A final glance toward Candace, Margie, Jon, Wendy, and Steve tells the story.

Their look is not of fire and hope but of apprehension. Just a few feet from shore, I am walking into turbulence and waves already three feet high.

Eight hours later, we are in an eight-foot sea. That's a measurement from trough to crest, so you are surging and dropping close to a one-story building with every wave. The wind is whipping, from due east. It's absolutely miserable. No, it's worse than miserable. It's disastrous.

I'm pitched up against the sides of the cage. I have already been violently seasick, vomiting at least once every hour since we started. Many on board are throwing up. I am swearing every other stroke when Candace and Margie call me to their perch on the left, port-side pontoon for a heart-to-heart. This is our Cuba Swim, they tell me. We all hate it, we're all mad. But we can't go back and wait for another start day. This is it. So, am I going to continue complaining and cursing on just about every breath, or am I going to somehow summon a positive attitude and give this Dream of mine all I've got? I don't utter one negative word the rest of the way.

The NBC media boat sinks at the twelfth hour, and all of their crew and gear have to be transferred to our vessels. I am apprised of all the problems as we hammer up and down the waves through that first day and into the night. At dusk there is a flurry of minor stings. Maybe an hour of unpleasant zaps all over the body. Those stings give me chills, and I yelp involuntarily with each rash of zaps, but never stop stroking. We all hope for the wind to slacken after sundown, but it just keeps blowing. It is a tough night for all of us. Toward sunrise I ask if the forecast is looking any more promising. Word is relayed to me from the navigation boat: the wind will pick up several knots through the day, continuing from due east.

Midmorning that second day, the tentacles wrap around my neck. Wow! It is Portuguese man-o'-war. Unmistakable. My doctor, Bruce Handelman, gets the epinephrine injection prepped immediately, his quick response rendering the symptoms fairly minimal. The pain at the site subsides by 10 percent every few minutes, so the worst lasts only twenty minutes or so. I do experience minor asthma and nausea, but within half an hour of the initial stings I am back to slogging through the waves.

I have no idea how much progress away from Cuba we have made.

I've tried hard not to imagine how little ground we've covered in these roiling, punishing waves; my attitude, after the meltdown of the first eight hours, has been that it will take us longer to get there but we will get there.

We struggle through the second day, I endure another round of stings at dusk, and in the pitch black of the second night I start to shiver. I have dropped much more weight than we ever anticipated, losing my stomach constantly with the heavy wave action, then largely unsuccessful at taking in much replacement fluid or nutrition while feeling so poorly. The Handlers offer my hot drink, but I am beyond replenishing what I've lost. The suffering is palpable this night. I am hanging on for the sunrise, but only by a thread.

Unbeknownst to me and the Handlers, the Navigator is aware that we have been blown desperately off course. From the first stroke, we have been heading northwest, into the Gulf of Mexico. This is close to a mathematical impossibility, with the Gulf Stream flowing hard to the east. But what we didn't know then is that we were caught in a huge counterclockwise eddy not far off the Cuban shore. Locked into the upper edge of that eddy, we were swept for many miles to the west. When finally out of it, we were actually north of the Stream. I was traveling north on my own steam and being pushed west by the wind until the Navigator, seventy-nine miles from Havana, deemed it impossible for us to make land. He had been grappling with our confounding course from early on without telling anybody. And we learned later on that he never did go out on those wind-reconnaissance missions from Havana.

The wind had been blowing hard to the west from the first step off that Cuban beach, and my strength was drained. My arms had been punching the resistance of wave walls for two nonstop days now, instead of clearing the surface effortlessly. The Navigator had his head buried in his charts much of that time, perplexed. No matter what the wind speed and direction, it couldn't counterpush a swimmer from being dragged east with the Gulf Stream. Current always trumps wind. Why in the world had we not traveled east? Well, none of us knew about the eddies, none of us had ever imagined we would wind up north of the Stream, not so early, still down near Cuba. The hard flow of the Gulf

Stream, our main navigational concern at the start, was never a factor this time out, an outrageously unlikely development.

Forty-one hours, forty-nine minutes. Margie and Candace call me in. They tell me the good news. We're seventy-nine miles from Cuba. Then the bad news. We're way the heck into the Gulf of Mexico and no land is reachable. I cry. They cry. I plead for another alternative. Florida is the Dream, but after this nightmare of a two-day valiant push on all our parts, have they thought of every imaginable landing spot? What about the Dry Tortugas? It would still be the farthest swim in history, shore to shore. Reality hurts. Margie tells me we're heading for Brownsville, Texas, and it's eight hundred miles away. It's over.

I am hauled onto the deck of one of our boats. The body is whipped. It's an interminable, uncomfortable trip to Key West, the hull slamming those unrelenting waves without respite for almost eighteen hours. At the hospital for an IV drip, I am weighed. I lost twenty-nine pounds in two days.

The spirit, too, is wounded. The journey had been arduous. So many gave so much. Cuba '78 is not to be. Yet already, in my semi-functioning brain in that Key West hospital, Cuba '79 is stirring. If the conditions had been optimal and it was me who had not had the right stuff to make it across, that would have been a different story. But it was the weather and insufficient science on the navigation that thwarted us.

1979 came around quickly and winter training was under way. I chose a navigator who had spent his life in the Florida Straits, someone willing to endure the many hours on the boat during my training swims. And I changed the training routine somewhat, adding a few very long swims.

I also dropped the shark cage in '79 because the asterisk issue for the record books had begun to rub me the wrong way. We went back to the plan of our Dive Team using sonar to scan the depths directly below and to about a fifty-foot circumference around me. If a dark body was spotted, the Shark Divers could quickly submerge. Most often it turned out to be a big grouper or some other fish. If it was a shark, or two, the Divers would position themselves between me and the animal, ready to poke their sensitive snout ampoules with a piece of PVC pipe should they come in aggressively, arching the back or flaring the teeth.

The expedition was coming together. We'd learned a lot from the previous year, but waiting on the government issues is as frustrating as ever. It got to be June 1 and we were still not cleared, from either side. It's taxing enough to prepare for a demanding endeavor of this scope, but when you're not 100 percent sure it's even going to happen, it's doubly difficult.

Closing in on July, the worst news comes through to us. We are denied entry to Cuba. No recourse, no alternative avenue of application. The blow hits us hard indeed. I have elevated this swim onto a pedestal far beyond an endurance record. In some ways, Cuba isn't even a sporting event to me anymore. It's a life quest. It's a symbol of how I want to live my life, believing you can touch magic if the Dream is worthy enough, if you're willing to sacrifice enough for it. I am crushed.

We can't let all this training poof into thin air, so we hash out our immediate options and settle on a Bahamas-to-Florida crossing. It will be approximately one hundred miles but nowhere near as challenging as Cuba. Here, the Gulf Stream flows due north. You are swimming west, but it really doesn't matter how far you are dragged north, as long as you can swim hard and fast enough to cross the Stream. Once you're out the other side, all the long coast of Florida awaits you.

I step off the island of Bimini on August 20 and expect to make it across, though no one has ever done it before.

Midday of the second day, I have a little tiff with Margie during one of the feedings. A few minutes later, I am utterly incensed to see her giving me the finger. What? I'm not allowed some boorish behavior after swimming all day and all night? I decide to punish her by breathing to my right for a while, to ignore her. The press boat, a big yacht with a slew of photographers leaning over the railings, looms high above. I think I must not be seeing well, way up there, but I take a longer breath to make sure. All these people, strangers to me, are giving me the finger! How judgmental! Okay, I lost my temper. I said some things I will apologize for later.

Then I hear the police whistle from Margie. That means I need to stop in my tracks. It could be a shark, so I should quit splashing the surface. I stop and look over. She signals me to lift my cap. I peel it above my ears, and now I hear them. My boats, the press boat, they're all chanting, index fingers pointing forward: "One mile! One mile!" I kick hard to get up and see as far forward as possible. It's the shore! Sand and palm trees galore. A welcome oasis. Hallelujah!

We land on the beach at Jupiter, Florida, in a time of twenty-seven hours, thirty-eight minutes, the day before my thirtieth birthday. There is a roaring crowd, the worldwide press reports our success, and I am surely proud and happy. The final distance, point to point, 102.5 miles, must be taken with a grain of salt, though, as the direct distance from Bimini straight across to Miami is sixty miles. On this swim, the Gulf Stream was my friend and added to our total distance.

It's a fine achievement for me, and my Team. It's a world distance record. My career is complete, at least in the eyes of the public and the sport's officials. It just isn't for me the heart swim that is Cuba. I am told it will again be tough to gain entry to Cuba next year. Thirty or thereabouts is the age most world-class athletes move on to the rest of their lives. It's time to say good-bye to swimming, for good this time. *Wide World of Sports* has come knocking, and it is my time to leave the athletic arena and enter the broadcast booth.

I am loath to let it go, but my beautiful magical Dream, the Cuba Swim, evaporates from a firm vision I was chasing with everything in me to a whisper of unfinished business, left to rummage around in a special corner of my imagination for many years to come.

I couldn't have possibly imagined then, at age thirty, that the Dream would ever live again, for real.

TEN

Athlete Identity Crisis

It's the professional athlete's tragedy: forced to retire at an early age, perhaps never again to tap into a talent well so deep, never to experience such a high level of achievement, such pursuit of passion. So here I was, thirty, retired from my sport, my world of discipline and focus and acclaim. It's not that I missed the long, torturous hours of solitude. What I missed was the athlete identity, the body-mind symbiosis. Just about every day of my life up to age thirty had been defined by intense training, chasing lofty athletic dreams, measuring my self-esteem by the truth of my commitment. Living a life of sports brings the comfort of clear black-and-white days. You can name your goal; you can envision it. You can map out your action plan toward that goal. You can concretely measure your success. Now I was immersed in the normal world of greys. And I was out of sorts. Friends pointed out to me that the passion I missed wasn't embedded in the sport itself; it was within me. My task was to redirect it. In my early thirties, even while trotting around the globe as an announcer for *Wide World of Sports,* from the World Table Tennis Championships in Tokyo to the World Water Ski Championships in London to the Lumberjack World Championships in Hayward, Wisconsin, I was hungry to be an athlete again.

Squash was my new game. I'd dabbled in it before. Since early days in the tennis mecca of Fort Lauderdale, I had been a huge fan of all racquet sports. Squash was referred to as "the thinking man's game," so that was enticing. I started sneaking into the private, male-only Harvard Club late at night, after midnight, and would spend three to four hours hitting forehands and backhands along the side walls. After a lifetime of legs dangling free in the water, I was not fleet of foot, to understate it, but I had a pretty good feel for shot making and actually qualified to play for the United States in the world championships in England.

I loved being back in training, although the combination of travel and my limited talents meant squash was never going to replace swimming for me. But it was the first social sport I had played, and I really enjoyed being able to laugh with an opponent after a funny mishap, where physical and mental pain weren't the game's backbone. But my alone hours on the court were intense, belting out obscenities of frustration if I couldn't hit one hundred perfect corner shots in a row. If I got to ninety-two and then missed, I'd go into a self-flagellating tirade and start back at zero again. It wasn't until many years later, deep into my fifties, that I stopped whipping myself. It's a common syndrome of sexual abuse, the victim taking on the blame and berating herself, the twisted psychology being that the self-hatred continues the cycle of abuse, something ingrained in the victim's inner core, and something the victim has since childhood deemed she deserves.

Every one of us knows heartache and hardship. It's the human condition to suffer at one time or another. Half the world's population doesn't have basic daily necessities. The suffering is great indeed, mind-boggling. For the other half, we have choices, some more than others. But we all suffer. All of us. Believe me, I've lived a life of overwhelming privilege and opportunity. Nevertheless, those crimes committed against me by my father and then my coach marked my interior world to a haunting degree. These early traumas were the cards I was dealt, and it pains me to admit, as a strong-willed type, how deep those wounds ran through my adult inner child for so very many years.

To this day, I dread the yearly appointment with the gynecologist. I hyperventilate in the waiting room, then tremble and cry through the exam. But that's the least of it.

Until I was in my fifties, anger and defiance and a drive to prove myself sculpted my interior universe. I guess the simple analysis is that when a child is sexually molested, she mourns the lack of respect for all she is beyond an object of sex. Now, having the perspective of years lived to look back at my twenties and thirties and forties, I realize I spent much of my time, too much of my time, in a determined rage to validate that I was more than a female sex-crime victim. I needed to hit those one hundred corner shots consecutively. I had vocabulary words strung out across my bathroom on a clothesline because I could not tolerate the precious time that would be lost standing there waiting for the hot water to run in the shower. In those younger years, the drive hinged on an imperative of proving my worth, to others and to myself. I found myself spelling out evidence to every stranger on a city bus as to what an impressive person I was. In later years, that drive didn't wane in intensity but derived from the joy of living a bold life. Hard-earned security evolved me from desperately needing to convince people that I was special to simply living a special life.

I was angry in the water throughout my teenage years and in the ocean in my twenties. Not angry every stroke, but often bursting with rage. I was tough on the streets of New York. If you glanced at me sideways, I might mow you down to the other edge of the sidewalk. And yet other days, I was like a member of the chamber of commerce, buoyant and charming to every corner knish vendor. We are complex beings, not any one way in every aspect of our lives. I would venture to say that most people who knew me back then—except Candace, who knew the whole me—wouldn't have had any idea this dark side of me existed.

Racquetball was relishing its heyday in the 1980s, with professional tournaments taking place all over the country, and a friend suggested I give it a try. If I had at least some flair for squash, none of my athletic skills were suited to the pure speed and brute strength of racquetball. I played my first pro match and lost before either my opponent or I could get a sweat going. I was miserable at the game. Another friend had told me to go see a certain player from Idaho while I was at the tournament. She was supposedly a fireball on the court, and quite attractive to boot. After my match, I showered and saw on the draw board that the Idaho player was on the main glass court. As I approached the stands, there was a raucous crowd, really into the match. I watched this Idaho woman make thrilling, diving saves, one hand on the floor supporting her entire outstretched body. She would plead with the ref for justice, tears standing in her eyes. She was pure charisma, this player from Idaho. I pointed to her and asked the guy next to me to remind me of her name. He said, "She's not from Idaho. She's from Connecticut. That's Bonnie Stoll."

That day, April 1, 1980, Bonnie and I began our friendship, which has expanded through adventure after adventure, traversed all these many life experiences, and grown in trust over all these many years. We were actually a couple for a short time in the beginning, but it was clear to both of us that we were better suited to being pals, like two golden retrievers romping around together, all over the world. Bonnie brought me onto her racquetball team as her fitness trainer. So I knew Bonnie as a great athlete in her prime, ranked No. 5 in the world, but we met just a few short months after my athletic career was done. Only a month or so before meeting each other at this tournament, she had seen me on *The Tonight Show* with Johnny Carson and had remarked that she thought we'd make good friends.

I personally don't believe in fate. But I do believe that brazen action, versus inertia, leads to people and events you couldn't have imagined. Racquetball wasn't a logical step on my life path. But at least I wasn't afraid to make a fool of myself and give it a try. There's a sublime quote widely attributed to Goethe: "Whatever you can do or dream you can, begin it. Boldness has genius, power and magic in it."

Out of my milieu, the ocean, I entered a number of arenas not particularly aligned with my abilities. I auditioned for *Saturday Night Live*. I wrote a couple of sitcom pilots with Candace. I hosted an inside-the-Beltway political show from D.C. I hosted a late-night entertainment television show. I failed and faltered many times, but I can look back without regret because I was never burdened with the paralysis of fear and inaction. I may have been floundering out of the water, but I was insistent on living a fierce life. I was bold. And there was magic in it.

It was during that time, after the Manhattan Island swim, at age thirty, that I wrote my first book. The hubris of penning an autobiography at thirty now makes me cringe, frankly. But the experience was a new adventure. I applied for and landed a coveted private desk in the Frederick Lewis Allen Room at the New York Public Library, a dedicated chamber of twelve mahogany desks, each with cubbies in which to store your pens and papers, each appointed with an old-school banker's lamp. This transition from athlete to "other" swept me away. Walking up the marble steps of that storied library every day, to slip into my regal leather chair, was a wonderful new world for me. Nancy Milford was working at the desk next to mine. Each day at lunch break, I'd have her do sit-ups and push-ups with me on the expansive Oriental rug.

I wrote another book at that time, with Candace, called *Basic Training for Women.* The book was done and we were in a meeting at a long conference table at the publisher's office. There was a timid knock at the door and a young woman sheepishly apologized for interrupting us but said she just found out Jane Fonda was coming out with her first exercise book, by a different publisher, the exact same day, in the spring, that ours was to be published. We all took that in for a moment and chimed in with a chorus of "Come on. Who in world would look to Jane Fonda for exercise?" Well, we found out soon enough that it wasn't a matter of "who in the world"—it was the whole world. Jane and I wound up at several book signings around the country at the same time, a few people politely gathered to see me; her line stretched out the door and around the block.

To add insult to injury, the night before that ten-city whirlwind book tour kicked off, I was sleeping in my Manhattan apartment when the phone rang. Reaching for the receiver, a tendon in my neck snapped. For the next two weeks my neck could barely support the weight of my head. I wore a neck brace until the very last countdown before all the television appearances, where they of course wanted me to demonstrate exercises. I found myself, teeth clenched, unable to swivel my head even one inch, saying to the various hosts, "Yes, Joan, that's absolutely right. Flexibility is the foundation of fitness." All the while, we'd see the crews setting up for Jane's demonstrations, where she'd toss her gorgeous legs, iconic leggings and all, to the sky, bat her gorgeous eyes to the camera, and just about the whole world was dying to follow Jane Fonda's fitness advice, including me.

Those were the days when Bonnie and I first started working out like maniacs. Candace and I gallivanted around the city. One night, snow covered the streets with a quiet, feathery blanket, and we walked all the way uptown, Candace crooning "Singin' in the Rain," doing a soft-shoe up and down the various stoops, swinging gaily around the lampposts, that imaginary umbrella held high. People fell in with us, and a mini–homage march to Gene Kelly was spontaneously choreographed.

New York—or I should say New Yorkers—were a constant source of wacky delight. I asked a woman on the subway platform one day if an approaching train was making a turn or going uptown. In her thick New York accent, she threw me a *verklempt* sigh and said, "What do I look like, the freaking commissioner of transportation?" I bellowed a laugh and said, "Oh, how I love you New Yorkers!" Then we both laughed and, typical of a New Yorker, she quickly walked me to the map on the wall and gave me a precise rundown of the trains on that line. These are the daily entertaining encounters out on the New York streets, where characters abound.

And little Tim visited me in New York. Those were the days a ten-year-old could hop on a plane alone, so, along with my visits to Liza in Florida, Tim also came up so we could pal around the city together. He was astounded that I didn't know how to cook. (The first time Bonnie came to my apartment, she was rummaging around the fridge and asked me what the Arm & Hammer baking soda was doing in there. When I told her the molecules of the baking soda were mixing in with the other stuff to keep everything fresh, she dryly remarked that one has to open the box for the molecules to do any mixing.) My ten-year-old nephew would take me to the grocery store, we'd come home, and he would make a beautiful meal for us. Tim has always been sensitive to other people's circumstances, and I do believe some of his empathy developed during those times we shared in New York, observing poverty and homelessness—and later, during his travels through many poverty-stricken areas of the world. I have never had my own children, something I've come to peace with, but having this special boy close in my life has put me in touch with the tenderness a mother feels for her child.

This was also the first time I had what you'd call a "real" job, although it's hard to call traipsing the *Wide World of Sports* a job. Being one of their announcers was an enviable way to make a living. I did work live events—the Tour de France, the New York Marathon, Winter and Summer Olympic Games—but the lion's share of that decade I reported on fairly minor sports from all corners of the globe, and it was a privilege to be witness to the best in the world as they pursued their excellence.

After *Wide World* there were a number of other shows where I hosted or reported, among them: foreign documentaries on exotic wildlife for the Outdoor Life Network; a travel program called *The Savvy Traveler; The Crusaders,* a cool citizen's social-work reality show; *America's Vital Signs,* a medical show; *Day's End,* a late-night news show; on-camera essays for the best show on television, CBS *Sunday Morning;* plus investigative work for Fox Sports, reporting long-format stories, à la 6o *Minutes.* I spent three years, for instance, on the scandal of performance-enhancing drugs at the Tour de France. (Lance Armstrong, to my mind, *did* win all seven of those yellow jerseys. He was no different from the other riders; it was a level playing field, and he was by far the superior among them.) The one job I would have gladly done gratis was interviewer at the U.S. Open tennis championships. Those were the days when we brought a player into the studio after a match for a long, layered conversation, such as the one I recall with Boris Becker. We quickly finished analyzing his match that night and the one upcoming and moved on to a discussion about the unification of Germany when the Berlin Wall came down. When not in the interview chair, I was out courtside, front row center, to watch the best in the world at that time. Evert, Navratilova, McEnroe, Connors, Agassi. You call that work?

I was, for the most part, an agent's nightmare, because as a broadcast journalist I gravitated toward the storytelling shows where the audience number was sometimes so low there was no accurate measurement for it.

Daily life episodes were often more compelling to me than reporting from the interior rain forest of Borneo. I was just back from a series on *The Great Cats of the World*—the snow leopard of India, the jaguar of Belize, the cheetah, leopard, and lion of Africa when a friend suggested I should call a friend of yet another friend in New York, Harriett. She was supposed to be cute, fun. She lived in the East Village and invited me over for some afternoon tea. We met out on her front stoop, exchanged some pleasantries for, oh, two minutes. Entering her small apartment, there were two club chairs, the tea service on a table in between them, a small Oriental rug in front. We have chatted on the way in and are now sitting in the chairs, Harriett starting to pour the first cup. Now we have been together, oh, a total of eight minutes.

Her cats, male and female, suddenly appear on the rug. And they begin the frightening, violent mating screams that we hear from the faraway alleys in the middle of the night. But here they are, literally a couple of feet from us. The female, from the side, opens her jaw to the hinges, the large incisor teeth the stuff of gruesome fairy tales. The male is not touching the floor. All four of his paws, claws out, are digging into the poor female's body. She is yelping a high-pitched, blood-curdling wail. His barbed penis is thrusting in and out with ferocious abandon. Harriett and I at this point have drawn our legs up onto the chairs. We are horrified. The episode lasts some five or six minutes. I don't think I blinked throughout. At the end, the male laboriously drags himself across the room and out of view into the kitchen. The female slinks behind Harriett's chair, breathing slowly and groaning in pain. We are trying to compose ourselves when Harriett reaches back for the teacup and asks: "Lemon?"

I traveled all over the planet to report on the magnificent big cats in their wild habitats, but two urban house cats were actually the most captivating of all.

On CNBC in its earliest days, I had a weekly half-hour show called *One on One with Diana Nyad*. It was a poor man's *Barbara Walters Special*. I'd choose any personality I found interesting—not only sports figures—go get a twenty-minute interview with them, and fill in the half hour with photos and video to tell the stories of their careers, their lives. I loved every minute of it.

For one, I approached Julia Child as a fan in a queue at a wine show in New York. She agreed to be the subject for one of my profiles. But on the scheduled morning we showed up at her town house in Boston, she answered the door, looming above us at the top of the steep steps, even taller than her already six-foot self, tears standing in her eyes. This was the first day her husband, in the throes of Alzheimer's, hadn't recognized her. I offered to set the interview for some other time, but she insisted making us breakfast would cheer her up. So we sat around Julia

Child's sunny kitchen as she baked a fresh loaf of sourdough bread, made us fines herbes omelettes, and regaled us with stories of her life in France, Asia, and the world of haute cuisine. And so it went with Ed Bradley and many other people I admired.

The broadcast work that brought me the most personal fulfillment in those years was a column for National Public Radio. It was called *The Score,* yet for the twenty-two years the weekly opinion piece aired, I never once mentioned the score of anything. NPR was an intellectual and creative playground, even though the compensation was rock bottom, $150 per week.

The poetry, the sociology, the history, the offbeat stories of sports that I tried to bring to NPR over the years—it was truly gratifying work. I found my niche, crafting a small, delicious story—beginning, middle, end—and unearthing rich anecdotes of little renown that might have otherwise remained buried.

There was the defiance of bricklayer Jack Kelly, father to Grace Kelly and the greatest rower in the world in the 1920s. He was denied entry into the most prestigious rowing race at that time, the Diamond Sculls of the Henley Royal Regatta in England. The blue-blood Oxford chaps thought it unfair that a common bricklayer, with his rough working hands, should compete against them, they being too busy with their erudite scholarly pursuits to train that hard. Kelly, a native Philadelphian and favorite son of the City of Brotherly Love, wore a Kelly-green ski cap every day of training, every race. Philadelphians knew when their Jack was gliding up and down their famous Schuylkill River, that iconic green cap surging back and forth through the early-morning fog. That cap was never once washed. After winning the Olympic gold at the 1920 Antwerp Games—and, by the way, defeating the Brit who was the then Henley Diamond Sculls champ—Kelly packed up his green cap, soaked heavy with a billion strokes of sweat, and mailed it to King George V with a note: "Greetings from a bricklayer."

So New York life in my thirties and into my forties was busy with work; it was flush with my deep and growing friendships with both Candace and Bonnie; it was about squash and reentry into the athlete's arena. And it was about love.

ELEVEN

Heartache

In my mid-thirties, at a neighborhood restaurant I visited frequently, the Popover Café, a young woman sat next to me and I was immediately smitten. Nina Lederman was her name. She was a recent graduate of Mount Holyoke College, now working in television production in New York, and I fell in love at first sight. If Candace was my first love, and Bonnie was my instant lifelong friend, Nina stole my heart. Our connection was intense. We rushed to be with each other. Day and night. Night and day. Nina had grown up in the Caribbean, coincidentally on the very island I would eventually call my training home, St. Maarten, and she was a dancer extraordinaire. She had the salsa and merengue rhythms of a true native. She led, I followed, and we were considered the Fred and Ginger of the lesbian crowd at the time. We spoke fluent French together, calling each other *"doudou."* It was a dazzling romance, Nina's and mine.

We started in New York, in 1984, and four years later moved to Los Angeles, bought a home, and were headed toward children and a forever marriage, right into the proverbial side-by-side rocking chairs (even though she is much younger). Nina's career grew and she became a television executive in L.A., while my work launched into a whirlwind of global immersion. We cried and fretted over being separated, but agreed these foreign trips were opportunities, and good money, that I shouldn't pass up.

I have always considered exposure to foreign cultures one of the grand privileges of my life. Starting with my parents' backgrounds, then my days competing around the world's oceans through my twenties, and further travel for work through my thirties and forties allowed me to embrace the world at large. Travel is a peerless professor. Those years of discovery laid the foundation for a fairly simple worldview of inclusivity.

At the core, the sandaled Masai tribesman wrapped in a crimson wool shawl and the slick Manhattan stockbroker in a $3,000 pin-striped suit are the same: We all want to love, to be loved, to laugh, to eat and drink, to feel secure, to contribute to our community. To dream.

For one documentary, I got to ride a bicycle the length of Vietnam, Hanoi to Saigon, elbow to elbow with fifty American vets and fifty Vietcong vets. As we swept through the rice fields, pedaled en masse through the villages, the women in their colorful *ao dai* tunics carrying huge loads on their heads—our marines largely macho and proud of their service to country, the army vets many of them ashamed of killing innocents in a war they couldn't defend—I myself was transported through a page of dark and critical history. I won't ever pretend to know the experience of war (and I rail against sportscasters pushing the metaphor of players taking the field as soldiers taking to the battlefield; a football game has no bearing on the anguish of war), but I got a privileged glimpse into that particular war.

I went with a few of the vets to a school one day after a 110-mile ride. Jerry Stackhouse, a navy man blinded by a grenade, wearing around his neck a photo of himself as a twenty-one year old just having arrived in 'Nam—handsome as heck—was doing our ride on the back of a tandem bike. A girl about age ten asked Jerry to share his worst experience in the war. Before he could take a breath, the girl blurted out that she wanted to recant her question. She said she felt foolish in asking it, that of course his worst moment was the grenade that exploded in his face.

Jerry said: "No. I've been to hell and back with this injury. Fifty major surgeries. A new face. A partial esophagus transplant. But I'm living a good life. My worst moment wasn't my own grenade blast. We came into a village one night. I was youngest so was sent ahead to make sure it was clear. We were wanting to spend a few nights recuperating from losses we had suffered the last couple of days. My heart was pounding. I was shitting in my pants. I am sweeping my AK-47 left to right in between the huts. Nobody was there. The village had been abandoned. Or wiped out. Then a little boy, he was younger than you, I think, came darting out from behind a hut. His gun was bigger than mine. His eyes were dead. And I blew him to pieces."

Jerry, holding his white cane, started to sob. "I've never forgiven myself. I saw that little innocent boy's head roll."

As Jerry wept, this little girl came over and wrapped her arms around his hips. She held him tight and then she gave a speech most politicians couldn't muster. "Jerry, we will never forgive JFK and Henry Kissinger and all those men who took our country from us. Agent Orange still lingers in our air. The birds have gone away to Lao and are not coming back. But, Jerry, I forgive you. You were a young soldier doing what you thought was right for your country. You can't forgive yourself but I forgive you."

I will never forget that moment, that girl. Neither will Jerry.

Climbing Mount Kilimanjaro slapped me into humility, my eyes opened firsthand to our American non-physical culture. On the second day up the five-day trek, I met up with an elderly woman, one would guess in her eighties, bent over with her spine parallel to the ground, on her back a huge bundle of tethered bark and long tree branches, teetering far out in front and behind her. When she stopped to have a chat in Swahili with my guide, I pointed to her bundle, gesturing that I wanted to pick it up, to see how heavy a load she was carrying up this mountain, the same mountain I was climbing, at less than half her age and with a guide to haul all my gear. When I struggled, huffed and puffed, and simply could not budge it, they had a good laugh. The old woman gave me a wink, bent down and got her little legs under herself, deftly swung the unruly mess onto her back, and started off. I found out later that she'd been hired by the Tanzanian government to carry building materials for huts up near the summit. Her salary? Five cents a day.

The fittest person in America is a veritable weakling compared with an elderly African woman who climbs and descends the continent's highest peak every single week.

The Ledger of Life looked pretty good for me around age forty. Solid friends, a life partner, money in the bank, a small but sweet family, work that took me around the globe on grand adventures of enlightenment. Those experiences, from the interior rain forest of Borneo to the wilds of Antarctica, taught me that we are indeed, all seven billion of us, equally deserving residents of the planet.

But life on the road has its pluses and minuses, as is the case for all lifestyles. Adventuring doesn't leave much time for nesting, and when I had my chance to make a sublime nest, I didn't do it well, not with full commitment. While on the road my home life suffered.

The unraveling started with all that time spent away, in New York and globe-trotting, when Nina and I were making our home in Los Angeles. It's of course not that simple. Dissecting the end of a marriage always reveals a complex web of issues. But our physical separation was the beginning of the end. I wasn't there to take care of her when she had a bad cold. She wasn't there to share my daily life. The telephone is an unacceptable substitute for looking into the other's eyes, for touch. I did fly to Los Angeles every free minute, one time literally just to be together for three hours—but those quick rendezvous threw us into a pressured, unnatural countdown. We'd be staring at our watches. Only twenty-two hours to go.

It was unfathomable, to us and everyone who knew us, that we wouldn't make it. But the beguiling dance came to a heartbreaking end.

Losing Nina may have been the most painful passage of my life. Why didn't I understand that commitment is the foundation of a relationship, when I knew so well, and lived it fervently in all my other endeavors, that commitment is the nucleus of all success? That devastating loss wrecked my inner sanctum for literally twenty years. After we split, I became abundantly clear about prioritizing—above all else—the people I've chosen to live this life with. In the case of Nina, I paid a heavy price for coming to that realization later rather than sooner.

The French have a saying: *"Si jeunesse savait, si vieillesse pouvait."* The translation: "If youth only knew, if old age only could."

A handful of little-watched television shows versus my marriage? If only I'd had today's clarity back then.

For a long while after I lost Nina, travel was filled with heartache.

The life lessons touched me as bittersweet. For a time, I deciphered every conversation with every stranger as a search for the truth. I was unmoored.

A man in Uganda raised his palm to me, when I asked him what he planned to do with his future, and answered, "It is not ours, tomorrow." That this day is the only day we can truly live was a message I really needed right then, when I was wasting my time on regretting too many yesterdays and lamenting too many not-to-be tomorrows.

In Thailand, a schoolgirl told me a parable many there are taught very young:

"An old man is slicing through a huge side of beef with a small knife. A young man asks: 'How can that small knife slide through this hide, this tough sinew, so easily, as if gliding through butter?' And the old man responds: 'This knife has been in my family for hundreds of years. And, like all the members of my family, this knife travels the path of least resistance.'" I still aspire to cutting through with less resistance.

At a holiday business dinner, everyone chatting about their plans for the New Year, I found myself next to an Indian, head of his company's Mumbai office. He didn't introduce himself, didn't remark how delicious the dumplings were purported to be at this restaurant. With huge dark eyes, he brought his face within inches of mine and said: "You know, when Siddhartha came from the forest, he ate *one grain of rice only* every day for the next seven years. He was so evolved that he could command all the water and nutrition needed for his body to function from *one grain of rice*." And that started this gentleman and me on a three-hour exploration of extending the body's potential through the power of the mind.

In the caves of Belize, chasing the elusive jaguar for the great cats series, I came down with malaria. Deep in the jungle, no quick way out to medical care, the Mayan shaman brought crushed leaves to my tent and made me a tea to reduce my fever. She came to check on me in the middle of the night and found me crying. She understood. She prepared a mud slush of some sort, opened my shirt, and massaged the mud into my wounded heart. And she cried with me.

To spend time with other peoples, from all walks of life, is to learn both how widely intelligent the human race is—and to experience the basic shared human attribute of compassion.

Through all these teachers, and through loving and being loved by my own closest friends and family, I have evolved. And my broken heart has healed. Nina is no longer my lover and life partner, I am a godparent to her wonderful children, and she is my cherished friend for life.

TWELVE

The Person My Dog Thinks I Am

You didn't find me complaining about thirty years' traveling the world, making my living as a broadcaster and journalist. Yet as those years on the road elapsed, I began to feel the mounting malaise of a spectator. I was a bystander, witnessing other people chasing their dreams. I was telling other people's stories instead of living out my own story. I was no longer a dreamer myself. I was no longer a doer. I was filled with an urgency to get back to full-throttle engagement.

True, I had met myriad impressive people, far and wide, but the bravest soul I ever met was Christopher Reeve. I met Chris just as my ennui over no longer being a person of action was churning harder and deeper. In a heartbeat, in a fall from his horse, the actor who'd played the Man of Steel was tragically relegated to playing spectator as his ultimate role. Despite his tireless activism for stem-cell research, he said so himself that being bound to a quadriplegic's life left him feeling a lonely onlooker. He adored sports and was particularly interested in the theme of retired athletes taking their intensity and passion over to the other aspects of their lives. One day hanging out backstage at an event, after we had talked about a few retired athletes we both admired, he asked me to tell him my story. So I told him the "Not a fingernail faster" tale from way back in my high school years. Chris loved it. He took a significant pause and looked me dead in the eye with those steely blues of his. He was still Superman to me.

"You said the day you walked out of that locker room as a teenager that you were going to live the rest of your life acting out that philosophy. 'Every day not a fingernail better. No regrets.' All these years later, have you carried out your promise to yourself?"

Now it was my turn to take a significant pause. I was at a loss for words. At this juncture in his life, Chris was a master at counseling others on not leaving any day with regrets and I wanted to give him an earnest answer. I asked him if I could get back to him. Well, Chris and I never did get a chance to resume that conversation. He passed away.

That encounter with Chris, in my early fifties, was the beginning of a period of soul-searching and critical examination that catapulted me toward a reentry chapter in my life, one of fierce immersion.

For me, the decade of my fifties was a time of full awakening. That teflon armor of self-protection from the sexual abuse trauma at long last was sloughing away. All the image making, the impressing, seemed silly and unnecessary. I was no longer outside myself looking on, judging, orchestrating a performance of sorts, even for strangers I would never see again. I could feel the pressure to prove myself fading away.

A contentment overwhelmed me, to be one whole entity, not fractured, not half-present. For so many years, I would come out of a movie theater, and while everyone else was discussing this or that aspect of the film, I would have no input because I had been in my head from the lights dimming to the end credits. Imagine what I could have achieved and experienced in those decades, had I been fully awake and engaged. It made me sorry, wishing I could have arrived at that place earlier. But that's perhaps normal in the course of human development. I'll probably look back, once in my nineties, and lament that I hadn't been more evolved and present in my fifties and sixties. We're back to that French expression: "If only I knew back then what I know now." That learning curve seems to leapfrog with us through each stage of our lives.

I reflected back on that speedboat racer I met in the Toronto hospital after the Lake Ontario crossing. Even in his dire pain, his eyes brightened while exclaiming how his entire being ignited to feel alive, alert, awake when he was behind the wheel. That's the high of engaging versus escaping. We all know the foibles of escape. Through fantasizing, food, alcohol, drugs, denial. It's a syndrome of the human condition, escape. And we learn, most of us the hard way, that we cherish our short years too much to spend them in any way other than alive, alert, and awake.

My good friends assure me now that, relative to most people, I was always engaged, always real, always In It. But it came upon me in a big way in my fifties, this nagging pressure of regret, of lost, half-awake time. I became determined to get to the bottom of any and all issues that were still keeping me from the passion of 100 percent engagement.

During this time, a friend who had suffered unspeakable abuse as a child told me he had been helped immensely by working via phone with a therapist in Tel Aviv. I was still in the bad habit throes of self-berating. Simply having to fumble with the keys at the door, bags of groceries in hand, would send me into a rage, lashing out at myself with the very words my perpetrator used on me. I decided to give the Israeli therapist a try. With all due respect to traditional psychotherapy, by this point I just couldn't tell the story yet again. The intellect had nothing left to process. My brain was acutely aware that none of it was my fault. But the emotions live at a cellular level. Sexual abuse carves a deep imprint into one's soul. Often a lifetime imprint.

The therapist worked with past lives. She knew that I personally didn't believe in any life other than this one here on Earth and assured me that my non-belief would not affect the session. She asked me to suspend my disbelief, however, just as a person could derive a life lesson from a fable that was obviously not true.

I was willing, so the therapist began. She said she had a strong feeling about a medieval village where I was a young man who happened to have a number of women friends. These weren't sexual relationships; it was that women related to me, trusted me, this young man. A warring tribe swept through our village, committing devastating atrocities; throats were slashed, babies were killed, and my particular torture was to be tied down and forced to watch as a number of my women friends were brutally raped. Sitting in the lotus position on my sofa in California, the faceless therapist across the world in Israel, I truly felt that young man's anguish.

The invasion ended, she said, and my village began its healing process. So the therapist asked me: "What did you do? Did you lash out at your women friends and call them 'Whores'? Did you tell them you were disgusted by them, that you could never look at them again? Did you berate them and punish them? No, you held them tenderly. You told them they were the innocent victims of barbarians. You told them you respected them as always and you would work to help them heal from the savagery forced upon them.

"So, why, Diana, can't you give your little girl a break? Why was the abomination that happened to her all her fault? Why can't you embrace her and love her and respect her, instead of demeaning her and perpetuating her unjust shame?"

Why, indeed? Deep imprints aren't erased in one phone call. But it's astounding how much we can take in and process, when we're ready. I was ready.

So my fifties was a time of soul-searching. While making the bed in the morning, I'd take a moment to look at the slogan on the crocheted pillow: "My goal in life is to be the kind of person my dog thinks I am." Silly, maybe, but there's a grain of truth in that perspicacious phrase. My dog holds the unconditional belief that I am a mensch of a human being, kind and loyal, worthy of his boundless love. Am I? The questioning all started with Christopher Reeve asking if I was living each day not a fingernail better. And it culminated with a specific, monumental moment.

October 28, 2007, 8:08 p.m.

That's the moment my mom took her last breath.

THIRTEEN

Dors Bien, Maman

I got the call in 1999. Mom had been driving on I-95 in Florida, in the wrong direction. At first they thought she was drunk. But it turned out she was just confused.

First Liza and I, then Candace and I, then Bonnie and I went down to Fort Lauderdale to pack up a life lived in a home for some forty years, the same home I lived in from seventh grade through high school. I was not only shocked to discover how far Mom had dropped out but also ashamed to have been unaware of her decline. I hadn't been down to Florida for several years. Mom always came to visit me in New York, with Liza and her kids joining us, and then later, she'd come out to California when Liza and I had both relocated there. She had not removed the dark, heavy, metal hurricane shutters for years; the house was walled in. There wasn't a scrap of food in the fridge or the kitchen cabinets. Her mail—after all her life being fastidious with beautiful pen poised atop expensive stationery on the desk—was stuffed unopened into the back of a drawer. In sifting through the stack of papers, I came upon a returned check made out to the firemen's league. Evidently, Mom had given $100 yearly to the association, but this past year she made a mistake and wrote the check out for $100,000. They kindly returned the error.

The neurologists told us Mom had Alzheimer's. They showed us the scans of her brain, the pathways of fluids beginning to shrink. In the end, for the millions of us suffering through the unraveling of our parents' and loved ones' minds, we are learning that the distinctions between Alzheimer's and various stages of dementia aren't easy to make. Most brain doctors say today that only an autopsy could reveal a definite Alzheimer's diagnosis. Sometimes I drift back to occasions, many years earlier, when Mom was not on firm ground, mentally. When I was in my thirties and Mom in her fifties or early sixties, we were driving on the West Side Highway in New York. Seeing a giant billboard of Whitney Houston—for her show at Madison Square Garden—Mom pointed and asked if we could possibly get tickets to see Judy Garland. I was impatient. I pointed back and sternly asked her, "Who is that, Mom? Is that Judy Garland? Is Judy Garland still alive?" But now that Mom was truly debilitated, I never again felt or expressed an iota of impatience. She was now the child. Liza and I were now the caring parents.

The thing that blew me away during those couple of weeks in Florida—Mom in a hospital, me down there selling her house and car and giving away all the beautiful St. John suits she would never wear again, Liza out in California researching assisted-living options—was that Mom had been driving to her ballroom dance lessons, and even still traveling to her dance competitions, in this unstable condition. I drove up to talk to her dance teacher one day. All he'd noticed was she'd been a little off balance the last few months. I suppose she felt such joy, such purpose, in her commitment to the dancing that it was the one place she was still nearly her full self.

When Mom took up ballroom dancing, I do believe it was the first time she understood me as a swimmer. Her genteel, artsy background kept her from appreciating the big muscles, the single-mindedness of my pursuit. But dancing in her middle-age years and beyond was her raison d'être and she was a dedicated athlete. She danced several hours every day of the week, prepping for competitions all over the United States. And Lucy was smooth on the dance floor. Her Viennese waltz was elegant, her fox-trot graceful, and she had perfect rhythm in all the Latin dances, the cha-cha and samba and rumba. I used to surprise her now and again and show up at her competitions. I'd watch secretly and then swoop in at the end of the night when she'd be presented with yet another big trophy. Mom was alive on the dance floor. And most of her time at home was also dedicated to her dancing. She'd watch her own videotapes, dissecting just what she needed to do to improve. And she'd study videos of the greats. I honestly believe, were Mom still with us today, she'd be blown away by my appearance, albeit brief, on *Dancing with the Stars,* more so than by my achievements as an athlete.

Those eight years, from that frightening day when she was driving north on the southbound side of a major interstate highway to the day she passed away, were of course not what I wanted for my mother's life. Romance, dancing, independence came to an abrupt end in one afternoon. Yet there was some admirable grace in Lucy being ready to let go of her life. She simply wasn't capable of the effort any longer. Once she got to California, with Liza and me tag-teaming to make sure one of us saw her nearly every day, instead of once a year, I believe she felt cared for, perhaps more so than at any other time in her life. And our relationship, our love for each other, found its heartbeat during those final years. We had never spent that kind of slow, patient, endearing time together, but now we did.

We passed the most simple afternoons—staring, for instance, at a strawberry, enchanted by its perfectly concentric rows of seeds. Mom would sit for endless, giggling minutes as my dog Scout wagged her tail across her face. We talked often about the love of dogs. We're lucky, any of us, to know all kinds of love. The love of a child, of a parent, of a friend, of a sibling, of a partner. But to love and be loved by a dog has its own very special tenderness. We were always dog people, our family, and when Liza and I brought our dogs over to Lucy's in those last years, it was probably a better mood elevator than any pill she ever took.

Mom and I loved to stride around the little putting green at her assisted-living home, where they'd had the genius to install magnets inside all the balls and in the cups as well. It didn't matter how off target Mom's shot was, it always careened around and fell magically into the cup. And she would smile that shy smile of hers and gloat: "Well, putting always was the best part of my game."

We had fun those last eight years together, despite Mom's mental decline. Liza and I were good partners in caretaking, surprising Mom with her favorite treats, always of a chocolate nature, piling up on her bed with our dogs to watch *Perry Mason* reruns, sneaking her out for chocolate-chip ice cream after lights-out and bed check. She might have seemed semiconscious, but when an outing for ice cream was uttered, she moved with lightning speed for her shoes. And Bonnie. All you have to know about Bonnie as a friend is that she visited my mom six days a week for eight years. Period.

From the first times I heard the stories of Lucy's mother's cruel double whammy, disowning her daughter twice, as a baby and again as a teenager, on some level I understood her pain and her shortcomings. Lucy wasn't a doting, cooking, caretaking mother. *Au contraire.* But I have no doubts that she adored me to the quick. From the moment she first held me in her arms, in New York City, August 22, 1949, until her last long gasp, when Liza and I held her in our arms, October 28, 2007, I rocked her world with delight and pride, and she rocked my world with unconditional love.

Lucy was brave in her final days. About a week before that last breath, she had a talk with me and Liza. It wasn't as direct as this, but she basically told us that as much as she lived to see our faces, hear our voices, none of it made sense to her anymore. She was in diapers. Couldn't walk on her own. Had to be helped with all body functions. She was drifting from her life, and she made the conscious decision not to eat. Sure enough, her resolve was evident. When gently offered a spoon to her mouth, she turned away. It was about six days. Lucy prepared, peacefully, to slip away.

"Dors bien, Maman." I can still hear you at the doorjamb. *"Dors bien, chérie."*

FOURTEEN

Sixty: Existential Angst

turned sixty two years after my mother died. I had never had a problem with age before. The cosmetics of aging—lines on the face, gravity tugging at the breasts—had never bothered me, hadn't even caught my attention. And at sixty, physical aging still wasn't my issue. It was the first true, staggering recognition of the end of this one-way road we're all traveling that hit me hard. So many days lived, none of them to be retrieved, no chance to live any one of them over again. I flashed back to that essay I had written in the fifth grade. If I had felt the stress of time fleeting at age ten, it was now scorching by at age sixty.

The life inventory began. On the people score, I gave myself a high grade. I may have blown the love of my life, but I had been fiercely loyal to my closest loved ones and, for that, I was at peace. My relationships are my lifeblood, and I nurture them with all my heart. If only my epitaph will read, "The best friend on Earth."

I have a friend who works as a hospice-care nurse. She has been sitting with the dying for thirty years. They are sometimes young people, tragedies, but most are old. And she tells me that never, no matter how successful the individual, no matter how many awards they've won, how much money they've made, they never talk about their careers during their last days. It's all about the people. Only the people.

I have my special family, small as it is. My wonderful sister, Liza, and I have become closer than ever in these later years. My nephew, Tim, beams at the center of my universe. I even got to join their mother-son dance at his wedding. Tim's wife, Karen, who is brains, beauty, and sheer delight all rolled into one, is now family, and that thrills me. Tim's sister Jennifer Julia, my niece, was a difficult relationship for me when she was a child. She was troubled, dark, hard for me to relate to, especially in comparison to the rocket of life-affirming light that was little Timmy. But Jennifer Julia has found her strength and happiness with her own loving family and she and I have made our way toward each other, too. At Tim and Karen's wedding, spring 2013, the emotions were soaring high for me, for everybody, as often happens when people you care deeply about revel in their joy. At the end of the ceremony, bursting with love, blind behind a sheet of tears, I sobbed an apology to Jennifer Julia for being such a lousy aunt. She might have been tough for me, but I was the adult. I was the one who could have led our way. She stepped close, looked me tenderly in the eyes, and said, "Why don't we start today?" The child leading the adult, as is often the way.

Starting with Candace in my twenties, then Bonnie and Nina in my thirties, these are the forever friendships that ultimately define my life. When one day sharing last breaths with my own hospice nurse, these are the tales I will tell, my time with these treasured souls of mine.

But if the people inventory at sixty was rich, the value I cherished of "No day a fingernail better. No regrets" had withered. It wasn't a question of a catalog of achievements. It was deeper than that. Had I become a person I could admire?

I became choked with existential angst.

One day during the month of that sixtieth birthday, August 2009, I was driving and the poet Mary Oliver's nonpareil rhetorical question flooded my brain:

"What is it you plan to do with your one wild and precious life?"

Oliver's commanding directive had guided me a couple of times before, but this time her words cut to the quick. I had to pull over. At the side of the road on a buzzing Los Angeles street, I was alone in silent contemplation. I was thirsty—no, desperate—to live with unwavering commitment. I needed the high, the inspiration, of chasing a star. I wanted every drop of my potential to be tapped. If genetics were to fol-

AGE SIXTY
BACK TO WORLD-CLASS ATHLETE

September 2, 2013
HAVANA to KEY WEST
110.86 miles
52 hours, 54 minutes, 18 seconds

She freaking made it!

TOP The thirty-five-year dream is realized. My two best friends, Bonnie Stoll and Candace Hogan, stand tall with me.

BOTTOM Bonnie at her Head Handler post. Every training swim, every minute of the Cuba crossings . . . eyes always on the Swimmer

TOP The Xtreme Dream flotilla. I swim next to the kayakers. They track my navigation boat *Voyager*, and the rest of our boats follow.

MIDDLE The Shark Divers prepare to protect me through the night: Caleb Bucci (left) and Ben Shepardson (right)

BOTTOM Fifteen-hour training swim in St. Thomas

TOP Bonnie helps with a thousand training details
MIDDLE My Kayak Team stays close by, the electronic Shark Shields tethered to the bottom of their boats
BOTTOM LEFT Bonnie, Shark Divers Captain Niko Gazzale, and jellyfish expert Dr. Angel Yanagihara meet before a dangerous night session.
BOTTOM RIGHT I am not allowed to touch the boat. Bonnie reaches out to drop pasta in my mouth. Handler Jon Hennessey on my boat dating back to 1978

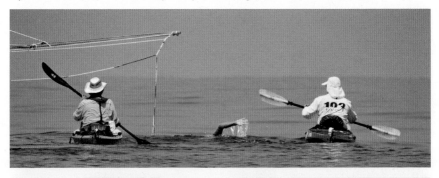

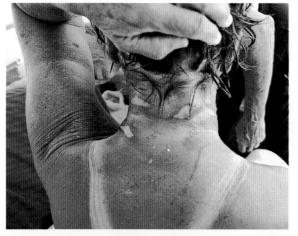

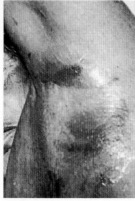

OPPOSITE, TOP RIGHT INSET As I would drift far out to the right, Bonnie would hold up an orange life preserver for hours on end to bring me back closer to the boat and safety zone.

OPPOSITE, MIDDLE My Team invented an underwater white streamer to help me keep on course when sensory deprivation took me far from reality.

OPPOSITE, BOTTOM The streamer would turn to red LED lights for me to follow through the nights. Kayakers Buco Pantelis and Darlene Meadows protect

TOP Chafing from ocean salt is painful

MIDDLE LEFT Biceps bruise 2012. Overtraining in huge swells

MIDDLE RIGHT Third-degree burns under arms from ocean chafing over long hours

BOTTOM The powerful Gulf Stream screeching east four to five times faster than my swim speed north toward Florida. The navigation is very tricky.

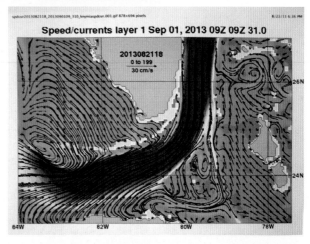

Speed/currents layer 1 Sep 01, 2013 09Z 09Z 31.0

2013082118
0 to 199
30 cm/s

TOP LEFT Maya Marchant: Expert concentration at the wheel. Winter/spring training Team St. Maarten

TOP RIGHT John Berry: Ops Chief 2013. Summer training Team Key West

MIDDLE LEFT David Marchant: my first Navigator. We talk strategy on Cuban shore. Summer training Team St. Maarten

MIDDLE RIGHT Kathy Loretta greets me at the end of every Mexico training swim, day or night, rain or shine. Also our Cuba Ops Chief

BOTTOM LEFT Dee Brady: Captain, Navigation Boat Drivers. Summer training Team Key West

TOP Mark Sollinger, Ops Chief 2011–2012. Chief winter/spring training St. Maarten (behind: in hat, Steve Munatones, independent observer, publisher of the *Daily News Open Water Swimming*, and Navigator John Bartlett)

MIDDLE LEFT Pauline Berry, number two Handler. Summer training Team Key West

MIDDLE RIGHT We swim into the night, Shark Diver atop *Voyager*

BOTTOM RIGHT John Bartlett, my ultimate Navigator. I swim just outside his windows.

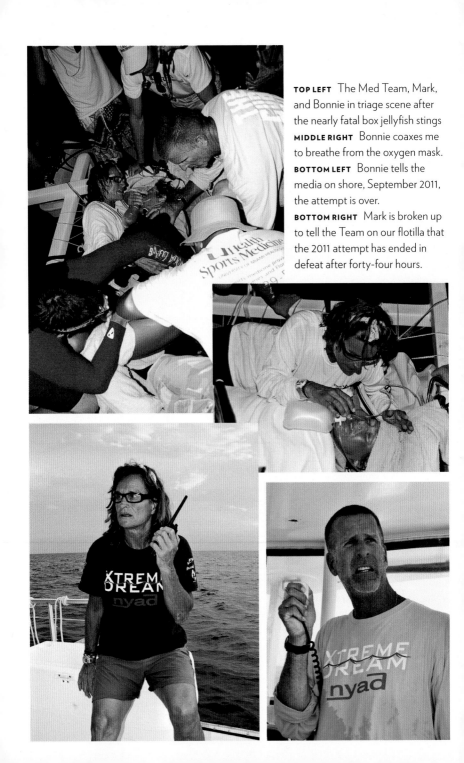

TOP LEFT The Med Team, Mark, and Bonnie in triage scene after the nearly fatal box jellyfish stings
MIDDLE RIGHT Bonnie coaxes me to breathe from the oxygen mask.
BOTTOM LEFT Bonnie tells the media on shore, September 2011, the attempt is over.
BOTTOM RIGHT Mark is broken up to tell the Team on our flotilla that the 2011 attempt has ended in defeat after forty-four hours.

TOP LEFT Bonnie tells me she's proud of my courage. We're going to find a way through those jellyfish.

MIDDLE The box jellyfish tentacles have left their sting marks. A life-or-death experience
BOTTOM RIGHT More rips of stings on my back

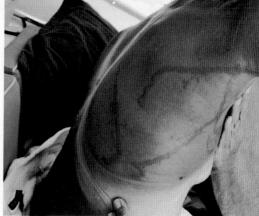

OPPOSITE, TOP LEFT Bonnie consoles me.

OPPOSITE, TOP RIGHT Mark understands my emotional pain.

OPPOSITE, BOTTOM RIGHT 2012 makeshift pantyhose jellyfish mask with duct tape

OPPOSITE, BOTTOM LEFT Niko Gazzale, Head Shark Safety Diver, and Angel Yanagihara, box jellyfish expert. They prepare for night diving. We use no lights whatsoever at night.

TOP Dr. Angel Yanagihara, world-renowned jellyfish expert

MIDDLE I pull on the silicone jellyfish mask. Took us a year to design and fabricate

BOTTOM I have to lift the head very high to breathe with the mask. It took months of training to be able to swim with it and always caused duress. But it was literally a lifesaver.

TOP With bugle at start of Cuba Swim, Marina Hemingway, Havana. Five times I looked out at that faraway horizon, each time brimming with conviction.

MIDDLE Navigator John Bartlett is thrilled with our progress on the fifth try.

BOTTOM Two hours from Florida, Labor Day, 2013, I give a thank-you speech to my Team.

TOP LEFT Candace cheers me as I head into the second night, fifth try.

TOP RIGHT Nina (Lederman) and Tim (Wheeler) come out to root me on with just a few hours to go to Florida.

MIDDLE Handlers Bonnie and Pauline share a light moment with me as we seem to be making it this time, at long last.

BOTTOM Bonnie and Candace in joy as I swim the last few of the fifty-three hours to make it all the way across.

TOP Thousands greet me on Smathers Beach, Key West. My first words: "Never, ever give up." Second thought: "You're never too old to chase your dreams." Third: "It looks like a solitary sport, but it's a Team."

MIDDLE/BOTTOM LEFT Bonnie guiding me to the official finish, where "no more sea water lies beyond."

MIDDLE RIGHT Bonnie and I hug. We've done it. Pauline and Candace and even the fans are crying.

BOTTOM RIGHT Bonnie, Tim, Candace, and I share the triumph.

low suit, and Mom died at eighty-two, I now had a fleeting twenty-two years to bust out and fully reach beyond my grasp.

Right there in the car that day, it hit me like a ton of bricks. Cuba. Cuba had always been the faraway Dream. The Beautiful Dream. The Impossible Dream. Cuba had always been about more than sport to me. Beyond setting an extreme athletic record, above achieving an historic endurance triumph, it was an epic challenge that took my breath away. From my mother pointing toward that mythical place when I was only nine, to the moment its shape on the world map enraptured me in my twenties, to the morning I first stood on the Havana shore to try that 1978 crossing, Cuba was my emblem for living large.

My adrenaline spiked. My eyelids widened, my pulse quickened, I sat taller. Would the shoulders come back, at this age? Would the will be there for such an outrageous, extreme endeavor?

Over those thirty years out of the water I had maintained a superlative level of physical fitness. I may have no longer been a world-class athlete, but intense training, every day, was a priority. And it always will be. I live by the credo that all life systems—brain, heart, relationships, career, energy, perspective, clarity, hope—function at a higher level when the body runs smoothly at a superior fitness level. In my non-swimming years, while traveling, I would forgo eating and sleeping rather than sacrifice my time for working out. I was a decent distance runner, until my knees had a serious talk with me at age forty-eight. I did a one-hundred-mile bike ride every Friday. Bonnie and I started a fitness business, BravaBody.com, which led me to yoga, which changed my life. I had for too long operated under the misconception that to be calm and quiet was antithetical to being strong and fierce. The composure of yoga amplified my inner strength.

Granted, while covering almost every sport on the planet those thirty years, as a retired ocean swimmer I was oblivious to the growth of open-water swimming around the world. Along with the popularity of the triathlon, long-distance swimming had become a draw to a fairly large population. I did, however, keep my eye on Cuba. I like to think myself a sporting person, but I will admit that each time a swimmer would make an attempt at the Cuba-to-Florida crossing and fail, I would do a little happy dance, alone in my living room. The Dream was still alive for me now, at age sixty, but I hadn't swum a stroke in thirty years.

FIFTEEN

The Dream Rekindled

Secretly, I started swimming in a friend's country club pool, August 2009, the month I turned sixty. Those first few days were a rude awakening. Not much of those three decades of other exercise was crossing over to the water. Swimmers in shape, with efficient and powerful strokes, ride high. I was slogging along, very low indeed. I started with a paltry twenty minutes of slow, easy freestyle, with fins to ease pressure on the shoulders. By mid-September, a month later, I was going two hours—still with fins, but the back and shoulders and triceps were stronger. I was finding my old stroke, up nearer the surface. I decided to graduate to a fifty-meter, Olympic-standard pool and drop the fins. By mid-October, I was putting in four- and five-hour swims. And having serious talks with myself. Bonnie noticed my developing raccoon goggle lines, Candace kept saying there was something different about me, but I simply said I had decided to add some swimming back into my regular fitness routine.

By November, I was going six and seven hours at a stretch. Most days, I would barely make it from the pool to my car after the workout. It was beyond falling asleep, it was passing out, slumped at the wheel in the parking lot for a couple of hours, before I could get it together to drive home. The body faced a daunting load of work. Yet the high road of commitment had me wild-eyed. This was going to take unknown physical dedication. It was going to come to emotional courage.

In December, Nina took a bunch of us on a birthday cruise. After four months of pool swimming, here was my first chance to see how I felt in the ocean. Docked at the Mazatlán port in Mexico, I went alone with my swim gear to a resort hotel and swam out around the beautiful islands just off shore. What had become grueling monotony to me back in my twenties was this day otherworldly hedonism. The water was lusciously warm, glassy flat. I could raise my goggles just a fraction of an inch and enjoy the island contours, the sandy beach coastlines. I was cruising around like a little motorboat, gliding from this island to the next. The shoulders were strong. My mind was happy. Four hours. Cuba still my secret. I needed what I considered a real training swim before I could be really sure, before I would be ready to share the vision with anybody.

Early January 2010, I went to Mexico for a couple of short swims. I stayed with good friends in Todos Santos, just north of Cabo San Lucas, at the tip of the Baja Peninsula; they were kind enough to arrange a fisherman to go out with me for a few hours. It was a brisk day, the wind whipping the air to a windchill perhaps in the low sixties. The water was about sixty-eight. My fisherman was at first a bit macho, as if he couldn't care less what we were doing. He just wanted to be paid what he would lose for not fishing that day. He wore a thick turtleneck fleece sweater. Our outing was the talk of the town, a first in these parts.

It was rough. Fast-moving, four-to-five-foot waves. I was shivering by the fourth hour. I swam in close to the boat every hour for some water and banana, and the boatman and I forged a bond that day. He got more and more involved, giving me emphatic hand signals as he changed course to try to work with the waves. He began to yell "Brava" whenever I'd start off into the whitecaps again after the short feedings.

At six hours, twenty-two minutes, I told him it was enough for the day. The waves into the beach were now rolling in huge swells, as high as ten feet. He pointed out the best landing spot for me and said he'd have to go farther down the beach to get his boat safely onto the shore. I was cold and motivated to get out, so I gauged a lull between the swells, put my head down, and swam hard. Trying to stand in waist-high water, the undertow was so ferocious I had to throw myself down onto hands and knees and power-crawl up beyond the surf. Shivering hard now, I saw the boatman sprinting down the beach to me with open arms. No longer the aloof macho man, he was weeping openly when he reached me. He gave me a huge bear hug and I burrowed into his body heat. He kept pounding his chest and exclaiming, *"Corazón!"* Heart.

My friend Linda rushed me back to her house and got me into a steaming hot bath. Her four-year-old daughter Ava, a precocious Penélope Cruz look-alike, sat curled up on the side of the stone tub, staring. She understood that I was in discomfort, so she didn't say a word. After about forty minutes, observing that my uncontrollable shivering had subsided and I was returning to normal, Ava put her little hand to her cheek, gave me a penetrating dark-eyed look, and asked, "Why?"

A four-year-old asks the germane question. Fair enough. I understand the answer is elusive to the outside world, but to me the spirit of the quest is grand. Inspiring. That first official training swim, just over six hours, was nothing to brag about, but I knew on the plane back to Los Angeles there was nowhere to go now but *onward.*

The hard-core training for Cuba 2010 needed to get under way soon, by mid-January, six months before the summer attempt. It was time to share my resolve with my five intimates.

I told Bonnie first. As is her way, she took in the news quietly, then asked to have time to think about it. This was a radical turn of events. She needed to go through a training swim first. Fair enough. Nina was over-the-moon excited, as were my sister Liza and my nephew Tim. Now Candace was a different story. Candace was the only one in my current life who'd been there, front and center on my boat, back in the 1970s. When I sat down with her for our heart-to-heart on this rekindled Dream, she wasn't happy.

"You've been there. Done that. To the *n*th degree. Why travel backward? That's not your way. You're the one who always leads us forward, onward. You're the progressive one. This is an old dream. You have so many talents. You've wanted to do your one-woman show for years now. Why this? I don't get it."

But once training in earnest and the push to organize for summer started, Candace caught the high I was living every waking moment of every day. She was in. I had hopes that Bonnie's spirit would also ignite. She would be my perfect Head Handler, in charge of all training, in charge of my physical and mental reserves on the crossing. But I knew not to push her. Leave Bonnie alone and she'll come to the right decision every time.

As for Tim, he was a recent star graduate of Berkeley's journalism school. I asked him if he would film the journey and he jumped at the chance, neither of us imagining a wide public would seize onto the guts of the mission. We simply thought it would be a shame not to have some archival video, chronicling the training and the Cuba Swim itself, for personal posterity.

None of us had reason to imagine this swim would be anything more than a private enterprise. It had been a long time since I'd been known as the maverick for the long swims I had done way back in my twenties. We're living in a different world these days. You hop on a treadmill at a health club and chat with the woman next to you for a moment and learn she's getting ready to climb Annapurna or snowshoe across the Antarctic. People are pursuing impressive ultra-endurance events in all corners of the globe, from running across the Kalahari Desert to rowing across the Pacific.

I couldn't be concerned with whether the public or the media would get excited about my personal Dream, except that fund-raising would be a challenge. Every major expedition runs on a hefty budget. I was going to need a Team of professionals in several areas. A Shark Team. Navigation Team. I told myself I'd figure it out. Much work to do but still, the heart of it starts with the athlete's singular rapture. That I could guarantee up front I had.

Mid-January, I went back down to Todos Santos, site of my first official training swim, and Tim accompanied me to start his filming. These weren't ideal training waters—too cold—but I hadn't established a permanent training camp yet. One more swim in Mexico and I'd have a location dialed in. Then Bonnie would be ready to try the Head Handler position.

This time, not only had the sea temperatures dropped a couple of degrees, but the giant squid migration south down the California coast had reached the tip of Baja. Thousands of four-foot squid were feeding in a massive frenzy, literally grabbing birds out of the air. I found my fisherman, who told me his buddy had lost his hand to a squid the day prior. We weren't going to be swimming here. We got some tips to drive a couple of hours up to the Sea of Cortez, on the eastern side of the Baja Peninsula. The water would be brisk, but at least we wouldn't go back to L.A. with nothing accomplished..

The Sea of Cortez is magical, a dancing sparkle of grey-blue as far as the eye can see, with soft curvatures of hilly land masses embracing the shoreline. Tim and I rented a small panga boat, sort of a large metal rowboat with a motor, and two young guys took us out. The first day was again just over six hours. The next day I swam over to an island and back, just over eight hours that time. I was chilled to the bone. Stumbling up onto the sand where some locals were enjoying live music on a Saturday twilight, a big man rushed out to greet me in the shallows with a welcoming wraparound towel. As I sat shivering, getting myself together, a number of the Mexicans came to me with tears in their eyes. It turns out nobody in their history had ever swum over to that island, much less swum over and back. *"Es mi honor,"* they would say. "It's such an honor to meet you." They thought that this was the goal I was aiming for. And why wouldn't they? It felt hard enough for me, too.

I put my head in my hands and cried on the beach that night. I told myself I better look deep inside and ask if I had this in me. The next six months were going to be hell. Would it be enough if my five dearhearts and a few volunteer experts were the only ones to ever know about this, if they were the only ones on that Florida shore at the end?

That night, sleeping restlessly under a three-story, hand-woven palm fronds of a Mexican *palapa,* I contemplated all these probing queries. No, it didn't matter if the public didn't wind up caring. The Dream of crossing from Cuba to Florida stirred my soul. This swim was the stuff of building character of granite. I had better steel my will now, tonight. This little swim in Mexico had been tougher than the first little swim. From here on, the journey was going to grow more and more punishing. From this night on, nothing could be allowed to rattle my faith. This night, the contract was made, and I signed on the dotted line deep within me. I had been yearning to be a doer again. I had answered the Mary Oliver question with the decision to go full throttle with this wild and precious life of mine. I was in it now. Full throttle.

SIXTEEN

It's On! 2010

A winter training camp took some research, in terms of warm enough waters, not too long a flight from home. I live in Los Angeles, the Pacific here way too cold to train for a two-day swim in the tropics. I started calling contacts in Hawaii, Mexico, Florida. January, February, and March, water temps in all those places are in the low seventies, okay for seven, maybe eight hours. But I was going to need to escalate up to ten-hour sessions, and higher, pretty quickly. I was never built for cold water. And even the best cold-water swimmers couldn't go the outrageous fifty to sixty hours this Cuba Swim would demand in anything but tropical temperatures.

I found a friend of a friend who managed a fleet of fishing boats just a bit south of Cancún. Kathy Loretta, who used to be the Barbara Walters of Mexican radio, interviewing every head of state who passed through Mexico for thirty years, had now semiretired to the charming little town of Puerto Morelos, on the Yucatán coast. She was instantly kind and organized, told me she could set me up with some of her fishermen for long swim outings but the water temps at that time were still in the low seventies and wouldn't warm up close to eighty until late April or so. We made a plan to reconnect then.

Nina had grown up on St. Maarten, in the Caribbean, and remembered her childhood friend Maya had married a major boat guy. She suggested I call them. That area of the Caribbean would be perfect, in that the water temperatures late January stayed in the upper seventies. And there were no dangerous sharks to speak of—sandy ocean floor, no reefs, so no good feeding for sharks—and there were no nasty jellyfish, either.

The last week of January I headed to St. Maarten, where Maya and David Marchant took me through the tough winter and spring of my first long swims in many decades. They were terrific. They had spent their lives on the ocean, sailed much of the world, raising their children port to port. They knew the sea. Even on a very windy day, hard to gauge my ability to cover distance with all the up-and-down action, David would turn us around many miles out, approximating that we'd reached the halfway point of a fifteen-hour swim, and, to the second, we would touch the dock in fifteen hours total. The Marchants were patient and caring. And they caught on to the magnitude of the mission.

David, an Englishman who grew up in the Bahamas, with flowing blond hair he likes to shake in the sea breeze, is both an expert sailor and a bon vivant who loves a good story, and a good meal. Sometimes I'd see him perched on the bow of our boat as I was swimming, looking like he was deep into some metaphysical thought and on the next feeding, I'd ask what his head was into. He'd say, "Oh, I was thinking about a seared tuna sandwich with a pesto sauce and some fresh lemon zest."

David spent countless hours researching the charts of the Florida Straits during these outings. Maya was expert at the wheel. Her concentration and ability to keep me directly midships, starboard side, so that we could both see each other easily every stroke, was remarkable. Maya still has a touch of a Dutch accent and fits the bill of the easygoing island woman, a good-looking blonde, barefoot and lithe. She's a great listener, and I so appreciated how she understood all the nuances of what I was feeling day to day and what it was going to take to achieve this. There was many an evening that I would be cold and seasick after battling waves all day long. Maya would run from the dock to get a hot bath started for me, get a hot drink ready, and then run back to the boat to help me walk up the steps from the dock.

David and Maya took me on my first set of three long swims, and on my next trip to St. Maarten, Bonnie came down to try out the Head Handler role.

From day one, Bonnie had all the right athletic instincts. She knew when to bring me in for an unscheduled feeding. She knew when I was approaching dehydration before I did. She knew when my shoulder was vulnerable and advised me, for example, to take a planned nine-hour swim down to six for that day. She understood just the right balance of work and rest for my body and the right tone to use, in and out of the water, to keep me focused and not lose faith.

Our routine was basically to spend eight days with David and Maya, doing three swims. Then I'd go back to Los Angeles to recover, gain the weight back, do some pool swimming, which was good for strength, and work on the details of the expedition. I was the CEO of an enterprise that was going to require some $400,000 cash operational funds, other services and goods donated, the management of some fifty people in all, and the logistics of several layers of permits to enter a country not readily accessible to an American group with several large boats and a slew of sophisticated electronics. Many friends coaxed me to find someone to take over all that organization, and I thankfully had a lot of help, but it actually relieved the stresses of training, to be in charge of the whole operation. Or maybe I'm just a control freak who believes I need to oversee every detail of anything that's truly important to me.

After some ten to twenty days at home, it was back to St. Maarten where we'd increase the hours. The first trip had been three eight-hour swims; the next was a thirteen, an eleven, and a ten. And we escalated through May until we were putting in eighteen-hour days in the ocean. The concept was to render fifteen hours a period I could easily handle. If the 103 miles between Cuba and Florida were to take about sixty hours—we estimated it at the high end to be conservative—that would mean four fifteen-hour back-to-back periods. So the goal was to make fifteen hours seem very little hardship for both my body and mind. Well, fifteen hours in the sea is always going to bring hardship. That's a swim duration that most marathon swimmers will never do in their lifetimes, and I was going that distance several times a week. Never easy, fifteen hours, but less and less miserable as we put in the work.

By late April, along with the excursions to St. Maarten, we also mixed in trips to Puerto Morelos and hooked up with Kathy Loretta for long swims in the Yucatán Channel. It was a refreshing change of scenery, although the splendor of St. Maarten and those azure-blue waters, is hard to beat. The huge difference in Mexico was the shark factor. Outside the reef, you are most definitely in shark territory, where they feed in the channel and at the edge of the reef. We were sent a device from Australia called the Shark Shield, about the size of the palm of your hand. Tied to our boat, its four-foot antenna trails out underwater, emitting an elliptical field of electricity that bothers a shark's sensitive ampullae (small nodes on their snout). CNN sent us footage they shot in the Bahamas of sharks swarming aggressively to take down chum on a string; with the Shield attached to the string, they come toward the chum but immediately arch their backs and pull away. That was reassuring. Experts we interviewed felt the Shields would not give 100 percent protection but would serve as a significant deterrent. In Mexico, we always had a Shield antenna dangling near me.

I came to associate the Puerto Morelos training with the familiar silhouette of Kathy Loretta, tiny at just over five feet, her silver hair all the way down past her shorts. No matter how late we'd sweep up onto the beach, no matter the middle of thunderstorms, standing there would be Kathy, devoted, with a big fluffy towel, waiting to envelop me and walk me to a comforting hot bath. Each Mexico swim, at that last quarter mile, I'd look up, and the sight of my sentry, standing loyal at the ready, would touch a tired heart.

My muscles responded well to the first ultra ocean training I had done in thirty years. Month by month, that winter and spring of 2010, I grew bigger and stronger and tougher. But the stomach was never happy. Bonnie would get me up at two a.m. for a twelve-hour swim, planned for sunrise to sundown, six a.m. to six p.m., so that I could eat enough and digest somewhat before the start. She'd basically have to force-feed me oatmeal and hard-boiled eggs and bananas and protein bars. I'm not a morning eater to start with, so facing lots of food at two a.m. isn't easy for me. She'd push me to drink the best part of a quart of cranberry juice I could get down in those predawn hours, efficient for hydration. I'd sneak back under the cuddly covers for even minutes at a time, in between bites and stretching, not because I needed more sleep; I was basking in the comfort and security of the cozy duvet to the last possible moment, knowing what a tough day lay ahead. I'd fixate on the clock: twenty-two minutes before I'd have to exit the snuggly covers and brace myself for the inevitable suffering to come. Seventeen minutes. I'd savor the smooth sheets, the weight of the duvet, as if the master of supersensory tactile powers.

It doesn't matter what kind of shape you're in. Twelve hours in the ocean is a day of discipline, every time out. While it's true that my confidence level grew throughout the spring, my body able to power through those long hours, I would still have to gear up for every training swim mentally. Bonnie and I would stand on the dock at five-thirty, waiting for Maya and David to swing around with the boat. It wasn't a light, frivolous mood. We weren't chatty. I'd get my cap and goggles on but wait until the last possible moment to take my robe off. Again, it wasn't that it was cold out. There was simply a desire to be wrapped in comfort, before the discomfort began. Bonnie would grease me down, for the chafing. She switched from Vaseline to Aquaphor, which lasted longer, but we continued to search for some substance to keep the bathing suit seams and the neck edge of the bathing cap from digging into the skin with the salt friction. We'd treat those bloody cuts at the end of each swim with natural aloe, trying to get them at least somewhat healed before the next outing. The chafing wouldn't keep me from making the Cuba Swim, or even from finishing any of these training swims, but those wounds surely were miserable.

David would give me a wind report, usually not welcome news, and he'd base our route for the day on that wind. We'd often try to hug the shore, tucked away from the wind, if we could. Our goal wasn't to get tough and swim in the highest winds possible. We'd be looking to pick the flattest optimum seas for Cuba. But we never canceled a training swim due to weather or winds, either. Storms rolled in, wind whipped up, but hell or high water, if we said six a.m. start, that's when we'd shove off the dock and take the first stroke.

Bonnie developed our nutrition program through those months, too. She'd try different goos and gels and ratios of electrolytes to add to our water bladders. It was easier for me to take a hose of a CamelBak bladder and then just float on my back, sipping at my leisure, rather than try to hold a cup above the surface, having to kick hard to keep salt water from contaminating the drink. Scissor-kicking to hold anything high above the wave action is an unintelligent expenditure of energy. Bonnie tried to prepare all my food in one-bite portions so I wouldn't have to hold things up in the air. Inevitably, especially on rough days, my stomach would become very upset. It was common for me to vomit violently at least a few times on a very wavy day. Bonnie would then get me to sip a bit of Coca-Cola, a good elixir for settling the stomach.

Many of the ultra athletes in different disciplines, climbing and running, talk about an iron stomach. We all know what it is to get the muscles in shape, to steel the mind. But often it's the stomach that makes or breaks an ultra adventurer's success. Whether it's at extreme altitude, or in desert heat, or in a saltwater medium, those of us who go long continuous hours under considerable physical duress have a hard time taking in any food or drink after a certain time. Bonnie would have to beg me to take in anything, then hope I would keep it down.

Along with the nutrition program, Bonnie put together a number of systems. Hand signals for day, whistle signals for night, an order of crew commands in crisis, the right words to get me through severe lows. I'm not one who responds to tough love. Berating does not work for me. Bonnie lets me know she can see if I'm in a world of hurt. She helps me up out of the valley, stroke by stroke, sip by sip.

Long about early May I am far from the rock-bottom exhaustion I collapsed into at the end of a twelve-hour day back in February. Those first few trips were pure hell. Now I am on a roll. My body is a lot happier, and I have developed systems of both counting and a playlist of eighty-five songs to get through the hours. I learned from my friend Emily Saliers, of the Indigo Girls, that all the songs on my list are in ⁴⁄₄ time. I had no idea. But those are the rhythms that evidently match the cadence of my stroke.

So I hear Bob Dylan's voice, all the nuances. I hear his harmonica, to the exact pitch. I'm not using headphones. I just hear the song in my brain. And I stroke, hitting the left hand at the particular beat, then the right at the next.

> Go away from my window
> [left, right, left, right]
> Leave at your own chosen speed
> [left, right, left, right]

Then the second verse. And the third. The metronomic precision of my stroke cadence serves not only to pass the time but to count hours and minutes with remarkable accuracy. Who knows why certain songs engage us, but I do know the ones that hypnotize me out there. I need tunes that my brain wants to engage in for hours at a time. And it is the melodies, not necessarily the lyrics, that put me under their spell.

I love singing Elton John's "Daniel" in the eerie middle of the dark ocean night:

> Daniel is traveling tonight on a plane

Lots of Beatles. *Revolver. Abbey Road.* Just for a short series, to get to the end of a feeding period, I go through a few hundred of "Her Majesty":

> Her Majesty's a pretty nice girl

Then through the short verse, Paul McCartney's irreverent voice and simple acoustic guitar delighting my ears, and on to the end.

> Oh yeah, someday I'm gonna make her mine

A nice short ditty that made my mind happy for many an hour. As I say, lots of Beatles. "Norwegian Wood." "Polythene Pam." "Eleanor Rigby." "Get Back." "Let It Be." "Day Tripper." Sometimes I'd try to run through as many Beatles songs as I could remember. I think I got up to 160 on one swim.

And there was Joe Cocker. I counted on "The Letter" for a lift when I was tired or cold. Around sundown, Janis Joplin's version of "Me and Bobby McGee" would breeze through my brain. And desperate times called for desperate measures. Three a.m., sunrise nowhere in sight, it was always Neil Young. People have kidded me that I should be out there singing "Hallelujah," not a song about heroin addiction. And "Hallelujah" was in there, along with James Taylor and Grace Slick and the Drifters and the Everly Brothers and Little Eva, but when I was low, running on empty, that Neil Young haunting falsetto put me in a trance, stilled my mind.

> I caught you knockin'
> at my cellar door

I'd go so far as to say the sound of Neil Young's voice, that song particularly, "The Needle and the Damage Done," enraptured me. It saved me a number of times when my body was on the edge of giving in. Delayed gratification has long been both a thrill and a strong suit of mine. I was sorely tempted to go to "Damage Done" in the lonely post-midnight hours. But I would stall, the criteria defined as dire straits, before I'd allow that falsetto to seep out and then ring through my ears.

Then there are times when you're childlike. You're not thinking clearly anymore. Your brain simply can't focus on something as complex and profound as the next lyric to "She loves you . . . yeah, yeah. . . ." I'd revert, without much conscious planning but from some spontaneous need for simplicity, to military calls ("I don't know but I've been told . . .") and walking chants ("When the streets are paved with gold . . .") and toddlers' songs. "The Itsy Bitsy Spider." And "Alouette," going through all the body parts, head to toe, in French and then in Spanish.

> *Je te plumerai le bec*
> *Je te plumerai le bec*
> *Et le bec, alouette*
> *Alouette, et le bec*
> *Alouette, gentille alouette*
> *Alouette, je te plumerai . . .*

I'd sing "Old MacDonald" in Spanish and then in French—not that I have any idea if they sing that song in those languages, or how they go. But I'd think of as many animals as I could.

Viejo MacDonald tenía un rancho
E-I-E-I-O
Y en este rancho tenía una mosca
E-I-E-I-O
Con un buzz buzz aquí
Y un buzz buzz aqua
Aquí un buzz, aqua un buzz buzz
Par todo unos buzz buzz
Viejo MacDonald tenía un rancho
E-I-E-I-O

(Some of you Latinos are laughing out loud right now.) Then in French:

Vieux MacDonald avait une ferme

On a hard ten-hour swim in Mexico, Tim, who was with me and Bonnie for a lot of the 2010 training, had brought his fiancée, Karen, to help with his filming. This day was rough as heck. They were in semi-crisis all day on the boat. The waves were mammoth, and we were in constant danger of smashing into the coral reef. I was mentally strong that day and fought hard, but we were all fried by sundown. The sea lay down the last couple of hours, so we could all finally relax a bit. I was actually enjoying the golden light streaming across the calm surface. Karen hadn't spoken to me from the boat all day. This was her first outing, and she didn't want to interfere. But near the end, when she could see I was happy to be almost finished, and proud of myself for handling demanding circumstances with no complaints, I came in for the last feeding and Karen asked her question: Am I out there thinking provocative thoughts about the meaning of life and such? "That's often the case," I said, but at that particular moment, I was engrossed in singing repetitions of the *Beverly Hillbillies* theme song.

Come and listen to a story 'bout a man named Jed
A poor mountaineer, barely kept his family fed

The shallow and the profound—those tunes became companions to me. I relied on them. They got me through many a tough hour. And, à la Pavlov's dog, I snap back to those hours every time I hear "Me and Bobby McGee" or the Bee Gees' "Stayin' Alive" or Gordon Lightfoot's "If You Could Read My Mind" or Simon and Garfunkel's "Bridge over Troubled Water" or "Scarborough Fair."

Numbers were even more a staple for passing and counting the time, when trapped in the solitary confinement of that protracted monotony. It amazes me to this day that for those thousands of hours, I never went to the same counting progression twice. The only constant was the sequence of languages. Whether the goal was a thousand strokes, counting only the left hand, or twelve sets of one hundred with a particular song in between sets, it was always English first, then German, then Spanish, and finish in French. The French brought hope: Nearing the end. Many hours traversed.

Similar to the songs on my playlist, "hearing" the sounds of the languages out there somehow teased my ears with pleasure. Starting with the hubbub of foreign inflections in my home as a child, languages from around the world have been one of the delights of my life. French, to me, is a narcotic to the ear. And I love the chauvinistic attitude one needs to truly speak and pronounce French properly. You need to pose the mouth in an assured pout, as if to say behind each word, "Well, of course, without doubt, this is an unquestionable fact; it simply can't be discussed in any other manner." If you've ever witnessed the French in an American buffet line, this is how it goes. They stroll from one end to the other, plates pristine empty white, shrugging, the mouths in full pout: *"Mais, qu'est-ce que c'est, exactement? Ce n'est pas du fromage, quoi. Il n'y a rien. Rien, je te le dit."* ("But what is this, exactly? This is not cheese, not really. There's nothing, I tell you. Nothing.") The precision of the vowels, along with the velvet consonants, makes for a potion of pleasure, even when what you're saying is unpleasant. French, even a French accent in English, is seductive. I admit I pull it out when I need to move things along. In a crowded store, I might call from the back, exaggerating the guttural *rs* "I'm sorry, I find ze blue one, but can you elp me wiz ze grey one?" The sales clerk runs to me: *"Ah, oui, oui, etes-vous de Paris?"*

So the French is the delightful dessert I save for last out there. I enjoy the German exactitude. *"Acht und zwanzig."* There isn't a lazy bone in the German language body. And when I come to the Spanish each progression, I am actually transported to a passionate attitude, pronouncing *"ochenta y cinco"* as if I'm standing enraptured in front of a magical Chagall.

Languages are one of the joys of my life. And they are key to my getting through many of the solitary hours at sea.

The sport seems at times a pure chronicling of masochism, so much physical pain and suffering, an unrelenting mental challenge. When you read about the foremost expeditions up the alpine peaks, you get the same sense. There is dire altitude sickness, rugged austerity in carrying the loads, heads down, each step agony.

Mountaineer Ed Viesturs, with many Everest summits to his name—all the noble way, without bottled oxygen—says he is so taxed above twenty-six thousand feet that he literally must stop to take twenty-five deep breaths with every step of only a few inches. I can't speak to the duress at the top of the world, but I am one of the few who knows intimately the eccentric conditions and demands way out off shore in the ocean. All the details smack of distress: vomiting from exertion, seasickness, hallucinations, hypothermia, dehydration, shoulder pain, the mind struggling for focus through the fog of sensory deprivation.

An outsider gets the distinct impression that the only joy for us extremists comes when we touch the summit or reach the other shore. But there is joy in the journey itself. To see the photos of Ed Viesturs on the Grand Couloir of Everest, to read his words from that vantage point, is to be inside his racing heart as he surveys a lunar-type landscape, elusive to most humankind. It's to join him in the poetry of our Earth.

For me, too, there's sheer awe of the planet itself. That awe filled me these recent years of chasing the Cuba Dream. It's a very different time of life, our sixties, compared to our twenties. The ego is not so fragile, the peacock feathers not so driven to strut. Add to that the realization that I swam many of those hours back in my twenties in utter rage. This time I was in love with our blue planet, whereas I barely noticed her when I was young.

The same heightened awareness held true for my body as well. The power of my shoulders, the über recognition of the mechanics of my efficient stroke, made me giddy with joy. I would catch resistance with the left hand, bend the elbow to let the biceps come into play, close up to the torso, rotate the shoulders for maximum position of fulcrum efficiency, zip the triceps press back toward St. Maarten, and literally feel myself catapulting forward toward the island of Anguilla. To feel this superior level of strength, to revel in this exceptional state of fitness, was simply sublime.

On one particular spring training swim I was in a semi-state of euphoria. It was a rare day of glassy calm. My brain was buzzing with all kinds of random thoughts. I was marveling at the exuberance I often felt cruising across the surface these days, unless there was a particular problem at hand, and I spent some reflective time on just how, through the years, I had worked through all that anger of youth to arrive at this plateau of authentic daily happiness.

On this magical day, swimming strong and fast from St. Maarten to Anguilla and back, perhaps echoing Ed Viesturs's exhilaration on Everest, out in the bluest of all blues, I traveled back to one of the most significant evenings of my life.

I had given a speech in New Mexico, an occasion where I had mentioned briefly my sexual-abuse story. I do talk publicly about that time in my life, because implicit in doing so is the message that going through that ordeal doesn't have to keep an individual from becoming a strong, happy person. It's important for me to address the epidemic and help create paths toward curbing it, even if only in some small way.

After the speech, I joined the group for dinner at a very noisy restaurant, where I was seated next to an older woman. Clearly the life of the party, she had a light in her eyes and was introduced to me as the pillar of their community. The clinking of glasses and silverware, the hubbub of other diners, and the poor acoustics of the room made it impossible to talk to anybody but the person immediately adjacent, so the two of us were a pair for the evening.

At one point she reached for her glass and the sleeve of her blouse pulled short to reveal the numbers etched on her wrist. I said, "Oh, you're a survivor." She nodded yes. I asked if it were too rude, the wrong time and place, for her to tell me the story. For the next half hour, the noisy din of the restaurant fell away. All I heard was this woman's voice. I was transfixed.

She was Polish and the roundup of Jews had already begun in her town. Her father declared that if they ever came to their house, they could shoot him. He wasn't going. They came. The family—this woman was only three, her six-year-old sister, her mother and father—were told they had fifteen minutes to gather some possessions. The father refused. They shot him.

An interminable train ride to Dachau, standing for more than a day pressed body to body with dozens of others, forced to urinate and defecate on the floor, they finally arrived at the camp. They descended onto the platform, the mother holding the six-year-old with her right hand, this three-year-old with her left. Once off the train, the mother and older sister were pushed to the right. This little one was taken to the left. She never saw her mother or her sister again.

On that day, and for the next two and a half years, until the Allies came in, this innocent child was forced into sexual slave labor. She became the little concubine of the SS officers. Oral sex, anal sex, intercourse. At age three, she was forced to perform these heinous acts many times a day.

I began to cry. I told her I felt deeply embarrassed to have mentioned my "little" story on the stage that night. She held my hands and pulled me close to say, emphatically, "We should never compare our pain to another's. You have every right to feel anger and grief for the loss of part of your childhood, at the hands of your perpetrators. It's your life, and you need to find your peace in whatever way you can." So I then asked her how, how could she have possibly lived a normal life, smiled at the sunrise, after what she endured as a little girl?

A family in Paris adopted her. On her first day with them, the mother took her into the garden, held her close, and told her it would be healing to speak it all out. She had no idea what she was about to hear. This little girl voiced every graphic detail. Then the mother assured her:

"You will never forget what happened to you. You cannot. And I will never replace your mother. I cannot. But you must believe that this is a beautiful world. People are basically kind and loving. You are going to live a wonderful life. You must take these memories and bury them deep in a corner of your soul. Don't live them on your skin. Tomorrow you will wake up for the first time in your new home, here with us. You will not wake up a tortured little girl. You will wake up a citizen of the world, deserving of a happy and meaningful life."

That evening in that bustling restaurant, this gentle woman and the intensity of her unfathomable story inspired me to a crucial new revelation within my own journey. And now I'm gliding across the sky-blue ocean of the Caribbean, soaring with joy, brimming with gratitude at this meaningful life I get to live, ennobled by this woman's strength and the strength of the human spirit in general. I'm not that angry, hurt girl anymore. I no longer live that abuse on my skin. And on my skin I am bathing in the bliss that is ocean essence.

Yes, it's true. At age sixty, I've let go of the rage. At sixty, in every way, including as an athlete. I am at the prime of my life.

Late May we are on the countdown. Six more long swims: three in Mexico and three in St. Maarten. The analogy to the countdown of each individual long swim holds true for the overview of the whole year's training. If you're going seventeen hours, you don't let your mind wander to imagine how hour fifteen is going to be when you're still on hour one or two or three. You need to use conscious discipline to keep yourself from projecting forward. This is the only hour you're swimming, this one. Halfway through, at eight and a half hours, it's a fool who celebrates in even a small way. There is no guarantee the second half will resemble the first. But when the end is near, those last couple of hours, you feel the relief seeping up. You feel the self-respect of having stuck with it. Now you allow some emotion to flood your tired mind.

Well, the same ratio of control extends over the entire season. Early months need to be steady. Just get the work done. Don't complain. Don't look ahead. Midway, in March and April, don't make any assumptions. But by late May, almost done, you allow the pride to swell. You didn't give in to the suffering. You didn't back off on the commitment. The relief is palpable.

When I see the Super Bowl team or the Olympic rower win, and they weep, I know well it's not simply because they've prevailed. It's because they've endured a long road traveled. It's been the miserable hours of cold and pain, overcoming the disheartening injuries. To endure is the stuff of living a vital life.

Early June I took my last long training swim in St. Maarten. I downed my last forced oatmeal feeding in the wee hours of the morning. The last reluctant disrobing at the dock. It was fifteen hours, and our goal of still being strong after fifteen hours, of imagining another fifteen right away, then a third fifteen, and then a fourth, in succession, was now reality. I was indeed proud of myself those last couple of hours. I filtered through all the memories of these ten months, since this Dream took hold of my spirit again, after all these years of lamenting having to leave it behind. It wasn't all that long ago that I'd slumped unconscious, over my steering wheel after only a few hours in a pool. I thought of these good people—Bonnie, Tim, Maya, David, Kathy Loretta—and all they gave of themselves. On the last feeding stop, nine p.m. and dark now, we found ourselves adjacent to a moored sailboat and got chatting with the captain. He said he'd seen another woman swim out of the harbor at dawn and asked if there was some race coming up that people were training for. When David told him this was the same swimmer, that we had been out all day and into the night, swimming around the island, he exclaimed, *"No way!"*

At the dock, Bonnie blew the whistle and waved both arms in a big arc. We were done. My little posse cheered, and I rolled over onto my back and sobbed.

SEVENTEEN

First Summer in Key West

All expeditions sequester in some small town while they organize and wait for ideal conditions. The Everest climbers hole up in Kathmandu, Nepal. For us, command central was Key West, and I can't imagine a haven more charming and friendly, a more idyllic place to spend a few anxious weeks. Our version of our very own Nepalese village.

Stepping off the plane onto the small Key West tarmac with Bonnie, ready to settle our training camp, round out the expedition Team, and get the Cuban and U.S. licenses finalized, I felt so strong from the year's arduous push that I could have walked through a brick wall.

From the moment we unpacked our bags there, early June 2010, and word was out that we were preparing for the Cuba Swim, the whole town jumped in to help us. Hotels gave us gratis rooms. Boat captains offered their vessels and crews for the crossing. Catering and water services put together our provisions at discount rates. It's the kind of place where everybody knows everybody and the entire community is ready to provide and assist.

One day, Bonnie and I were standing at the counter of our favorite sandwich shop, saying to each other we needed to get a kayak team together. The guy bent over fixing the espresso machine popped up to say, "I'm Buco! I'm a paddler, I've read about you guys doing this thing, and I know just the team you're going to need." Only in Key West. Buco Pantelis became a central and valuable Team member from that day. He put together our Kayak Team, six kayakers who would accompany me in two-person shifts, the Shark Shields attached to the bottom of their boats. And Buco put in many nighttime training hours off Key West when I needed safety precautions.

We quickly enlisted a Shark Diver Team, led by world-renowned expert Luke Tipple, who told us this is dangerous territory and we couldn't use white lights on any of our boats at night because they attract jellyfish and baitfish, followed by sharks. Red LED lights would be okay, proven to not draw a curious shark, although they come to the low-frequency surface vibrations made by my swimming more so than to visual stimuli. The divers in the water would also wear and use only red lights. Luke assembled a team of six guys, the concept being for three to work a shift, two in the water and one standing sentry on top of my escort boat. The other three would rest on their mother ship until time for their shift. Luke repeated to me what other shark researchers had told us: that we humans are not their food. It would have to be a hungry animal, one that hadn't eaten in a week or so way out there in the wild, to come up and take me, especially in the middle of a flotilla of boats, with electricity buzzing from the Shark Shields under me. But, he added, he didn't want to lie to us. Sharks are also unpredictable, especially the aggressive oceanic whitetip.

Luke is a shark conservationist and will never kill an animal. As was true of our Cuba Expedition back in '78, our Shark Team will use no lethal weapons on the crossing. They will dive with triangles of PVC pipes, with a tennis ball at the tip, ready to nudge an intruder's nose.

Shark expert Dr. Patrick Rice also helped us. Dr. Rice had developed a potent agent called Shark Repel, a canister the size of a can of shaving cream. When shaken and dispersed in a mini-explosion, sharks zip as far away from that smell as possible. My Divers will be the first line of defense. The Shark Shields serve as second line, and the cans of Shark Repel will be on hand for dire emergency, life or death, although that can't help me with a surprise attack in the black of night. My guys will literally put my life before theirs and swim between me and the luminescent pairs of eyes of predators below.

We started to do some night swims off Key West, Luke's Shark Team and Buco's Kayak Team getting in their practice, Bonnie implementing her crisis-communications system with them, and David Marchant starting to work with the Gulf Stream currents.

We picked a date, July 10, to do a twenty-four-hour training swim with full Expedition. This would bring me to my peak, which I would then maintain with shorter swims until an ideal weather window came our way. It would also give us a valuable "dress rehearsal" for the entire crew to perform seamlessly in the exact milieu of the real swim. David plotted a course, taking our fleet out to what he determined would be our halfway point coming across from Cuba, about fifty miles from Key West. This way he'd get to see how much progress we'd make and problems we'd encounter with the Gulf Stream. The escort-boat Drivers would learn to follow David's course, at the same time keeping the boat at an explicit distance and speed for me. The Shark Team would have the full night-dive experience. The Kayakers would work in shifts, two by two, Shark Shields attached to the bottoms of their boats. They would also follow me and bring me back to the escort boat if I happened to drift out to the right, which I tend to do. The only problem we had to keep working on was the Kayaker to the right of me paying very close attention so as not to hit my hand with his or her paddle. Even as slowly as we were traveling, two miles per hour, if my hand was coming forward and the paddle was sweeping backward, that collision could injure my hand, perhaps even break bones.

Bonnie and her Handler Team would take me through the normal feedings as well as any specific issues that needed immediate attention, from nausea to prompting mental clarity. Bonnie was in charge. And she brought onto her Handler Team not only Candace but Jon and Deborah Hennessey, the three of them my old Handlers from back in the '70s. It was such a kick to look up and see those familiar faces. My sister Liza and my good friend Heidi Horner rounded out Bonnie's Team.

As for jellyfish, we expected the Portuguese man-o'-war would be the worst of it out there. The Kayakers and Shark Divers would look out for the blue floating bubbles best they could daytime. If I were to be stung during the night, our doctor had epinephrine and prednisone and bottled oxygen, to open the airways, as well as some topical pain relievers.

Saturday morning, July 10, the Team met at the docks and started motoring out about fifty miles to David's chosen start point. We didn't realize the irony of it at the time, but that twenty-four-hour swim made us swoon under the spell of what is called the classic doldrums. A surface tension so flat and still, in every direction as far as the eye can see, that you sense you could set a dinner table on it and it wouldn't go under. The ironic part is that we never once saw the doldrums again in all our time through this adventure. That perfection was wasted on a training swim. There wasn't so much as a whisper of wind. The joke throughout was that we should just bust over to Havana, stealth, without the government licenses, and get this thing done now. Alas, we had to believe those doldrums would come our way again over the summer.

The twenty-four hours went reasonably well. What surprised me was that I didn't have to dig down much for backbone. After warming up the first few hours of the morning, I was cranking from about noon to sundown. And for a little while I got lost tripping out on the stupefying Gulf Stream. I would venture to say there is no bluer blue on our blue planet.

Working out in a gym one day many years before in Manhattan, Al Pacino approached me, and in his inimitable intense rasp, asked what was the most beautiful ocean I had ever swum in. I've swum them all. The pale blue Indian Ocean off Tanzania, the dark blue Pacific of Hawaii, the green-blue of the Aegean, the grey-blue of Patagonia, near the Antarctic Circle. But none of those wow your senses as does the striking, vibrant, bright blue of the Gulf Stream between Cuba and Florida.

I was pretty darn together the whole swim, except for one stretch of dizzying hyperthermia. These waters were much hotter than in St. Maarten so, even though I had been doing short swims here for over a month now, I became dehydrated under the blazing sun. Bonnie bumped up the water intake in a hurry by hot midafternoon and then made a note in her swim journal to recalculate, with my doctor Michael Broder, how much water-electrolyte mixture I'd need during the Cuba Swim.

The night was largely uneventful and Bonnie blew the finish whistle at nine a.m. on Sunday. Big cheers all around. Candace cried. They were proud of me. I guess I didn't look or act especially rugged at the very end. I vomited for a couple of hours and needed an IV. But I proved I was ready for twenty-four hours, and that swim boosted my conditioning level another 50 percent, once I rested. Every faction of the Team learned a lot, and we debriefed on Sunday afternoon.

The Shark Team didn't like their lack of visibility at night. They were frustrated with not being able to use any lights at all, to sweep the area under me. Luke developed a new protocol of taking an underwater white sweep light and swimming a wide circle around me, about fifty yards away at all times, pointing the light away from and under me. White light added risk but Luke just had to have at least a minimal view under there.

The escort boat right next to me had been too big. I had to lift up to my left breathing side too high to see Bonnie and the Handlers. The boat was also too powerful and just couldn't cruise parallel to me at my speed. I was constantly searching for it ahead of me. David went on a statewide hunt and came back with not only the perfect boat, a thirty-eight-foot kayak excursion boat named *Voyager,* but two sterling people. These two immediately clicked with the pulse of the expedition.

Dee Brady was owner of *Voyager* and all in for what we had now come to call the Xtreme Dream. Dee was about my age, a hippie all the way. An ex–New Yorker who reads the *Times* cover to cover every day, who worked her butt off and retired early to freewheel around the world on her boat, an aficionada of small-venue live-music events, ready on a dime five cents change for any and every adventure. Any given day of the year, Dee can be found house-sitting a villa in Tuscany or guiding folks on kayak trips through the Bahamas or hanging out in little Mexican fishing villages for the winter. Her travel bag, no matter the length of stay, is the size of an egg carton. To this day I can't tell you what color Dee's eyes are. None of us have ever seen her without her navy blue tinted glasses. Dee was a calm, steady voice from the day we met her. Not only did she become our main Driver for *Voyager* but she became our Team mediator. She keeps quiet and listens. No dramas, no gossip. Dee is just cool.

The other fellow hippie who joined us with the arrival of *Voyager* was the boat's designer and, we would soon discover, a veritable genius, John Bartlett. Also about my age, Bartlett was a handsome guy. He turned heads, especially with his unassuming way. He was low-key, no dandy. But he was enthralled with the universe. From physics to engineering to art to bass guitars, every conversation with Bartlett was a deep, detailed probing. He talked with his fingers animatedly bouncing, chest high, as if he were tickling a brisk ragtime tune on the piano. Once we were all settled together, we'd sometimes play a game after dinner at the Team house. The game involved using names of famous people throughout history and the only rule was that everybody had to know every name. Every single time, the names Bartlett would throw in the hat were the most arcane—a seventeenth-century composer of harpsichord music or a botanist who'd prepared a tea remedy for the first astronauts. Bartlett's mind was on fire.

Our mission fascinated him. And he knew the Florida Straits like the back of his hand. He dived right in with David, offering his considerable knowledge of the Gulf Stream, coastal currents, and tide issues that would affect our crossing.

I quickly fell in love with our two new Teammates, Dee and Bartlett, and I also fell in love with my new escort boat. *Voyager* had a low, surface-level transom off the starboard side, my breathing side, where Bonnie and her crew could work down at my level. And I could see them with a normal quick sip of air, not having to make the effort to lift my head. All it needed was a change to slower propellers and a reconfiguration of the steering wheel. *Voyager* was our boat. Dee was our Captain of the Driver Team. Bartlett was our new all-round consultant. We had hit pay dirt with them.

When we looked at the computer GPS track of our exact course during the twenty-four hours, we saw that I had made two full loops at night. Literally swam twice in a complete circle. We all assumed those loops were the result of my swimming, oblivious, out to the right too far and taking too long to hear or see the signals to get back to the boat. We needed a system to keep me constantly parallel to the escort boat. If this swim was to be minimum 103 miles, every fifty yards off to the side and fifty yards back adds up. And I couldn't for the life of me concentrate on the boat and keep a constant, parallel distance from it. I had trouble not drifting off in bright daylight and was hopelessly, constantly, way out to the right at night. This was the case all through training, Bonnie spending most of her time either daytime holding an orange life preserver high in the air to signal me back to the boat from where I had veered, or nighttime whistling persistently, again to get my attention and bring me back close to the boat.

It might be hard to understand how the state of sensory deprivation takes you into an interior world, renders you incapable of focusing for long on a glimpse of reality with each turn of the head. You simply cannot keep it up. You slip into the recesses of your mind, and it's frustrating for the Handlers and the Kayakers to almost every minute have to bring you back to the real world.

Not only did all that veering way out to the right, sometimes as many as a hundred yards off course, blow up our total mileage unnecessarily, but being that far from the eyes on board the escort boat meant they were now ineffectual to help me, should a shark or jellyfish attack. The Kayakers tracked me no matter where I went, but the Shark Divers needed to stay near *Voyager*.

David and Bartlett and our paddler Stuart Knaggs from St. Maarten had a solution. They constructed a pole, kind of a skinny gangplank, that lowered from the bow of the boat out to the right, twenty-one feet from the starboard side. Hanging down into the water from the end of that pole was a chain, about ten-feet deep, with a little rubber triangle that would hydrodynamically undulate as we traveled forward. And furling back from that planar was a four-inch-wide streamer of white sailcloth that would trail back ten feet underwater and remain twenty-one feet parallel to the escort boat at all times. Now I had myself an underwater lane line. In the brilliant blue Gulf Stream, that white streamer was visible from a long way away. Even if I drifted out to the right, when I saw Bonnie's orange life vest, held up high against the sky, I could quickly spot the streamer and make it back to position. At night, Bartlett rigged a string of red LED lights along the streamer, which he powered from a generator on board. They were an eerie yet comforting companion, those red lights at night, to both me and my crew. We also decided after the twenty-four-hour to attach a red LED flashing strobe light to the back of my goggles. On a night with no moonlight, Bonnie couldn't see me from twenty-one-feet away. She relied on the splashing of my hands, so the red strobe helped her pinpoint me.

Mid-July, we were working on all kinds of refinements while waiting for the U.S. Treasury Department license to travel to Cuba, as well as the Cuba permissions to enter with our crew and flotilla. We were terribly frustrated, getting no response from either side.

July 28 was to be a normal, fairly short training day in Key West. But the phone rang early. A friend of my brother's in Boston in a few sober words reported that my brother Sharif had smothered in his pillow during the night. He was only fifty-seven. I left the Team to carry on and flew to Boston.

EIGHTEEN

Sharif

My brother Sharif (born William but called himself Sharif from his early twenties) was a schizophrenic. Had he grown up in today's era, his childhood symptoms would have been diagnosed. But in the 1950s and '60s, we just considered him an asocial, supersmart book-worm. He had a vast tree snail collection and even wrote a book about them when he was only eleven, titled "The Jewels of the Everglades." Science teachers around town would bring their students on field trips to our house, where Bill would lecture to them about the wondrous creatures he both knew and somehow understood.

The air-conditioning vents in one of our homes connected Bill's room to mine, and I could hear him up all night, talking to his imaginary characters. In the morning he was too tired to go to school. We didn't find this alarming. I also spent many hours with my imaginary charac-ters, usually locked in the bathroom, in fear of my father.

He went away to college in Boston, and even in those first few years there, we mistook his mental illness for a hippie drug phase. He came to stay with me in New York City occasionally, sometimes sitting in the lotus position on my living room floor, a blanket over his head, not breaking to eat or drink for spells of more than twenty-four hours at a time. His talk was gibberish. I thought he was high on something heavy, maybe angel dust.

When I went to visit him in Boston, usually a couple of times a year, I would ask the homeless in Kenmore Square, his preferred hangout, if they'd seen the Pied Piper lately. Any fringe type knew Sharif. They'd tell me just where to find him. They had nicknamed him the Pied Piper as he would help them with their medical, legal, and family problems. He read, from train station and hotel garbage cans, *The Washington Post* and *The New York Times,* both in their entirety, every single day. His mind worked at warp speed. He could discuss—even outargue you on—any topic under the sun, including your own area of expertise, but when it came to perspective on his own life, he was unable to grasp even the simplest of realities. He told me he was playing sax for the Boston Pops, that his medical research was being published at Harvard, and that he was backup quarterback for the Pittsburgh Steelers, which infuriated him because he didn't want to have to travel to Pittsburgh all the time.

I offered him rent money for a small apartment many times. He declined. He liked his life, his friends. I'd try to hand him a wad of cash every time we'd get together. He'd refuse but say he was grateful for the gesture.

On my visits to see Sharif, I got to know some of his posse. They were for the most part just like him. Off-the-grid individuals, extremely intelligent, who were never going to be able to work a steady job or take on any standard responsibilities. I'd ask if he wanted to go to a nice dinner, eat some lobster, but he preferred the soup kitchen. He wanted me to meet his buddies.

I knew all his pawnshops. He had a thick clump of pawn slips in his pocket, literally a couple hundred tickets. But he knew just which one was attached to which alto saxophone at which shop. We'd sometimes spend all day traipsing around from shop to shop, retrieving this guitar, putting down more cash for that harmonica.

He had a child, on the streets, with a drug addict. And he gave up drugs and alcohol the day Shawnee was born. Kate also got herself together once she became a mother. I have come to know Kate and Shawnee, and they're warm, caring people.

Life on the streets takes an undeniable toll. Sharif was tall, six foot two, but by his fifties, he was stooped and walked with an uneven gait. His eyes were furtive, from watching his back all the time. He died in a little apartment that Liza and I had found for him the year before, one of the few actual residences that got him off the streets over the years. He had had several epileptic-type seizures, and that's what evidently happened the night he died. He smothered facedown in his pillow at fifty-seven, but he was an old fifty-seven. When I first heard the news, I can't say I was surprised. Still, my heart wrenched at the hard life he had lived, all that magnificent brain potential unfulfilled. I had just seen him the year before, and it wasn't that I foresaw he wasn't going to live a long life. It was that I knew old age would be particularly wearing on him, more than most. He cut a tragic figure, shuffling down the street, never a dollar in his pocket, especially on a brutal day in Boston's windy winter. And yet he was unmovable from his routine. He had created his own family. He counted on them. They counted on him.

Liza, Tim, and Tim's fiancée Karen and I hurried to make the funeral arrangements. We went from the shelters to the soup kitchens to the pawnshops to tell his friends, and a very respectable-sized crowd showed up at the service. In a tiny rental car, the four of us stopped to pick up the blind man to whom Sharif had taken dinner from the soup kitchen every night for twelve years. And the young woman he had been mentoring. And the guy he played sax with on the subway platforms.

At the funeral home, we met with the minister. We had taken advice from Sharif's friends that he would have liked a minister to say a few words. He asked us for three words that best described Sharif. We consulted Kate and Shawnee:

Kind. Selfless. A leader.

I briefly addressed the gathering, mostly to say that this was a very informal occasion, with no prescribed order of speakers, and that anybody was welcome to say anything at any time. And if later, when we would be having coffee and cake (that raised quite a few eyebrows in this crowd), anybody wanted to speak up then, that would be just fine.

So the preacher began his short bit, using the three words at his disposal, and then proceeded to say that Sharif reminded him in many ways of Jesus Christ. Liza and I exchanged glances.

At this point a guy with wildly disheveled hair and a tremor in his husky voice jumped up. "Hey, wait a minute! That's what I was going to say! I'm the one who always called Sharif our very own Jesus Christ! We used to philosophize on the beach at sunrise, and he'd tell me how he was going to help some poor bastard who was in trouble that day!"

Another mourner: "Shut up and show some respect. The preacher's talking."

The guy with the husky voice: "You shut up. That lady said we could talk anytime we wanted to."

And so it went among the disenfranchised, Sharif's posse.

Leaving the service that day, I was oddly serene. En route to Boston, I had fully expected to spend our time there in sorrow, not over Sharif's death but over his life. His beautiful mind never reached a whisper of its potential. He had never been on a vacation, after childhood. I asked him once if he ever took Shawnee up to the idyllic lakes and mountains of New Hampshire and Vermont, and he doubled over in laughter at the prospect. I don't think he ever soaked in a hot bath as an adult. I surely wish he had known a more comfortable life and had had the wherewithal to tap into his many natural talents, but the truth was, I came to admire him that day. His friends worshipped him. He showed up for them. I've been fortunate to meet many impressive individuals in my life but Sharif is certainly the only one I've known kind enough to deliver dinner to a person in need every day for twelve years. Rest in peace, my brother.

Sharif's funeral was the first time in a year I had let go of the singular fixation on the Swim. That flight back to Key West gave me an encapsulated four hours to think about my brother. He got sober literally the instant his daughter was born. He never again gave his days away to drugs. Any dollar he happened to come upon, he gave to Shawnee and his street family. Even steeped in mental illness, his ultimate choice was not to escape but to engage. I may be driven by near-impossible dreams, but the ethic that arches broader and moves me even more than reaching for the stars is simply: engaging. To me, life in retreat, a stagnant life, is not life well lived. What I admire is pushing forward—onward. Sharif spent forty hard-knock years homeless on the streets of Boston. But he never gave up. He never stopped engaging, no matter how hard his life was.

NINETEEN

Back to Key West

The instant the small plane's landing gear touches the tarmac in Key West, the mission floods back. Back to obsession.

In the car from the airport, I fixate on the surf, the horizon, the flags blowing from the east. Bonnie urges me to take a short swim that day, to clear my mind.

The sense of time pressure is now approaching urgent. We are a month past our twenty-four-hour swim. John Bartlett sits with us one night to go over the thirty-year history of wind patterns in the summer through the Florida Straits. On average, there have been two days each June, two each July, one each August, and one each September when wind direction and speed would have allowed a swimmer to chance a crossing. June and July are past now, and we are already into August. If all that weren't depressing enough, he then launches into the rarity of the Gulf Stream laying out with a northerly component, what a swimmer sorely needs to keep from being dragged too far east to be able to make shore in Florida. Bonnie and I walk home from the Team house close to despondent.

Along with swimming and weight training and more Team meetings the next couple of days, I am pressing in every direction imaginable to secure both our OFAC (Office of Foreign Assets Control) and Department of Commerce licenses. We earnestly discuss going over to

Havana stealth, middle of the night without the licenses and paying the price when we get back stateside. But the punishment is as serious as jail time, plus fines upwards of several hundreds of thousands of dollars. Even if some of us are game, the boat captains aren't going to risk having their vessels seized.

The Cuban permissions dishearten us even more. We have no means of direct contact there. Delegates of the Cuban Interest Section in D.C. assure us the minister of sports in Havana is aware we are desperately waiting, but he's been on family holiday and away from his desk for a couple of weeks, unable to tend to paperwork.

One pressure cooker has lifted at this point, though, and that is funding. We have our main corporate sponsor, Secret, firmly behind us. They don't want me to tout the brand but rather to participate in their online campaign called "Fearless." Women are featured, and a vibrant conversation online confronts fears and encourages a fierce approach to life. A new state-of-the-art sports training center in Geneva, Ohio, called Spire, also backs me, and quite a few donations start streaming in online, mostly because CNN is following us full-time.

Sure enough, on August 8, the nightmare we all dread becomes real. That elusive weather window comes and goes but we don't have the government permits. Our meteorologist, Dane Clark, calls to tell us a number of factors—high ridges moving down through lower latitudes, a storm front heading up the eastern seaboard and thus dragging some calm across the Straits behind it—are coming together. He's predicting some pretty darn calm seas August 11 through 14. Dane's wife, Jenifer Clark, an expert Stream analyst who goes by the nickname "Queen of the Gulf Stream," tells us that the axis of the current is in a fairly good position as well. We have both weather and current on our side, yet we sit in Key West, sick with exasperation, and watch four days of glassy calm evaporate before our very eyes. I literally feel I am developing an ulcer.

We riff on many a potential other swim throughout the Caribbean. We even imagine my jumping off a big floating dock twelve miles off Cuban shores. But all that is useless. Cuba's the Dream. It's got to be Cuba.

In desperation, I take a long shot and call a politically connected friend in D.C. It turns out Hilary Rosen is a colleague of Hillary Clinton's, the current secretary of state. The Treasury license we need falls under jurisdiction of the State Department. Much to our surprise, Hillary Clinton sends a message that she will intervene on our behalf. The license comes through within twenty-four hours.

I have a hard time letting go of my rancor over that calm window we missed. But *Onward!* is the Team credo, and *Onward!* we go. We are back to daily training, fine-tuning of technical aspects, calling around for any creative avenue of communication with the Cubans, and waiting for weather. Again. Still.

As end of August approaches, my anxiety level grows. People always think the training is the bear. And it is. But at least you have control. You know what you need to do and, punishing as it is, you put your head down and push. This waiting, not knowing, having no control, is worse. I long to be back in St. Maarten, putting in fifteen-hour days. Friends and strangers alike are sending me all kinds of quotes and adages about the virtue of patience.

Well, I was down with those platitudes back in July, with seemingly plenty of time to get the mission under way. But now Labor Day 2010 has come and gone, the water temperatures will begin to lower below my threshold of comfort in about a month, and my concern is acute. Bonnie and I drag ourselves every single night over to Vanessa Linsley's office, where she pulls up for us literally dozens of various computer models. Vanessa, a former world-class ocean sailor, is our Xtreme Dream Fleet Captain. She will pull the boats and crews for the expedition together. These vessels are what we call our mother ships, and their crews will take care of the core Teammates as they come back for rejuvenation in between shifts over on *Voyager.* Every night Bonnie and I huddle behind V's computer while she shows us the North Atlantic Gyre and, depending on its position off U.S. shores, how it is affecting wind speed and direction. She takes a look at wind patterns all through the Caribbean, from the Virgin Islands, tracking them below Cuba, and all the way over to the Yucatán. We look at the Gulf of Mexico and then the jet stream pattern and where the high and low ridges are sitting north of us. So many weather factors come into play across the Straits, and that's why it's so darn hard to predict the weather out there. You begin to see the world as one connected ecosystem when you closely study weather in one little area.

One night Vanessa takes Bonnie and me out onto the docks. The east wind is blowing, as it has steadily for almost a month now. She instructs us to stick our tongues out. What do we notice? We both report crunchy granules of salt, assuming the wind is picking up surface ocean spray. No, the crunch we are detecting is actually sand from the Sahara Desert. They call it "Sahara dust." The winds off Africa travel east all these thousands of miles uninterrupted, carrying desert sand to this faraway strip of the Florida Straits.

On days when the gusts are too strong and the ocean waves are massive, Bonnie and I go to a lagoon near the community college. Bonnie sits on the dock with her book and my cooler, and encourages me through long winding laps around the lagoon, about a half a mile in diameter.

I'll never forget our first day over there. As we pulled into the parking lot, a prehistoric-looking lizard, monstrous in both size and appearance, came scooting right in front of our car. Another followed. We screeched to a stop and were scared to death to get out. We locked our doors as several more brazenly marched through the grass, out of the bushes, across the blacktop. We pictured ourselves as in *Jurassic Park,* imagining one of these lizards leaping onto our hood and smashing our windshield with a colossal whipping tail.

We called animal control and whispered: "We're in the parking lot of the community college on Stock Island and there are gigantic lizards threatening us. Do you know about these animals?" The next thing we hear is unabashed laughter on the other end of the phone. Then we hear this man calling to a colleague: "Jeff, you won't believe this"—and he stops to laugh out loud again—"there's a woman on the phone scared to death of some horrifying huge lizards at the community college." Very funny. We soon find out that these lizards are common and entirely peaceful. The whole island of Key West eventually heard about that one and we were teased mercilessly.

These damn east winds. By now I know every flag on the island, around the marina, out on the piers, and they seem to be in a perpetual state of flapping motion. Day after day, we can't catch a break. These east winds will not put the brakes on. The doldrums of our twenty-four hours July 10–11 are now nothing more than a mirage of a distant memory. The trade winds coming from the east slap up against the

Gulf Stream current pushing to the east—which makes for a nasty set of high, stiff peaks out there. Our only hope is a hurricane. In August and September, those storms that form off the west coast of Africa and travel across the Atlantic wind up in a variety of positions. Circumstances are sometimes such that they simply peter out and go from hurricane to lower force status. Sometimes they continue west with full power. That's when the Caribbean islands, Cuba, Mexico, Southern Florida get slammed. And sometimes—what we are hoping against hope for—they make a turn somewhere out in the Atlantic, close enough to the eastern seaboard, and head north. That's the situation when the force of the storm drags the winds out of their normal east pattern and the winds in the Straits die down.

Going to Vanessa's office each night is akin to lambs going to slaughter for Bonnie and me. We are willing hostages to every scenario she paints, believing new promising patterns are surely going to develop. We succumb to pipe dreams with each report of a new storm brewing off Africa. Dane calls every three or four days to say there is a maybe, maybe, maybe window potential. But then he calls it off a couple of days later, and it hurts him to report that window has fallen apart, knowing how dejected we are. The emotional roller coaster is wearing on my nerves.

Truthfully, we have been so neurotic about the weather window that we almost forget the license from Havana. But an overnight package of documents is sitting on our doorstep September 10 from the Cuban Interest Section in D.C. We are cleared.

Training is really tough at this point. Bonnie, Dee, David, Maya, and Bartlett never let me see them sweat. But we grow into a quiet operation as the weeks ooze by. Nobody seems to have a sense of humor anymore. We are now approaching end of September, meaning that last big twenty-four-hour training swim, July 10–11, my peak, is more than ten weeks behind us. All this time since then we have struggled with the daily swim schedule: When we put in a longish twelve-hour practice, are we risking my being tired, should our window materialize in a hurry? But two weeks of doing only four-, five-, or six-hour swims won't suffice to keep me in the sixty-hour shape I had reached back mid-July. So we throw a long one in every now and then. Flirtations with possible windows come and go, at least once a week. The uncertainty is wrenching. As soon as I believe we might be on our way to Havana, I get the mind-set steeled. I start the imagery of the hours, surviving the various crises. I can literally feel the hormonal surge of adrenaline rise in my veins. Then we're called off, and my spirit nose-dives. My swim bags stand fully packed at the door, where they've been for two months now.

The nights are cooler now. Even Key West has a slight change of seasons. None of us says it out loud, but we fear fall is making its way. Several people tell us, knowing full well what we are hungry to hear, that they remember the years when they'd sit on their decks in early October and enjoy the flattest calms of the whole year stretching out to the horizon. We hang on their every word.

Bonnie has coached me through shredded nerves for more than a month. And I've been buoyed by her steady strength. But I'm growing desperate. I am losing sleep. Several friends send me this quote: "You never know how strong you really are until strong is the only choice you have left." I repeat it under my breath all day long like a madwoman.

It is October 1, 2010. We are heading out for a four-hour swim. The flags are blowing at the marina. The breeze is brisk, from the east. I take the usual plunge off the starboard Handler's station of *Voyager*. But this day isn't like the others. I don't immediately surface and start swimming. I turn over on my back. When I look up to *Voyager*, there they are, my steadfast Team: Dee, David, Maya, and Bartlett with forearms on the rail, offering me sympathetic eyes. Bonnie stands down at the transom, hands on hips. I give them the slit-throat sign. The water temperature dropped at least a couple of degrees, overnight. It's over.

Packing up the expedition, facing the unreal prospect of training another full year, keeping the faith—this is a tough pill to swallow.

Bonnie, Dee, Bartlett, David, Maya, and I box and label all the gear we so carefully innovated over the summer. We are securing everything with Vanessa at the marina when it begins to pour. Perfect. A cold, driving rain says it all.

As Bonnie and I are driving back to look into a flight home, Dee calls us to return to the boat. Two manatees are playing between the hulls of *Voyager*. It's technically against Florida rules, but we take the liberty to all get in and cuddle with them for a couple of hours. They're like giant water doggies, affectionate and playful. We interpret that moment together with the manatees as our sign of good things to come. It's either that or we leave each other crestfallen in the chilly fall rain.

TWENTY

Buck Up, Another Go: 2011

Back in California, my huge duffle bags of gear loom as a reminder of unfinished business. I am as unsettled as my swim stuff, shuffling aimlessly around my house. The dozens of pairs of goggles, the suits hanging on hooks, the caps, the tubs of grease, the huge canisters of protein powder, the red LED night-lights that clip onto my goggle straps, the big training towels from Mexico. All that stuff is sitting there, not begging for final stowaway, but at the ready, still in play. And, as shoes are so often symbolic of events throughout our history, there are my specific flip-flops, white, only used for walking down to the dock or the beach for training, only for slipping on after training, only for the start in Cuba, the end in Florida. These are definitively not shoes for casual wear. When those white rubber flip-flops sitting by my back door catch my eye, my body receives the signal the brain is sending. If I truly want to do this thing, it's time to buck up.

I ask myself now those same questions that pressed me a year ago. Will I have the strength of body and mind to endure what it takes to get ready for this long haul? Yet there is one glaring difference this time, the fall of 2010. Last year it had been thirty long years since I had been engaged in the sport. My body memories had faded and it was truly a brand-new experience. This year, I know only too well what suffering lies in wait.

It took that month of October 2010 to wrap my head around putting it all together again, especially the training. The entire year of extreme physical exertion, the steadfast focus, was all driven by the Dream. We had been building to a crescendo. No matter how tough the going got, the underlying resolve was impenetrable. But there was one twist of the plot I didn't take a nanosecond to prepare for. And that was not even getting to give it a try.

One has long debated the journey versus the destination. When focused on a difficult, long-term journey, it's the goal itself that dangles in front of you, that makes you dig deep, that keeps your pursuit strong, even in the face of tremendous adversity. For me, the question has always been whether the journey itself is going to be a worthwhile way for me to spend my precious time, destination or not. The catch-22 is inherent. You wouldn't take this journey without the destination always looming large in your imagination, driving you onward. But I need to be clear that the work, the wearisome path, is honorable, edifying, and renders me proud in the end to have taken every punishing step, perhaps short of the final step. I never earned my PhD. But I don't regret those years of study, those dialogues about the philosophies and the writings of Europe's great nineteenth-century authors. My marriage to Nina failed in the end, but I don't lament the years we spent in making a life together.

Once back home in Los Angeles that October, to rise above my disappointment at the destination's remaining untouched, I earnestly tried to extract the positives we had built along the way of our expedition. This was imperative, not only for my own well-being but as the leader of my Team. They deserved to feel proud of all they had given, all we had discovered.

But I am human, and being all aglow over the journey wasn't the overriding truest inner emotion in me that October. Hard as I strived to walk tall, it was a down time. The vision had been so very real. Just as a high jumper's eyes track along the steps she's going to take, then her eyes lift over the bar, a preview of what her body will do, I had fixed in my mind the persistent strokes all the way across. To have it all vanish into thin air was now unreal. I thought for sure that right about now I'd be reveling in the yearlong intense experience. I'd be packing up all my swim gear for posterity. I'd be getting photos of our Team on the finish beach enlarged. I'd be satisfied and content. I thought I'd be looking back at the effort now, concluding that it was right to have spent a precious year of my life chasing this old Dream of mine, and finally seizing it.

I gave myself the month of October off. Time to reconnect with friends and family. Time to get my house together. I had moved into a fabulous 1924 Italianate home the year before, with scant time to unpack, so it was nice to be a homebody for a little while. Time to take my dogs for sunrise meditation walks on the beach. (They walk. I meditate.)

That first sunrise stroll was otherworldly. Staring out at the chilly Pacific took me right back.

I remembered vividly that day in June in St. Maarten, rolling over onto my back and sobbing. I would never have to do another fifteen-hour training swim in my life (even though that was naïve, given the twenty-four-hour in July and the subsequent, unexpected three further months of training in Key West). Now my head wanted to move on, but my heart was still heavy. It was too much to process in a hurry. I needed to work my way through it.

On maybe the eighth or ninth sunrise walk, I felt a brightening. I remember the exact moment. Teddy and Scout were romping and I sprinted with them along the surf's edge. I was happy. My body was happy. The positives started to roll.

I was in the best shape of my life—something to hold high at the age of sixty-one now. Instead of fixating on the hardships of the training, I allowed some of the delight to come wafting back. Some of the sensual memories sparked those occasional moments of outright exaltation. On a glassy day, there was palpable pleasure in gliding way on top of the table-flat surface for hours, a swimmer traveling distances known before only to boats.

A smile would come across my face underwater, literally, when I'd see Bonnie standing strong, facing me all day long from the port side. Her deep tan, her muscled torso, her cool wraparound sunglasses. Some days she wouldn't sit at all for the twelve or more hours we were out there. Her eyes on me were a comforting constant. She's a warrior, Bonnie. I was safe, physically and emotionally, with Bonnie on guard.

Our learning curve in so many aspects of science, from the facets of that particular ocean to the rigors of getting a body and mind ready for such an undertaking, had been both steep and gratifying. The Team fellowship, founded on trust, was strong and true. And I had been successful as "CEO" of a major operation.

Mine was a highly unique situation, to be an athlete at this age, working with loved ones who never knew me as an athlete the first time around. It's rare to come back to world-class performance later in life, but here I was at sixty-one, attempting to do something I had tried and failed in my twenties. And here were the closest people in my life, in it with me for the first time. Nina, too, had come into my life after my early swimming period and now would join the expedition on the friends-and-family boat.

Years before, at the U.S. Open tennis championships, Jimmy Connors electrified the crowd on one of those manic nights in New York when he played the comeback match of his career. He hadn't been at the sterling top of his game for several years. His eleven-year-old son Brett knew that his dad was some big deal, had won Wimbledon and such, but all that had happened before he was born and when he was still a baby. This night, when Jimmy rocked the house against Aaron Krickstein, the crowd on their feet in a zany frenzy throughout, Jimmy pumping fists and screaming up close into the courtside television camera, Jimmy found his champion form and spirit one last time. Brett was courtside. At eleven, he witnessed his dad in his full glory. Jimmy, not prone to tears, cried at the end, Brett in his arms. If not for that match, Brett would have always known his dad's mastery only via secondhand stories and old press clippings.

In my case, Tim was born September 1978, one month after I had tried Cuba the first time. Tim had been the kid who told friends his aunt had once been this great swimmer but he really didn't know that much about it. Filming one day in Mexico, he came on camera for an interview with me. He's not much of a crier, but he broke down when he said the thrill of his childhood was when Aunt Diana was coming to play with him. Then he cried again when describing what it was like now, to have this champion he had always read about come to life before his very eyes.

Bonnie, whom I had met a few months after I had retired from swimming, was now leading my Team. Bonnie's a stoic type. But I thought I saw her crying on the side of the boat one day. I stopped to ask if she was all right. Through her tears, she said it was so moving to watch someone do what they do best. Just as watching Bonnie with any kind of racquet in her hand, elegant and smooth as butter, had brought me to awe on many occasions.

So Bonnie's in charge, Tim an integral part of the expedition, Candace back with all her history and perspective, Liza and Nina involved. It was a glorious time of life for me.

Those walks with my dogs over a couple of weeks brought me around. The despair turned to hope. After all, that was my goal at the core. If engagement is what I honor above all, I had just spent a year engaged with unwavering intensity. These are the values of the journey, without the destination. And the journey isn't over yet.

My spirit renewed, I took a quick trip to Havana before getting back to training. Dee, Kathy Loretta, Tim, and Karen came with me. This was a crucial move, as we made friends with Commodore Escrich of the famous Club Nautico at Marina Hemingway. The meetings were long and bureaucratic, but we now had an ally. We had a direct contact who could get to the minister of sport on our behalf, who could green-light our entry in a matter of twenty-four to forty-eight hours. There would be no stress from the Cuban side of travel next year.

I must admit I wasn't in the most jolly of moods. We weren't there on vacation. But still, for me, anytime in Cuba is to be captivated by the island's charm.

I had gone to Cuba a half dozen times over the years, since my attempt in 1978. Bonnie and I had made the trip for sports exhibitions, me giving stroke lessons in Havana's only training pool, where you had to be careful not to cut your hands on the jagged and broken gutter tiles; Bonnie teaching racquetball on their only court, one of the side walls exposed where large slabs of concrete had chipped away. The Cuban Olympic Training Center blows your mind, given the world champions they have produced in track and field, volleyball, and boxing—not to mention the baseball greats. There is one, only one, stationary bicycle, with a right pedal that you cannot budge and a left pedal that has been stripped, so it flies around out of control. The athletes train à la Rocky, throwing each other bags of gravel and sprinting up and down sand heaps.

I have always tried to be sensitive to the Cuban Americans, especially given my childhood on Florida's Gold Coast, knowing the Cuban exiles there had had just a few hours to gather what they could, get to the bank for some cash, and leave their homeland. And respectful of course also of the hundreds who escaped on makeshift rafts, some dying during the treacherous crossing. But there are many who defend the Fidel regime, saying he took Cuba from third-world to second-world in one generation, creating a high level of education for everybody, rendering homelessness a rarity, and training arguably the best doctors in the world. My love of the country doesn't come from a political place. I'm not defending socialism. All I know is I always was enchanted by the Cuban people. I always wanted my swim to serve as a literal touch, a metaphoric reach, shore to shore, in the hopes that we would be open to each other again one day.

I had been there for NPR at one time and was just floating around the streets, recording sound. I approached a nicely dressed man at a busy corner in Old Havana and asked if he knew the American cars streaming by. He said, "Well, I am *cubano*. Of course I know the cars very well."

He took the microphone from me and delivered a textured, delightful, unedited six-minute soliloquy.

"Ah, here is coming now the Ford Fairlane. This you can see is from 1956, and the ornamentation on the hood tells us it is from late in the year 1956. *Dios mío,* now is coming the love of every *cubano.* The Cadillac Sevilla." *(Gasp.)* "Look to see the exquisite bucket seats, white leather with black piping to match the exterior."

And on he went for fifteen or so pristine blue Oldsmobiles, cherry-red Chevrolets, and sea-green Buicks. An editor's dream, he finishes off with: "So, as you can see, to stand on the street corner in Havana is to be in a moving car museum. Have a nice day."

People from all walks of life, all corners of the globe, find Cuba a special place. I'm just one among thousands. Of all the foreign travel I've been privileged with over the years, Cuba may be my favorite place of all. I most definitely wanted to make a statement with this swim, that the embargo had gone on quite long enough. It was time for us to reconcile, on both sides. And this trip only strengthened that vision for me.

But during this trip, there was no doubt I was on edge. My year had just collapsed, and I wasn't there for salsa dancing. Our license to bring the expedition into Havana, summer 2011, was now a fait accompli. I needed to get back to Los Angeles and get focused.

TWENTY-ONE

Guts Before Glory

When you give your all, it's true that you don't leave room for regrets. Yet when you get a second chance, you always realize you can do better. I've heard umpteen grandparents say they've done a finer job of parenting their grandkids than they did their kids. Every major expedition in major Mother Nature elicits a learning curve. Whether you actually reach the summit or you come close to dying while trying, you return with ideas of what to improve on your next attempt.

So here we were, having taken October off and getting back to training in November for a 2011 summer attempt, Team Xtreme Dream busy taking new strides toward contemplating the science, the technology, the nutrition, and new thinking on how to tap the inner core spirit.

One thing I decided to change this year was my land-training routine. I had developed a two-hour rotation of yoga, core work, and upper-body calisthenics last year that I would do every non-swimming day. This year I worked with Bonnie to both lengthen that routine to two and a half hours and to increase the dumbbell weight increments to add a degree of bulk to my frame. If I was swimming at 136 pounds last year, Bonnie wanted me at 145 this year. A couple of tough swims had left me too slight. I was motivated by the challenge of a change-up.

The swimming itself, both pool and ocean, had been right last year, so come November I started back to long hours in the pool. The Rose Bowl Aquatics Center, in Pasadena, became my home base, and management generously dedicated one outside lane for me so that I could plop my cooler on the edge and go eight, nine, or ten hours uninterrupted. Bonnie, a self-admitted tanorexic, would sit poolside in her deck chair and whistle me to stop quickly for drinks and food. A scoop of peanut butter with a few gulps of our electrolyte drink this stop, half a banana the next. My stomach wasn't in turmoil in the pool as it was in the sea, so feeding wasn't such a nasty proposition. Bonnie's a voracious reader, so she would whisk through novel after novel as I splashed through lap after lap. Meantime I got into books on tape. Listening to the entire biography of Steve Jobs in one ten-hour pool session was a delightful diversion. I never did turn to headphones for music or books in the ocean. In the ocean, for one, I wanted to be aware and fully in the medium. Also, with the surface rarely as calm as a pool's, the sound would come through to me intermittently, so I'd miss many words, whole paragraphs. Well, you don't mind missing a phrase of a familiar Simon and Garfunkel song, but you're miffed when the narrator says, "The phenomenon of black holes . . ." then twenty-five seconds of static, blurred words, and gobbledygook, picking up with ". . . so you can see why we call this the ultimate mystery of our sky."

It might sound extreme, ten continuous hours in a pool. But I had all my counting goals lined up before I'd turn off my car early morning in the parking lot. No gabbing. A quick walk to the locker room. Quick undress. Quick shower. Quick slathering of sunscreen. Focused, I would walk to my lane, place my cooler within reach, and immediately begin. All the swimmers at the Rose Bowl—and several former Olympians train there—were incredibly supportive. They knew I wasn't there to chat. My legs would be so darn stiff at the end of a really long session that I could barely bend them to tuck into a flip turn at each end. But, as in the ocean, I never cheated myself out of even one minute. If the goal was ten hours, it was a true ten hours.

I thought it would behoove me to meet with some of the great long-distance swimmers of our era, do some communing with them, so I attended the Global Open Water Swimming Conference. It was wonderful to mix in with my peers who share my passion for these quests. Martin Strel had swum the entire length of the Amazon River, and he shows the scars from piranha bites across his back as his battle wounds. Jamie Patrick holds the record for the gutsy double crossing of chilly Lake Tahoe. Shelley Taylor-Smith (Shells), to my mind, and in the minds of many, the greatest competitive marathon swimmer in history, faster and tougher than all the men she raced against, eclipsed many of the big records in her day, the 1990s. I spend a wonderful day exchanging stories with Shells and the others, but even these intrepid adventurers tell me at the conference that they can't quite conceive of sixty sleep-deprived hours in the ocean. Especially not that ocean.

By late December 2010, I was strong and content. The foundation laid last season was now paying off. I was just a few weeks away from the start of ocean training and already way ahead of last year's schedule. CNN's reporting had made our fund-raising easier this time around. The U.S. government permits would go smoothly, too, as we had been recently cleared for 2010 and had new contacts.

My only concern was a nagging ache at the front of my left shoulder. Both shoulders had felt strain from the very start, coming back from the thirty-year hiatus. But I had found ice to be the miracle cure. My car looked like a cryogenics lab. As did my home. Ice packs of every size and description were constantly within reach. I traveled with ice chests, packed my shoulders in ice going to sleep every night, ate all meals with ice compressed around each shoulder. One day napping in my car after a very long workout at the Rose Bowl, ice packs heaped up on both shoulders, I awoke to a tap on my window. A senior shuffling out from water aerobics in her bathrobe asked if I was a football player. I told her yes, linebacker for the Oakland Raiders. An homage to my brother and his mythical days with the Steelers.

But in early January 2011, that slight ache on the left side escalated to a sharp pain on every stroke.

The first orthopedic doc I saw said I would never, ever be able to swim any further without surgery. He said the biceps tendon at the front of the shoulder was shredded. It was significant. He assured me no physical therapy, no injections would repair that tear. Only surgery would allow me to swim again without the tear widening. That tear splitting any wider and the pain would be intolerable. Well, I certainly didn't have time to recover from shoulder surgery and then get in shape for the summer. Not in January. So I did what all athletes do: I went to a different doctor to get a different diagnosis.

The next orthopod took his own set of images and gave me the same bad news. Bonnie was in the room with me when he told us that he had treated several swimmers with the same tear. None of them could resume their careers until surgical repair allowed that tendon to function fully again; especially given the extreme demands of this ultra-training, I needed surgery right away. I didn't like this guy's answer, either, and Bonnie told him he had no idea what this particular swimmer was capable of.

Our third stop was an old friend, orthopedist Jo Hannafin, at the Hospital for Special Surgery in New York. She took a look at my MRI and told me the tear wasn't all that bad. She was sure that with three weeks out of the water, a gentle set of exercises to calm the tendon down, and an injection to bathe the tendon with anti-inflammatory cortisone, I'd be able to resume training full tilt. She was right. And she got me working with the medical team in Los Angeles who took care of my shoulders from then on: rock-star orthopedist Dr. Neal ElAttrache and superstar physical therapist Karen Joubert.

I also got invaluable advice from the great freestyler Ous Mellouli, the first African male to win Olympic gold in an individual swimming event. Ous had the precise same biceps tendon tear in his shoulder. He was given the same advice the first two surgeons gave me. Surgery was imperative. And, like me, he didn't have the time to recover from that kind of operation and find his form again for the 2012 Games in London. But he had figured out a way to change his stroke rather radically, to protect that tendon, and he showed me his new form. Instead of keeping the elbows high at the entry phase of the stroke, the classic freestyle, he taught me to enter the hand very close to the head and to lower the shoulder as the hand extends forward underwater. It took me a while, talking to my hands on every single entry, to change my old ingrained stroke habit. But Ous, along with my caring and expert med team, got me back to swimming long sessions, pain-free.

Late January, the trips to St. Maarten, what we now called Camp

SXM, were back in swing. David and Maya were at the ready. Even with the shoulder setback, I was in far better shape than this time last year. We escalated to longer swims right away, rather than having to build up slowly.

Maya introduced me one day to a guy who would become key, Mark Sollinger. From day one, Mark and I spoke the same language, were cut from the same cloth. He had run a few marathons, was a lifetime devotee to the martial art of bando, had always been involved in intense fitness training, and for twenty-five years had owned the water-sports program at La Samanna hotel on the island, which became one of my sponsors. I met Mark at a time when he was primed for throwing himself into something tough yet inspiring. He was my guy, the kind of guy who simply steps up, every day, in every way. Mark, at six feet three inches with marine buzz cut, his wife Angie, also superfit and gung-ho, and their eight-year-old daughter Sam opened their home to me and Bonnie and all the Teammates who came down for training at Camp SXM.

David was still my Navigator. Maya was still our main course Driver. But Mark and Angie took over SXM training. It's one thing for me to press on with the three a.m. force feedings, for me to find the where-withal to punch into the waves over these protracted hours. This is my Dream. But to watch Bonnie getting all the gear ready at that same three a.m., to see Mark heading down to the dock at that hour to get the boat prepped, for Angie to slide a pillow under my head that night on the shower floor when I can't stand any longer and can't even make it to the bed—their dedication brought me unspeakable comfort. None of these friends ever got paid a dime. They were in it. All in. They were true Teammates, and I will never forget the magnitude of their sacrifices. Sometimes when I was low, Mark and Angie would lean over the side on one of my feeding stops and sing me a duet.

> And I can take you for a ride on my big green tractor
> We can go slow or make it go faster

They would drag out Angie's West Virginia accent and go full-on country. I loved it. Bonnie would joke and point to the St. Maarten

French Bridge as we approached it. When we first heard of the French Bridge, we imagined it looming huge above us, akin to the George Washington Bridge across the Hudson. So we laughed uproariously to see this quaint little structure you could reach up and touch from the deck of our small boat. When Bonnie would signal me the bridge was just a couple of strokes away, I would call out, "Bonjour, le Pont Français." Every time. It was the little tender habits we developed that brought us all so close.

We had both funny and deep conversations during many a feeding break. Training swims found us telling stories, trading observations about the universe. Mark and I shared a host of wow moments. At the ninth-hour feeding of an eleven-hour swim:

"Mark, I was reading last night in Stephen Hawking's *A Briefer History of Time* that most astrophysicists today believe all the matter and energy of this universe, on the precipice of the Big Bang, literally existed within the dimension of a millionth of a millionth of a penny. Come on, Mark, all this in a millionth of a millionth of a penny! Doesn't that just blow your mind?"

Then Mark and his buddy Fred would lighten things up with their imitations of Arnold Schwarzenegger: "Yah, yah, that was incredible, the Big Bang. Und yah, she has very strong biceps. She is a badass schwimmer for sure."

As winter—such as winter is in heavenly St. Maarten—turned to spring, we again mixed in swims at Kathy Loretta's Mexico training camp. In St. Maarten we had choices, coves and coastlines where we could tuck away on heavy wind days, but the Yucatán coast was unprotected. With big, blustery winds, it was better to swim in close to shore, but the reef stretches along parallel to the beach and very close to extreme shallows. If the waves coming toward shore are big and tall, the crew has to be on intense guard all day, not to let me either slam into those sharp corals on one side or constantly get slammed onto the sand on the other. Tim was with me instead of Bonnie one set of swims. He was the filmmaker, but he always dropped his camera when I needed him. The morning surf was over ten feet, huge. That was a harrowing fifteen-hour day, Tim's voice so hoarse from yelling all day at both me and the boat driver to keep me from crunching down onto the reef or the shore, he could barely speak.

Another not-so-ideal day in Mexico, we swam outside the reef, careful to tie our Shark Shield to the boat. The wind was screaming to the south. Usually we go in one direction for a calculated time, then turn around and come back, always trying to finish close to our start beach. We don't want to finish far from home. It's not as simple as dividing the time and distance in half. Wind, currents, and tides have to be considered. It takes experience to judge the turnaround point each time out. After a grueling day in the sea, the last thing I need is to then be on a small boat for a long time, feeling poorly, as we motor back in. The crew also needs that punishment like a hole in the head. But this day I have no chance of making any progress to the north. We decide to push south, thinking the wind might switch or die down later. But it blew like heck all day long, and we flew south. At the feeding stops, Bonnie told me the shore was zipping by; we were zooming past hotels, little towns, jungle areas. At the end of that twelve-hour day, they pulled me onto the little aluminum panga boat, and it took us close to seven banging, hellish hours, straight into the stiff wind, to get home. I sat shoulder to shoulder with Bonnie, silent with our heads wrapped in uncomfortable wet towels, that hard backless metal bench unforgiving at each slam into the waves, eyes closed all the way. I actually cried that late night, to see Kathy under the moonlight on the beach, towel in hand.

On that same Mexico training trip, I was cruising fairly smoothly one day when I literally felt my stomach flip. I had never had that experience before, or since, so was alarmed the moment it happened. I stopped abruptly and yelled up to Bonnie that my stomach had done a full somersault and it was still flipped. She coaxed me to dog paddle toward the boat, asked if I was in pain. I wasn't. I dug my fingers into the skin of the thorax, grabbed the area and pushed the lower end back toward my spine until I felt the flip back into the right position. Bonnie and I looked at each other, having no idea at the time if this was normal or dangerous or not. We didn't say a word and I swam out the rest of the session. Ah, the eccentricities of extreme sports.

Bonnie and I determined a twenty-four-hour wasn't necessary this year. But we went back to SXM for one eighteen-hour session. The wind was whipping. We all knew we were in for a tough day.

End of the training season, my mind was close to numb with trying to come up with new singing and counting progressions. As I took the plunge into the big St. Maarten lagoon, where we would warm up through the forty-five minutes out to the French Bridge and then into the open ocean, I decided to put my mind to something new. I was going to go from city to city, as I could think of them on a map, all around the world, singing that army ditty that goes:

> I don't know but I've been told
> Streets of Bogotá paved with gold
> Sound off! One, two
> Sound off! Three, four
> Sound off! One, two, three, four.

I'm going to start with South America and see how many hours it will take me to go through Africa, Asia, Europe, and then move on to North America if the eighteen hours are still not done.

Colombia first: Bogotá. Cartagena. Cali. Medellín. Pereira. I can picture each on the map, this one on the coast, this one in the bamboo forests. By the time I get to Venezuela, my mind is starting to drift with memories. I've often joked that each long swim is akin to six months on a psychiatrist's couch. Your life floods your brain, one random image, one pointed voice at a time.

Sure enough, at Caracas, I am taken back to my "wedding" to Nina there. It isn't legal, or formal. Just our little private ceremony, our exchange of vows on our hotel balcony. We both speak a fluent French and for a time ignorantly considered Spanish a simple language. Our chauvinism runs so deep, we think we can learn all the basics on the flight from Los Angeles to Caracas. We are cocky when we enter the jeweler's shop, to order our wedding rings. A squat man emerges from the back and folds his short, thick forearms across the glass counter. We start chatting, very impressed with ourselves and our breezy nuances. We want diamonds and emeralds, a channel setting, here are our sizes, we can only afford this much, we need the rings by Friday for our ceremony. The jeweler looks from one of us to the other throughout this performance, takes a big sigh, and says to us in his New York accent, "Look, ladies, I'm a busy man. Why don't youse just tell me what youse want and I'll go in the back and make it for youse, okay?" I find myself literally smiling underwater as I recollect our foolishness. And as I remember our sweet, low-key wedding.

I am drifting off with that memory. I have not heard Bonnie blowing the whistle for a feeding. There it is. After some bites of a peanut butter and ginseng sandwich, she wants me to try something new. They're little square jellies called Shot Bloks. They deliver electrolytes slowly into your system as you suck on them. But Bonnie has also heard from Jamaican free divers who have contacted us online. They dive all day, cleaning the bottoms of boats, and wind up with severe swelling in the mouth, from the saltwater exposure. They heard about my problems with mouth-tissue sores and swelling after long periods in the ocean, and they have told Bonnie that they suck on dried papaya while swimming. An enzyme in the papaya has evidently helped prevent their tissue from swelling.

Dried fruit has too sharp an edge for me to keep in the mouth while swimming. But the concept gives Bonnie the idea to try these little jellies, not so much for their chemical properties but to literally put a barrier between my teeth and my cheek, not allowing salt exposure at least in that little area. It works. Bonnie sticks a Shot Blok in my mouth at the end of every feeding, and the mouth sores are at least somewhat abated.

I've had some sandwich and, Shot Blok lodged between cheek and teeth, I'm back out and stroking and return to the army ditty. I go through Peru, Brazil, Chile. When I come to Argentina, after Buenos Aires, I get to Patagonia, scene of one of the grand experiences of my life. For perhaps the next half hour, I am frolicking with the whales once again.

I had been sent to Patagonia for a documentary film, where we'd swim technically below the Antarctic Circle latitude line. And I was allowed to bring Candace with me. Our protagonists were the "right" whales, named long ago because they were the "right" ones to kill, given that they travel relatively slowly, unlike other species that can dive and swim distances quickly, thus remaining elusive for long periods of time.

The daytime air temps are mid-thirties, the water temps about the same, just above freezing. We swim in the thickest wet suits made at that time, a thickness so unmanageable that it takes Candace a couple of hours at dawn each day to yank and drag and squeeze me into that thing. Our guide to swimming with the whales is Armando, playboy of Argentina. Armando has shoulder-length, bleached-blond locks and wears a shocking-pink wet suit with diamond studs down the lengths of his arms and legs.

We patrol in small Zodiac rubber boats in the early morning, the whales bouncing and breaching and playfully slapping the surface with their mammoth tails. Armando signals me to get ready. We slip over the side of the Zodiac and, hand in hand, move slowly toward a female who has flipped onto her back to give herself a break from nursing her baby. I whisper to Armando, "I've always heard you don't go near an animal with nursing young'uns around." He says we'll be okay, the baby splashing around on the other side of Mama at that moment.

I follow Armando up onto Mama's stomach. Her flukes are waving slowly toward the sky as she rolls slightly side to side, making a contented creaking noise. I am scared out of my mind. My pulse climbs close to 200. We are lying on the belly of a sixty-foot, 120-ton animal, her baby frolicking just a few meters away. Armando motions me to be silent.

We lie there for maybe six, seven, eight minutes, a singular experience, to understate it, to basically be hugging a living, breathing mammal the size of a tanker. The whole month, swimming with whales below Patagonia, is forever carved in my memory and was the trip of a lifetime for me and Candace.

Perhaps the only glitch is that I am evidently on camera imitating Armando's thick accent. I don't know about you, but I start to speak in broken English exactly like the people I'm engaging with, subconsciously figuring that I'm communicating better if we're both using the same language. The director yells, "CUT! Diana, why are you talking like that?"

"Talking like what?" I ask, oblivious.

He replays a piece of video, and I am shocked to hear myself: "Arrrmahndo. Whhhy we not see zee whales over zehr?"

Again, now maybe ten hours in, I find myself smiling, pretty much on automatic and unconcerned with the pounding waves. I press on with the army tune, mapping out the cities as I can remember them, continent to continent. I'm pretty good on Africa, dismally remedial on Asia, really good on Europe. And that game takes me through the travails of what would normally be a hellish eighteen hours.

It is mid-June, and the long months of guts before glory are behind us. Just as I did last year on the "last training swim," I cry my eyes out when I hear the final whistle. We are again ready to move the expedition to Key West.

TWENTY-TWO

Red Alert

Bonnie and I are at home in Key West now. Everything is familiar. We stroll the beautiful neighborhoods after dinner, the locals chatting us up from their extended porches, the foliage stunning, the roosters crowing all hours of the day, the historic architecture a mix of Bahamian style and Victorian influence. We know most of the merchants, all the staff at our favorite hotel gym, where to get our morning newspaper. Bonnie can't help herself and winds up coaching just about every tourist on vacation through better workouts and develops routines for them to take home. Our neighborhood is largely Haitian and I speak a patois with them along the sidewalks. *"Eh bonjour, madame. Tute munde c'est meme bagail, n'est-ce pas?"* (Everyone the same under the blue sky, isn't it true?) Madame laughs back and makes a swimming stroke motion to me. We even know most of the dogs in town; we always have a bag of dog treats with us. It's an easygoing island pace in Key West.

Dee Brady and John Bartlett bring our escort boat *Voyager* down, and we get into the routine. John has now engineered the "lane line" streamer to perfection. I rarely stray from parallel to the boat anymore. We put in short hours, usually six to eight, mixed with the gym workouts. An eight-hour outing seems like kids' stuff now. We have

Team meetings, usually over a barbecue at the Team house, once a week. Bartlett is always up for a discussion, his blue eyes dancing, his fingers playing that imaginary piano with gusto, from the crafting of Leo Fender's guitars to the drift factor of an object such as a swimmer in a fast current. Mark, Dee, David, and Maya get the boat ready for each outing, check the weather for our best wind direction, fuel us up, and we shove off the dock with military precision, Bonnie down at her station, all hands on deck. We do a few night swims to get the Shark Divers into their rhythm. We finish a long day swim, without our shark guys, at the tail end of dusk. Out of it, in the usual trance at this point, I am alarmed when something strong and solid and alive hits my hand. I yell up to the boat. "Was that a shark?" Not a moment's hesitation, Mark plunges in and slaps a big disturbance all around me. We'll never know if that was a shark or not, but I do know what a solid friend Mark is.

July comes and goes, which makes me a bit nervous. The good news is the government permissions have come in early this time. All we need now is that weather window. On one hand, there is plenty of summer left. On the other hand, I am traumatized by how the east winds had refused to lie down last year. But Dane calls on August 1. He likes what he's seeing. A high-pressure ridge is sliding south down the latitudes into Florida. Another couple of degrees and we might just have a terrific setup for light winds out through the Straits.

We have an alert system. If Dane gives us a "maybe" five days out, we put the Team on amber alert. Everybody needs to be packed. Passports, personal gear, at the door, travel plans made. Most of the thirty-five-member crew are with us in Key West. The whole SXM Team is here. Mark, Angie, David, Maya, two of our Kayakers. Several others will come from different parts of Florida and can get to Key West in half a day. Luke Tipple, Liza, and a few others are out in California, a couple of Handlers will come from Vermont and Colorado. Tim and his crew are with us. The boats need a good twenty-four hours to clear U.S. customs and get over to Cuba and clear customs there.

Dane's forecast is promising enough to issue the amber alert. He monitors all the conditions, from all his various sources. We then check in with our other sources, to verify. Three days out from the potential window, Dane says he's confident the window is going to hold. Gulf Stream expert Jenifer Clark isn't crazy about the positioning of the Stream. It's tugging hard to the east, not the northeast that would be ideal for us. We might not like where we wind up, way up the Keys, with a Stream strong to the east, but we'll never make it without low wind and a southern component to the wind. We move into red alert. Everybody mobilizes in a hurry to Key West.

I am not going to tire myself out, or subject myself to seasickness, with the eighteen or so hour boat ride over to Cuba. Bonnie and I fly a charter out of Miami. Kathy Loretta, our Mexican buddy, acting as our Cuban Ground Ops, has been in Havana a couple of days already and has secured a few rooms at the lovely Hotel Acuario (sarcasm intended), made all the diplomatic stops with Cuban customs, the dock managers, and arranged an efficient timeline with the Commodore of the marina, in an effort to allow our boats in with a minimum of bureaucracy. It is not unheard of for American boats to take eight or more hours to clear customs, the search routine thorough to the point of dismantling the boat bow to stern. A quick turnaround is paramount for us, and Kathy has greased quite a few palms toward that goal. The Cuban way.

Dane's last report, before we left Miami, called for a pretty good-looking stretch, under ten-mile-per-hour winds from the south-southeast, for the next four days. Then back from the east at fifteen miles per hour. We aren't in a panic, but we have no lollygag time in Havana, either. We simply cannot be out there in an east wind. Deal breaker. The boats will be in tomorrow, August 6, and clear customs by nightfall. We will have one last Team meeting. I will have time with Bonnie, Mark, David, and John, as well as some private soul-searching with Candace. Then the Team will fan out to explore Havana a bit, and get themselves organized for the start, set for dusk the next day, August 7.

I go into my prerace regimen with Bonnie. We take all my goggles to the hotel pool, test every pair, once again label them in order. We meticulously empty and repack my two gear bags. Bonnie knows where every item is, how it is labeled. Then she goes over all of it with her Handler Team.

Yes, I'm nervous. Maybe even scared. I am confident that training and Team prep have been undeniably meticulous, but I still know it's going to be a long, rough couple of days. And the yearlong buildup has been emotional for the Team, too. We just want to get started.

The Commodore hosts a press conference at the marina. Big turnout. The Cubans have seen quite a few swimmers from around the world, going back more than sixty years now, jump off their famous shore, with their sights on The Other Shore, the United States. They are versed in the issues to address. The sleep deprivation, the sharks, the meaning of the quest. And, of course, there is the unspoken matter of countless Cubans fleeing these very shores that we now render an athletic starting point. They even call the Florida Straits the Cuban graveyard, so many Cubans have not survived the crossing on flimsy rafts in the middle of the night.

When I first met with the Commodore, José Miguel Escrich, a big bear of a humanitarian who has long been surprisingly open about wanting to normalize relations and travel between our two countries, he told me that our swim would be vastly easier to approve, on the Cuban side, if we would swim from Florida to Cuba, and not set an image that reminds people of the many who have fled or tried to flee. Not only would the Gulf Stream make such a southerly route impossible, but I wanted to finish in my own country. Regardless that the direction of the swim was not what the Cubans wished, the Commodore became our greatest ally there and diplomatically pushed through every request we made, including speeding up the customs process for our boats.

Just before Bonnie and I flew over this time, I couldn't sleep and went to a twenty-four-hour drugstore in Key West, to pick up some gum. There was only one other customer in the store, and he got to the cashier right before me. He turned around to me, gave me his soulful Cuban gaze, and said, "I don't know what it is, but something means a great deal to you right now."

He could see it. I was heavy with hope. And fear. He then opened his wallet and carefully extracted a pristinely folded two-dollar bill. His face was close to mine now, his eyes penetrating. "The night we left Havana, in a leaky raft, my grandmother hugged me tight and told me she had decided not to go. We both cried, aching with the fear we would never see each other again. She took this two-dollar bill, told me an American gave it to her, explained to her it meant good luck. She told me to hold it close to me, to help me survive the trip. And she told me to one day give it to someone who might really need some luck. My uncle died from the hardship of the trip across. And I've never seen my grandmother since that night. But tonight I know it's the right thing, to give you this good-luck bill. Hold it close to you. Find your way, as I did. And one day you must give it to someone at just the moment of their need."

We embraced for a long moment. I cried. He cried. We never exchanged names. But that man, his grandmother's two-dollar bill ever since crisply folded in my wallet, ready for me to give one day to a person I sense in true need of it, represented to me the Cuban people. They are warm and unhesitatingly giving. This is true of the big bear Commodore. True of all the Cubans I've ever known. As I've said, I wanted to make this somewhat of a goodwill crossing, signaling the day when we will travel freely back and forth, when our two peoples will enjoy each others' cultures, unrestricted.

On August 7, the press conference ends at about noon. We call the start for six p.m. Bonnie runs around doling out cash to Kathy Loretta for dock fees, customs "tips," ice (which was dumped onto the dock in a huge single block, reminiscent of turn-of-the-century deliveries in the United States; we will have to chip it apart), and fuel. I get ready.

Candace spends an hour with me, such a calm soul. She helps me ease the adrenaline flow from a roaring river to a steady basso. Candace is a natural healer. An old-soul wisdom flows through her eyes, her hands. I've seen her touch people when they were hurt or sick, first above the skin, passing her hands gently along their energy pathways, then directly, and alleviate at least some of their pain. And I've seen her do the same with animals. In some regards, Candace lives on a higher plane of consciousness. I've never known her to gossip or spend foolish time on people who are not moving ahead with positive force. Here she is now, as she was with me on these very shores way back in 1978. And, as she did back in the day, she again imbues me with an inner peace. Her hands are warm and firm and steady. She asks me to inhale as she presses my neck, exhale as she strokes the length of my back. It's a meditation of unfazed composure. Before she leaves, she sings the song we've always agreed she will sing when we finally see that other shore. Her voice is pitch-perfect, soft and melodic.

The lyrics of "When You Wish Upon a Star" are like an elixir to me. My interpretation: When you reach for the stars, if you're willing to be that bold, your dreams will one day come true.

Bonnie brings me a last meal, around two p.m. The usual. Hard-boiled eggs. Oatmeal. Water, water, more water. The overwhelming excitement of the start is going to be dehydrating. So is the urge to crank too hard over that first mile. Over those last few hours, in some regards the clock seemingly frozen, the feeling so surreal to be finally near takeoff, in other ways the hands of time whizzing by, the pressure of the moment mounts to a pulsating peak.

By four p.m. our boats have all cleared customs out and are hovering by the rocks at the marina entrance. Some Cuban boats, ready to accompany us to legal international waters, twelve miles out, are mixed in with ours. At five-thirty, Jorge, a local we have befriended over our short time at the Hotel Acuario, comes to pick us up in a golf cart. Bonnie and I climb into the cart, silent, Kathy Loretta with us, for the ten-minute ride to the rocks. I feel my heartbeat pounding in my wrists. All four of us look to the horizon. It's twilight calm. Hope is alive.

The Cuban press corps is both huddled and spread along the starting point. Unlike the American press, they are polite. They don't yell. They respectfully observe and wait as Bonnie and I get my robe off, the grease-smearing process going, the cap and goggles set. Then I turn to them for a few last questions. Again, they are refreshingly sensitive. I hug Kathy, then the Commodore. I blow the bugle, my signature tune, "Reveille," meaning "GET UP," "GET GOING," and the Team screams "ONWARD!" from the boats.

Time to get to work. I am a professional. It's time to settle down and get swimming. Time to put into motion what I've worked so hard for. Bonnie and I embrace. She whispers in my ear: "Onward!" Tim is there filming, one eye on the viewfinder, giving me his beautiful smile with the other. I see Candace out on her boat, arms high and encouraging. Liza is waving and smiling, along with my old Handlers, Jon and Deborah; Heidi and Jesse round out the new Handler Team. Mark is tall on his boat, pumping his fist, yelling "ONWARD!" There's Dee at

Voyager's wheel, thumbs up. David and John stand side by side, hands on hips, facing me. Luke is way up on *Voyager*'s roof, already on the shark lookout.

The French version of *Courage!* is the last word I say. And we're off. I jump and start swimming toward *Voyager*. Dee is waving me to sweep in next to the boat. John and Mark have now lowered the streamer, and the water is so clear that I can see the white cloth underneath from quite far away. I am pressing toward it, reminding myself to pull back on my stroke count, trying to reel in my excitement and refrain from busting out on all cylinders. Bonnie and Tim jump from the rocks into little rubber inflatables for rides out to the flotilla. We all can barely grasp that this is finally happening, yet with that first stroke, it is real. We're ecstatic to at long last have our mission under way.

TWENTY-THREE

Unprepared for the Unexpected

The surface is so calm, I am so fresh, I can see everything. Bonnie on the Handler's platform, hands on hips. Dee at the wheel. David at his navigation station. Luke up top, surveying for creatures. The blue below me is dazzling. I'm trying to decide: Is it azure? Sky blue? Baby blue? Ultramarine? Whatever a colorist would name it, its heavenliness makes me giddy. I take a glance backward on a breath every now and then, content to see the Havana skyline receding fairly quickly.

What's this? What the hell is this? We are not two hours in when I wince with a dagger pain at the front of the right shoulder. I don't tell Bonnie yet. I deal with it for about half an hour, trying to change the hand entry by a few centimeters in various positions, thinking I can find relief. How can this be? First of all, it was only the left shoulder that ever gave me problems, and that has not been an issue for many months now. I've never had even a twinge on the right side. But it persists. I have to tell Bonnie. You ride a fine line out there. You have to be tough and not give in to complaining about every little ache. But when something is, or could develop into, a game changer, Bonnie needs to be aware, so she can have a chance to come up with solutions before it escalates. She'll bring in her Handler Team and then the doc, if necessary.

Bonnie's approach is never tough love. No matter what I suffer, she assumes I am pain tolerant and would never complain over a minor hiccup. She gets me to do some shoulder stretching in the water, suggests I've been going too fast, too high a stroke rotation, and tells me to slow it way down for the next ninety minutes, to the next feeding. I don't stop and grouse over those ninety minutes, but the pain is there every stroke. I'm truly exasperated. Did I not warm up properly? That's not it. I went through the exact same routine I do before every long swim. Did the adrenal surge off the rocks push me to an exertion beyond what the shoulder was warmed up to handle? After the hundreds of hours, the hundreds of thousands of strokes logged these past two years, how could a lousy couple of hours strain this shoulder? I'm too strong, too fit, to have this happen, too prepared.

Just when you think you're prepared for every possible setback, wham, the unexpected pummels you and you're unprepared. I do plenty of kvetching those first few hours, so Bonnie calls me over for a heart-to-heart.

"Look. This is a shame. We can't figure out why the heck it's happening. But it is. You're not going to quit because of this shoulder pain. I don't know how you're going to do it, but you've got to rise above it. It's draining you to keep your focus on it. Let me call for your Tylenol from your bag, and we'll hope to pain manage at least to a degree. But you've just got to funnel your attention elsewhere. Think you can do that?"

I promise Bonnie I'll quit complaining about it. I'll find a way.

As I carry on, Bonnie rifles through my two duffles over and over. The Tylenol isn't there. I am so damn fastidious about my gear, went over the packing list a thousand times, but I somehow forgot my Tylenol. I'm highly allergic to all other forms of pain medicine. Asthma comes to me quickly with aspirin or Aleve or any other product, over-the-counter or prescription. Bonnie and our doc put out the word to all the other boats. No Tylenol on board. Everything but. The doc has injections of pain meds but is reluctant to send me into an asthma episode.

It's night now. Pitch black. The seas are quite calm. Not glass but not a struggle, either. Except for that right shoulder, I'm moving at a decent pace. The Team is upbeat. We are making progress. I sometimes wonder if the shoulder is going to rip right out of the socket. Bonnie assures me that won't happen. Tendons might be straining in there, but we discuss that the shoulder must be strong as an ox at this point. Just get through it.

I count all night, rather than sing. The counting seems to get me off the pain more than the singing. Six thousand strokes in English, one count every four times the left hand enters the water. Then six thousand backward in English. Then the same progression in German. Then Spanish, then French. Bonnie lets me finish counting to a number easy for me to pick up with when she whistles me in for a feeding. If she whistles and I'm at 4,689, I give her a "wait a minute" finger signal, so I can make it to 4,750, and then swing in for the feeding.

She asks me about the shoulder every stop. That's all I need out there, to know that Bonnie is aware of what I'm dealing with. Even if we can't do anything about it, the compassion goes a long way.

At daylight, she brings the Team doctor over to talk with me about the shoulder pain. He doesn't want to inject the shoulder directly with medication. That requires a precise entry; he would need an MRI image to gauge it properly. And he's concerned about an allergic reaction. But he has discovered one of our St. Maarten crew has a bottle of something that, in French, sounds like the exact ingredients of Tylenol. I take two capsules. Only twenty minutes later, I start feeling the constriction of the throat. I'm having an allergic, asthmatic reaction.

Our doc starts me on puffs of Ventolin. Many puffs over the course of the entire day. And he sets up a nebulizer at Bonnie's station, low to the surface. It's not easy to manipulate from the water, but he has me grab the mask and hold it over my mouth. He counts me through several deep breaths. I take a break. Then several more. He also has me take a few sips of oxygen every hour or so. My breathing passageways do open somewhat by midafternoon, but the many puffs of Ventolin have made my heart rate speed up. I still can't get my breathing under control. I take less than one hundred strokes and the oxygen fuel to the muscles is depleted. I am weak. I need air. I roll over onto my back, clutch my lungs, and take a few minutes of deep breaths. When freestyle is too taxing, I start with a modified breaststroke, with dolphin kick. I can get more air this way, my head up more often and for a longer beat on each stroke. I'm unfortunately not making good headway, but my breathing is more under control. I can go this modified breaststroke for as many as ten minutes before needing a break for treatment and deeper pulls of air.

I keep thinking we will get there, it will just take a lot longer. Mark, Angie, David, Maya, Dee, and Bonnie keep my spirits up. Candace and Tim visit Bonnie's station and give me their eyes, caring and hopeful. "You're doing better than you think," they tell me. The other Handlers, as they come to the platform for their shifts, encourage me the best they can. I know them all so well—Liza, Jon, Deborah, Heidi, Jesse—and their kind eyes comfort me. But I can also see David's body language. He huddles over his charts and then comes on deck and shakes his head while talking to Bonnie and Mark. He's in constant contact with Bartlett over on his boat. We must be tugging too far and fast to the east. I don't ask. It's never a good plan for me to know if we're making measured progress or not. I can only do the best I can do.

Sundown. Insult is added to injury. Huge swarms of moon jellyfish rise up beneath me. Each is a beautiful, opaque whitish disk, sort of the shape of a shuffleboard puck, but thicker. And they're larger than what we're used to seeing in close to shore. Each seems to be more than two feet in diameter. They are clustered together, a veritable sea of jellies, in every direction, not too far under the surface. No matter how shallow I try to stroke, I am swiping these animals with every hand push. The moon, to the touch, is not gelatinous as are many jellyfish. It's a fairly solid, weighty feel, much like a thick steak. I don't usually see much below, but I can plainly see the layers of these jellies, a massive bed of floating circles. Perhaps beautiful under different circumstances, this evening they are an unwelcome complication.

Mark sends our little inflatable "taxi," which normally buzzes from boat to boat, transferring crew from work shifts to rest periods on their respective mother ships, to scout the width of the moon army. Too wide for me to skirt, way out to either side. A couple of miles, minimum. So we plow through.

The surface tension of the jelly gives when I paw it, but the animal stays intact. I sweep them behind me with each stroke. But as I begin to feel little whips of pricks, I suspect that my touch is breaking them up to a degree, and I learn later that's when they defend themselves and emit their sting. Each one alone is not excruciating pain, but the collective effect, perhaps thousands of stings for that twilight hour or ninety minutes, makes me grit my teeth between yelps as the pricks continue all over my arms and legs and face. I yell out several times. Bonnie and her niece Jesse see them everywhere. Relentless, persistent stings.

By the time we are into true darkness, the jellies now having dived deeper, I am wheezing with pulmonary distress from the multiple stings. This on top of my pulse still racing due to the huge volume of Ventolin in my system.

Perhaps bizarre, the shoulder pain disappears as suddenly as it had materialized. It lasted just about twenty-four hours, and now it is entirely gone. Yet because of the pulmonary trouble, I no longer have freestyle in me. I can't take in enough oxygen to feed my muscles for the contractions demanded by freestyle. The only forward progress I can make is with this oddball breaststroke with this undulating kick, like a wounded dolphin. David is telling Bonnie that I need to get some more speed going to keep from heading straight out east toward the Bahamas. Bonnie conveys this to me on several stops. But each time I try freestyle, I am winded in just a few dozen strokes, whereas I can sustain the slow breaststroke and keep trying.

From dark to past midnight, I hear Bonnie's voice on every single lift of my head. Fifty times a minute, from seven p.m. to one a.m. Except for the short stops for drink and during my gulps from the oxygen mask, Bonnie yells to me. She doesn't take a break. I'll never in my life forget Bonnie's voice that night. During that half a second before the downstroke that takes my head back underwater, I hear my buddy: "Come on!" "That's it!" "You're doing great!" "That's the way!" "Awesome!" "You're so tough, Diana." Fifty times a minute for six hours. Eighteen thousand times.

At about one a.m., I come in close so Bonnie and I can have a quiet, intimate conversation. It's so dark that I can barely make her out, just a foot away from me, but I can tell she's been crying. I say that I keep hoping to recover and get back to breathing normally, but we're going onto a total of some eighteen hours of pulmonary distress now. She doesn't inform me exactly how far off course we are but does share with me that, even if I can soon get back to a steady freestyle, and stop taking all these treatment breaks, our total distance to Florida is now a much bigger number, we have traveled so far to the east.

I go back to the intermittent freestyle with the breaststroke taking over the majority of the time. After several hours of that wounded breaststroke, trying everything I can to get my lungs working again, Bonnie's voice now hoarse, I come close to her at the Handler's station again. She pulls in David, Mark, and John, and they run down a quick assessment. Not being able to give strength to our northerly course, we have been dragged far off to the east. I tell Bonnie that if we were just a few miles from the Florida coast, I wouldn't care about trying to make it via a debilitated breaststroke. Hell, I'd dog-paddle the rest of the way. But now, with perhaps two full days to go? I'm not going to make it. Not this way. Not this day.

This is a tough moment, but Bonnie and I agree we are no longer in a noble pursuit. To slowly breaststroke for some necessary recovery time, during various crises on the way across, would be one thing. But to swim almost the entire time slowly and injured will not take us to Florida shores.

It's not a long discussion. We all agree. Bonnie pulls me up onto the surface-level transom, and we just sit there together, stunned, for a few minutes.

There are no tears. There isn't much talk. They quickly move to get me onto an inflatable transport and over to a bigger boat for the long, silent ride back to Key West. Dr. Michael Broder inserts an IV, and I lie on a couch for what seems eternity. Teammates come to take my hand, exchange a knowing look. Candace holds me close. Bonnie hugs me, and now we do cry. Bitter tears, after trying so darn hard. That photo, of our desperate embrace, moves me to tears each time I see it. It speaks to our solidarity, as if our hug, if we held it long enough, would keep us from having to abandon our unshakable faith. We trained together. We put the expedition together. Now we suffer disillusionment, together.

That was August 8, 2011. Fifty-eight miles. Twenty-eight hours, forty-two minutes.

The arrival at the docks in Key West is like attending my own funeral. A number of friends had come in from various parts of the country, thinking they'd be heading out on boats to accompany our flotilla for the last few miles, to victory. I come out onto the stern of our boat, not yet allowed by customs to step down onto the dock. My pals and a few press reps, along with CNN and Tim's film crew, applaud me and our Team. They know how deep the effort ran, but all I can feel is crushing failure. I say a few words, mostly a twisted exasperation of disbelief and sorrow. My last public statement that day: "My beautiful Dream, Cuba to Florida, is not to be."

It's the tough stuff of life, profound disappointment. When we summon the guts to put ourselves out there, to reach for the highest star, when we march unafraid into dangerous territory, unwavering in our preparation, brimming with hope that we will succeed, the letdown, when it all comes crashing down in defeat, is colossal. They say we shouldn't contemplate the deeper issues of our lives when sick or exhausted. But my despair is at too wretched a level on that dock to mine down to common sense. This Dream lived somewhere in my imagination for thirty years, from the first spark of magic to it when I was in my twenties. There was again magic to it, in this unlikely story of coming back to a long-ago Dream all these years later, especially as an athlete in her sixties. So now I've tried twice. Failed twice. The emotional toll is heavy, these twenty-four hours after sitting on that transom, devastated, with Bonnie. It's so painful that I cringe, to remember sitting there with my legs dangling in the water, no longer in the ocean kicking, no longer swimming for another thirty hours, as we had envisioned it. One minute you're making an heroic effort. You're not one to ever quit. The next moment it's over. The reality is a lot to take in. I hate it.

I'm not sure where perseverance comes from. Do we inherit a will to push on? Do we survive a childhood ordeal that makes us gritty? When you hear the stories of most leaders and people who have attained high levels of success, meaning also nonfamous people who have triumphed over hellish circumstances, they can speak of natural talents, and experience, and good fortune, and timing, and mentors. But they collectively agree the critical denominator to any individual's succeeding is perseverance.

A man once told me he had a grave illness as a child. From the age of only fifteen months, he was confined by a full-time hospital stay for many years. He said, almost from the beginning, when he was very young, he was determined to live a vital life, not to spend all his days a weak, sickly person. This man's interpretation of his victory over his physical challenges was that it was the illness that sparked his spirit, that he was actually grateful for the illness. To play devil's advocate, I asked him: "What if you were born with that forceful drive? What if it was your innate strength that has served as the lifetime foundation, from the day you were born, to rise above any hurdle in front of you, including that grave illness of your childhood?"

I've been asked this all my life. Was it the trauma of my younger days that drove me? I will not give credit to molesters, as if to say they in the end help us become more powerful individuals. I am confident I was this fierce person long before those events. At two, three, four, I believe I heard some version of "Reveille," in my spirit, at the crack of dawn, and went to bed exhausted at the end of each day, having put out so much that there wasn't a fingernail more to give.

Yes, of course, we react to respective situations we encounter; we develop patterns and syndromes in our anger and our fear and our disillusionments . . . and our joy. But there is a base personality. A parent can observe a very young child constantly delve down and press on, while another passively allows whatever situation is occurring to rule. But I can easily argue the other side of the Nature vs. Nurture debate. Regardless of our genetics, no matter the bad luck of our circumstances, we choose our courses of action. The traits of will and perseverance aren't so easy to trace, such as the color of our eyes. And, to go back to the Nature side of the argument, perhaps it is part and parcel of the human condition, that we all have the potential for drive. It's up to each one of us to summon what is within.

All I know on this dock, at this moment in time, the Cuba Swim once again relegated to myth, is that I am crestfallen. That low haunts me about twenty-four hours after that last weak stroke. But at the thirty-hour mark, I feel the surge of the mettle within.

We organize a Team party that next evening. We are upbeat, happy, proud. And we're not faking it, just to lift each others' spirits. We achieved a lot. We learned a lot. I call out each valued individual at the party, add a couple of funny stories along the way, but mainly thank every single one of them for all they contributed to our quest. Not one of these Teammates was paid a dime. They dedicated themselves in the name of adventure, history, and friendship. It's been a magnificent journey. We can't throw the majesty of the mission, all the expertise and passion we've injected into it, down the toilet just because we didn't make it all the way across. It's a life lesson. The journey has been inordinately worthwhile, the destination be damned (for one night anyway).

That night after the gathering is surreal. None of the core Team can sleep. We are all desperate for sleep, but we are churning with emotion. Bonnie and I walk down to the ocean about three a.m. and sit on the beach for an hour, talking about the training swims, the characters, trying to make sense of what has just transpired. Mark is roaming the streets by himself, and the three of us stroll together for about half an hour. At dawn, Candace and I sit on the little porch of our condo for a while. The frame of mind is undeniable. We are all already talking about putting it together again. But right away, not next year. It is early August. I will need about a month to recover. Bonnie says six weeks. Let's take a chance on another window before the cool water sets in. Let's not go through yet another long, long year of training. If perseverance is the backbone of success, no matter where it comes from, we are standing tall, my Team. We refuse to give up.

TWENTY-FOUR

Whisper of Hope

I head home to Los Angeles and start hammering away at the details for another crossing. Dane is on the weather lookout, although we need at least a few weeks for me to recuperate. It was not only the hours of swimming. Struggling and fighting through those many hours of asthma took a different toll. And the weight loss, about fifteen pounds, is not only fat. Muscle tissue has been eaten away also; it takes time to build that tissue back.

I'm swimming lightly, doing also a light version of my dry-land routine, while Bonnie and I are discussing what we can improve upon. We are an intelligent group of individuals, our Team. We have been conferring on countless subjects for two years now. In debriefing this attempt, we ask ourselves how the jellyfish experts could not have warned us that we might run into a pod of jellies this thick, this far spread, impossible to swim around? How could I have forgotten one of the staples of my gear bag, Tylenol, after packing, repacking, and taking inventory of that bag dozens of times?

How could I have thought my Med Team, out in this unsafe environment, should consist of one research gynecologist? Michael had done his best, no doubt. But it was poor judgment on my part to not have a team of combined ER and sports medicine docs out there. Those multiple doses of Ventolin were wrong. But the bottom line is that no medical team could be truly versed in the full array of issues that can crop up on this crossing. It's virgin territory out there. It could well be one of the planet's last unexplored frontiers. Nobody, but nobody, had experience in the full gamut of this expedition's complications. When Bonnie and I had discussed the nutrition issues with A-list sports-science PhDs, all of them had said nobody in the world had empirical data to inform what the body will endure on this unique, extreme venture. Similarly, we certainly found out too late, on the third attempt, that even a crack ER Med Team had no idea what to do about the potentially fatal box jellyfish sting.

We had done many things right. After consulting a number of endurance sports scientists, Bonnie had deemed a minimum of twenty ounces of fluid every ninety minutes our strategy for hydration. Michael Broder was astute, also, in his assessments of necessary fluid intake. Dr. Timothy Noakes, a sports scientist from the University of Cape Town, had told us I would never starve out there. Food wouldn't be the ultimate issue. But dehydration in salt water could be dangerous.

We line up a medical unit from the University of Miami's sports medicine department for an attempt in September.

And we have another gap to solve. I am clearly the "CEO" out of the water, and Bonnie is expedition boss when I am in the water. But Bonnie is too busy managing me. We need an Ops Chief. Mark Sollinger is the obvious choice. He knows every area of the operation, commands respect, and communicates in short, direct phrases. "Copy that" is one of the standard Mark ends to a telephone conversation.

I also decide to switch Navigators. Never for a moment disrespecting David Marchant, as David is as competent as they come out at sea, but John Bartlett spent thirty years living in the Florida Keys, navigating the particular eccentricities of the Florida Straits. And he's more of an empirical type. He devises mathematical models, plotting my speed against current and eddy readings, many different scenarios, as all of that input data changes constantly on the way across. David is more of an instinctual sailor. All kinds of expeditions switch out crew members, ask team members to change roles. I ask David to step down, and he is such a team player that he offers to help John in any aspect of the mission. Bartlett is going to take us across.

Bonnie is annoyed that my chafing along the bathing suit lines is bloody and painful. It's the least of my problems, but it's true that the salt grinds along those lines and becomes a constant, nasty discomfort. We have tried all kinds of remedies. We've injected Aquaphor into the seams of the straps. That quickly oozed out and was unwieldy to try to reinject once in the water. A friend made me some silicone pads, which she sewed around my straps. The silicone did rub less than the straps, but the new thickness of the strap area pulled the suit out of position on every stroke.

Bonnie is now determined to find a substance that will stop the friction rubbing and she calls Steve Munatones, the founder of the World Open Water Swimming Association. He tells her that some swimmers these days use anhydrous Australian sheep lanolin for friction. We order some and start training with it immediately. After years of enduring these bloody wounds in the salt water, we now have the magic potion. My chafing days are over. Hallelujah.

The ultimate irony is that this dashed attempt of early August lands me on even a higher plateau of physical conditioning than where I was after the twenty-four-hour of July 2010. Nothing can get you primed for a sixty-hour swim like a thirty-hour swim. Right after Labor Day, we move the expedition back to Key West and put the boats, the crew, the Cuban paperwork back into motion.

Sure enough, we don't wait for long. Dane reports that several patches of calm have flirted across the Florida Straits during our recovery time. And on September 19, he calls. His forecast is so good that he tells us to skip amber alert and go right to red. We are a well-oiled machine by now. Kathy Loretta is on her way to Havana to get customs and docking, fueling and ice squared away. Vanessa is rounding up the boat captains and provisioning. The whole crew is making their way to Key West. Bonnie and I arrange for flight plans again. And now here we are again at Marina Hemingway. The Cuban press conference. The prep rituals. The Med Team can't meet us until we reach international waters, but we'll only be a few hours without them, and our competent EMT, Jon Rose, also one of our Shark Divers, is up to speed on the asthma possibility, has all medical protocols ironed out from the Med Team, and we feel confident our same mistakes will not be repeated. My Tylenol is zipped in its special compartment.

The chanting grows in volume.

"Where we swimming TO?"

"FLORIDA!!!"

September 23, 2011. 6:05 p.m.

The start, the plunge, the otherworldly box jellyfish stings only two short hours in. An endless night of suffering. A full day of weak progress, an attempt at recuperation while injured. Bam, the box resurface to kill again the second dusk. Am taken on board by the Medical Team for a short time. Then a second night and half of another day, swimming hurt.

Forty-four hours, thirty minutes, an otherworldly eternity.

Two Homeric voyages in just over a six-week span. And now the end of September marks the end of our journey for 2011. As we gather for another Team rally in Key West, Bonnie and Candace, Mark and John know only too well what's churning in my mind.

Any explorer, on any expedition, if still alive and with even a hint of strength left, at the desperate moment of having to turn back, remains hopeful. If it's Mother Nature's furor that has brought you to your knees, there whispers still the perhaps illogical optimism that more knowledge, further innovation, a bit more luck will mean success the next time up the mountain.

That whisper is gusting through my brain now. When we figure out how to get through these killer jellyfish, when they are no longer the issue, if then I break down and simply can't go on, then I'll be done with this quest. But not now. I've tried and failed three times. Yet I'm not done.

TWENTY-FIVE

The Last Hurrah: 2012

It's been said many ways. It's far better to have tried and failed than never to have tried at all. To wit, I found October 2011, in the aftermath of two failed attempts that year, far and away easier to live with than October 2010, when we never even got to Cuba.

There is no surreal disbelief this time. No moping. The path is clear. But that's *my* path. What about the others? I am reading all kinds of expedition tales, and it's no surprise that when a solo athlete pursues a dream over prolonged failures and postponements, his support crew rarely are able, practically or emotionally, to hang in there with him. So far, I'm lucky. The Team is solid.

Mark and his family stand ready to operate Camp SXM again. That's huge. Come January, Bonnie and I are again living in their home, interrupting their lives, and we're often in dire straits after a tough day. But Mark puts his head down and comes through. As does his wife Angie. By now, we're tight.

And it's always great to have a kid's perspective when nerves run high. Their daughter Sam is ten now. Part tomboy, part magical girl. Early one morning after a very long session, having vomited much of the night on the shower floor, I drag myself back to bed. At some point,

I open my eyes to see Sam, her long legs folded near my pillow, her clipboard and pen in hand.

"Good morning, Diana. Our class is collecting donations to help the people through the tsunami recovery in Japan." The tragedy was a year prior at this point. "My mom is giving twenty-five dollars. Dad is in for thirty. What can I count on from you?"

We all play Hangman with Sam on a big white board after dinner on non-swim days. The Sollingers make what can seem like months of torture fun and easy and loving.

I do a little presentation at Sam's school. Sam's introduction of me is better, more articulate, more dramatic, than most CEOs I work with. The whole elementary school is engaged. A third-grade boy keeps waving his arm wildly. When I get to him, this is his suggestion:

"Why don't you train a school of fish to swim right in front of you? Then when the jellyfish grabs one, he'll be very busy and you will swim by. Then the next jellyfish will grab another fish, and you'll swim by. Of course, it will be sad for the fish, to see their brothers and sisters sacrificed this way, but they are your dedicated army. And when there is only one fish left, he will accompany you right up to the shore."

Me: "Oh. So what I need is a suicide army of fish!"

The boy: "Exactly. That's what you need."

Actually, that was the best idea we had at the time.

John Bartlett came over to St. Maarten where he, Mark, Bonnie, and I would meet on all kinds of improvements. But the jellyfish always led every discussion. We tried a dozen thin types of stinger suits—allowed in the sport, as they don't provide either flotation or warmth. I wore one paper-thin suit for a long outing and I should have known better. The suit ripped under the arms on the very first strokes, and I felt the digging from the exposed edges of the material. I knew it was going to lead to nothing but bad news, but I made the mistake of persisting with it the first eight hours of the day. By the time Mark and Bonnie reached over to peel it off me, the dark red third-degree burns under each arm were outrageously painful, especially in the salt water. When home in Los Angeles, my physical therapist Karen Joubert treated the burns for several days with infrared light therapy. That mistake kept me out of the water for ten days.

Bonnie, my rock, is seriously worried. Unless we find a solution to safely plowing through those box jellies, she simply cannot put herself through that trauma again. Without hyperbole, she thought she might be forced to watch her best friend die before her very eyes. She felt helpless out there, not easy for an alpha leader.

That's where Dr. Angel Yanagihara enters our story. Angel has dedicated her illustrious career to the study of the box jellyfish, and she is now considered the world's leading expert. When our Team approaches her for an education, we have no idea what a brilliant mind we are about to encounter. And from our first conversation, busy as Angel is, traveling around the world's oceans in pursuit of more knowledge about these animals, she immediately agrees to dive into our project. We conduct a summit in Key West, getting the Team together for the 2012 attempt. Angel holds us spellbound with her first lecture to us:

"Jellyfish belong to the oldest group of animals with a defined body structure on Earth. They've been around for six hundred million years, since an age when the continents were essentially one large land mass and our atmosphere was composed of mostly methane and carbon dioxide. The most specialized of class in this amazing ancient group that includes corals, anemones, and jellies is the box jellies. Over thirty species are known worldwide. Box jelly venoms contain the most potent and rapidly acting toxins of the animal kingdom. They are the only jellyfish that have eyes like our own, with a lens, retina, and iris. Remarkably, these animals have twenty-four eyes with virtual 360 degree vision, since there is an eye stalk on each of the four corners of the bell body and each eye stalk contains two lensed eyes, as well as four more sets of six more primitive light-detecting visual organs.

"Box jellyfish are also powerful directional swimmers and use their vision to hunt prey at over four miles per hour. Most box jellies are photophobic, meaning they come up to hunt at dusk. They're efficient predators, feeding on tiny larvae and fish as large as the box jelly itself. The fastest known event in biology is the explosion of thousands of tiny hollow venom-filled hypodermic tubules out from the tentacles upon contact with the prey or unlucky humans. The potent venom is instantaneously injected into the prey, leading to massive cell destruction and instant death."

Now we know for sure that it was the box that stung me and Jon Rose on that September 2011 crossing. We have seen the pictures of this transparent blue creature, about the size of a sugar cube, with fairly short tentacles for a jelly, about three feet long. One short shard of tentacle the length of a human forearm fires 300,000 tiny harpoons of venom into the skin and begins its work of cell destruction and paralysis. The wounds on my skin, once I was out of the water, revealed those thousands of tiny box pinpricks. The tentacles had wrapped around both biceps, the right forearm, the back of the neck, the entire back, and both thighs.

Top predator species are being lost in the oceans, due to global warming, oil spills, mass killings, and other factors. We learn from Angel that fewer fish and turtles can mean more jellyfish. With upsets to the balance of life in the oceans, box jellies are proliferating wildly in tropical spots around the world. They've long been known to be a danger in certain Australian waters. After I was stung in 2011, someone sent me a YouTube video of an Australian reporter standing in knee-high water. The woman begins her report and is stung right there on camera. She screams in pain, tumbles into the shallow surf. The cameraman leaves his post, and you can hear him yelling into his phone for emergency help as she wails. Well, that woman died. It was the box and she never even made it to the hospital. Many people stung away from shore by the box do not make it back to land before they die.

We learn that the optimum time of month for one species to surface en masse is eight to eleven days after the full moon. But we can't just take those four days each month off our calendar for a potential start, when we have so few weather opportunities. And, by the way, there are at least twenty-nine other box species that we could potentially encounter that surface other evenings, or even in the daytime.

Angel joins our Team officially, in part because she is inspired by our quest, and in part because she has in me a public guinea pig for her protocols. She is working in many places around the world with combat units and special forces operations, their divers having now suffered the box stings.

We also quickly learn from Angel that, while epinephrine is the right procedure for most lung-distress syndromes, it is absolutely not what we should have used for the box symptoms. Box venom accelerates with adrenaline boost. Actually, having Angel on board is the most intelligent Medical Team recruit we could have, with our ER and sports docs more than anything out there to handle noneccentric swim issues such as extreme nausea, as well as emergencies for crew members. What if someone falls and splits their head open? That's where the ER team would come in. But the true life-and-death circumstance we now know to be out there will be better addressed by a box specialist.

Angel has compounded a green gel, to smooth out over the skin, that gives a chemical signal to the animal not to release its venom. The gel also contains ingredients to inactivate venom if a sting does occur. There is a scientific name, but she simply calls it Sting No More. We see a video of Angel's proof that the gel works. In her lab in Honolulu, Angel spreads the Sting No More all over her right inner forearm. She then lays a live, whole box jellyfish on her arm. You see the prehistoric-looking animal rhythmically contracting on her skin. The vibrant pink tentacles pulsate on her arm for four minutes. She pulls the jelly with forceps up and down her forearm, ensuring every opportunity for a sting. But it doesn't sting.

There is high drama in the lab. To prove the efficacy of her compound, that these freshly caught jellies will sting, Angel then takes another and, without blinking, lays it on her bare left arm. A medical team stands by. She is stung instantly. The video shows bright red inflammation on the skin, in the outline of the jelly's bell and tentacles. She records her pain scores for ninety seconds, until the pain is not bearable (rockets to a 10 out of 10). The symptoms of spinal paralysis and pulmonary compromise accelerate. She quickly uses her own Sting No More on the sting site and records the pain scale each thirty seconds until it falls below a 2 on the scale.

Needless to say, Bonnie and I quickly gain total confidence in Angel and the substance itself. The quandary is in how to apply this substance, now mixed into my own anhydrous lanolin, over every square inch of my body. There is no goo that will remain an integrated coat of coverage as I splash and move forward through the water. It's going to quickly wash away. And I can't cover my face with goo. The seal of my goggles is critical.

We hatch a plan. Angel will be on board, close to the Handler's station throughout the night, ready with her gel to mitigate stings. But we decide I need what you might call full combat armor. (Angel may one day develop a strategy to apply the gel head to toe so that it maintains a smooth coat for many hours of swimming action but not in time for me.) The swim-tech company Finis will make me a custom stinger suit, this in accordance with the rules of marathon swimming. No neoprene or any fabric with either flotation or warming properties allowed. With each prototype, Finis will send the suit to Angel in Hawaii, and she will test it with the actual animals. Once we have an impenetrable fabric, Finis will fabricate suits for me with exactly the right tension to last all those hours and with nonchafe material at the neck and under the arms.

I try a number of gloves, all of which make my hands very tired. It's hard to believe a thin latex glove can make swimming so much harder, but it takes me six months of constant training with the gloves—in the end a certain gauge of surgeon's latex—for my hands not to ache after a long swim.

As for the feet, we wind up using a pair of Finis Lycra booties. The trick with the gloves and booties is to somehow get a secure wrap of duct tape around the wrists and ankles, to ensure no gap of skin is exposed between the wrists of the stinger suit and the gloves or between the ankles of the stinger suit and the booties. The rules of the sport forbid any aid in either moving forward or keeping afloat. But Steve Munatones educates us about variable rules in life-threatening circumstances that exist around the world. Even though, for example, most legal swims must end with the swimmer walking out and onto a shore, all the way to absolute dry land, there are certain areas, such as the Isle of Jersey, where for safety reasons you may simply touch the rock wall for completion. Other areas, some swims in Japan, allow for shark safety protocols. Steve tells us we are literally writing the safety standards for swimming in the life-or-death environment of the box jelly.

In this case, we are allowed to have a Handler wrap my wrists and ankles with duct tape, a task simply impossible for me to do on my own. But I can't exit the water for the wrapping, nor be propped up. I need to tread on my own steam.

Early going in practicing all this, it takes me forty-five minutes to put all that jellyfish gear on, and even the seventeen minutes we finally whittle it down to is extremely tiring. Getting the suit on is okay, although it takes me dozens of tries before I can separate the legs out in the water and prevent them from swirling around each other. But to take a wet hand, raise it above the surface, usually a bumpy surface, pat it dry without dipping down again, then work millimeter by millimeter to get that tight latex glove over partially wet skin, kicking hard to keep the hand above the surface those many minutes, then continue to keep the hand above water while my Handlers secure the wrist with duct tape, without holding me up but just working the tape around the wrist—that took such intense concentration and effort that going back to swimming became a welcome enterprise. We would find out how much more arduous my working those latex gloves on was to become after many hours into the Cuba Swim itself, when my fingers would become numb and I had diminished tensile strength. And the booties are even tougher. I could have auditioned for Cirque du Soleil after mastering that move of kicking hard with one leg to hold the extended leg above water, trying in surging waves to keep the ankle as dry as possible, long enough to have it wrapped with duct tape all the way around.

It takes months to develop the Stinger Suit and get the right gloves and booties and then be able to get all that gear on and then train with all of it to gain the endurance and strength to swim with it through the night hours. I would get mad, frustrated by how much it slowed me, tired me out; I bemoaned the loss of swimming free, unshackled. But, as the sport dictates, life-or-death circumstances require life-or-death measures.

It was the face, specifically the mouth, that presented a conundrum. Last time, after the attack of the first night, I'd worn the cotton hoodie the Shark Divers had fashioned for me. Not only was it heavy when soaked, making my head a dense bowling ball, hard to lift on every stroke, but the hole they had cut for the mouth left my lips and some skin under the nose exposed. We this year escalate to a highly scientific material, heavy-duty panty hose, tighter to the face, and cut the mouth opening as small as possible. Then Angel smears a handful of Sting No More all over my mouth area, the only place I still need protection, and hopes that the constant mouth action during each breath won't wipe the gel away too quickly. In training, we reapply the gel on every ninety-minute feeding stop.

The Team confers with Angel on dozens of possible plans. One is a flood of red lights all around me underwater. The box evidently do not swim as effectively under exposure to certain red LED lights. They even go to sleep. But I couldn't see the logic of swimming quickly into and out of a field of these animals, hoping that their sudden exposure to our red lights would instantaneously make them sleepy.

There is a groove to it all now, our third year at it. A couple of hiccups delay training, a week here and there. Later in the spring of 2012, on a huge wave day in Mexico, I feel my left biceps straining. This was one of the few swims Bonnie couldn't make. Tim, and my old friend and 1978 Handler Jon Hennessey, are on the boat, and I mention it to them a couple of times. At the end, fighting monstrous swells all day long, that biceps is bruised a deep black and blue from the elbow to the armpit. Once home, Dr. ElAttrache puts me through an MRI, tells me the biceps tendon I had injured the previous year at the shoulder insert is now seriously strained. The entire biceps, the length of the arm, is inflamed. Is this the end? I panic. But day by day, ice pack by ice pack, my fear abates. Another two weeks out of the water. But the arm recovers.

I must say I am proud of my body over these extreme training years. Physically, I am a better endurance athlete in my sixties than I was in my twenties. I was faster back then, but in this era I have more brute strength. If I was somewhat of a thoroughbred in my youth, I am now a sturdy Clydesdale. I recover more quickly from radical workouts. I bounce back from muscle and tendon strains and injuries. I think my constitution and my immune system are stronger in middle age than they were in youth. For one, I weigh more now. If I was 125 pounds back then, I'm now 145. I'm sturdier. There is bulk to back up the extreme caloric burn during the long hours out there. I'm not as sensitive or delicate emotionally, either, so I suppose the mental calm and perspective that comes with age contributes to being more robust in this new incarnation of my athlete self.

In my sixties, I am far more patient, with myself and my crew. I used to berate myself ruthlessly if I were to have trouble with leaky goggles or had veered way out to sea from the boat. And I was tough on my Handlers, harsh on them if they for instance handed me a cup without the mouth opening facing me, so that I had to maneuver the container into position while tired and kicking hard to keep it above the surface. I was also far too self-pitying back then. Every piece of bad news got me down, and mad. This time around, I am measured. I take hard knocks in stride. I am a mature person now, and that translates into being a more mature and hence better athlete.

Early June 2012, we decide to add in a twenty-four-hour swim before packing up for Key West. Instead of putting the whole Team together to swim off Key West this time, we go low-key in St. Maarten. Mark and Angie and their crew, Bonnie and our Handler Allison Milgard take me out. I start at nine a.m. sharp on June 7, 2012.

It's rough going. We wait for favorable conditions when attempting to cross from Cuba, because there's no other way, but in the case of training, even for a long haul such as twenty-four hours, we go whenever we've planned it, mostly to be considerate of the crew's schedules. The waves are slapping hard, and even our tricks of snuggling in against the coast bring little relief. I'm pretty darn seasick all day long.

Come nightfall, we get me into the full jellyfish regalia. The cumbersome gear makes surging up, over, and through the waves even more awkward, certainly more demanding. By midnight, I am fried. I've lost my stomach too many times and not been able to replenish the calories or electrolytes. Bonnie and Allison are asking Mark to send for ginger ale, melba toast, anything they can think of to settle the stomach and get some modicum of strength renewed. Angie takes the support boat middle of the night to scour the island for ginger ale. She won't take no for an answer and comes back with the goods.

By the next morning's early hours, it is probably around three a.m., I am whipped. I can't remember ever being this depleted. My brain is confused. My arms don't want to lift anymore. We would finish our twenty-four hours at nine a.m., but that seems forever away at this moment. Bonnie comes down close to me and asks me to look her in the eye. She says we are going to forget about the number twenty-four. All she asks is that I put my head down, drill down to some deep level of purpose, and find fifteen more minutes. I roll over onto my back. I'm too weak to cry. I'm just floating in another world. Bonnie blows the police whistle. As if returning from a faraway place, I look to the sound. Now she is whispering, a motherly tone.

"Diana, I know you're hurting. It's just a training swim. You've gone eighteen tough, rough hours already. But I know you don't want to pack it up. Look at me. Can you hear me?"

I nod.

"Okay, I want to see you do five strokes. I mean it. Only five strokes. If you just can't do it, we're going to call it quits. Do you have five strokes in you?"

"I think so."

"Let me see. I'm going to count. Go on now. One . . ."

I'm slow to put my head down. I am half aware, half out of it. Left arm, right arm. One. I can do it. Five strokes. I stop and float on my back again. I'm falling asleep. The whistle jars me awake.

Bonnie: "Let's try five more. Come on. Five more."

One, two, three, four, five.

"That's it! I know you don't want to quit. Five more. You're doing great. Come on."

This time I am heartened. The rhythm comes back. I get all the way to a hundred, counting only left-arm entries. I stop and look to Bonnie, thinking I'll get some big praise for that effort. She wanted five and I gave a hundred.

"Diana, come here. Listen, what do you say we just go to first light. We're not that far away. As soon as we see the first flicker of daylight, we're going to call this one. What do you think?"

I'm not sure the body is going to agree, but I nod yes.

Bonnie has motivated me to feel proud of myself for not quitting. And now she knows what she's doing when she asks me to shoot for first light. She knows what hope the sunrise brings. Every breath to the left I'm looking at a black sky, stars by the billions. I have no idea where east is, but I occasionally roll the shoulders a bit more than usual, to get a peek at the right-side sky. Pitch black. I try to settle in and not look frantically every stroke. I decide to count sets of two hundred, left-arm entries only, and take a gander up at the end of each set. Two hundred English. Pitch black. Two hundred German. Still black. Two hundred

Spanish, two hundred French. Has time stopped? Where is that damn sun?

Now I go through the same routine, same sequence of languages, but I count backward down from two hundred. When I look up at the end of the Spanish set, is it my imagination? The stars are not so plentiful. There isn't light per se. But the stars are definitely fading. I finish the French and look again. Now the black has melded with a deep midnight blue. I go into a series of counting to one hundred. By the end of the fourth series, the French, my heart soars. It is first light.

The sunrise is uplifting for all of us. Since I was a kid swimmer, always up before the sunrise, I've not wanted to miss it. There is power, promise, in watching the light emerge and bathe the Earth. And that's what's happening to me now. My energy, my entire being, literally surges. Bonnie did know what she was doing. Get to the sunrise and we'll get to the end. It's a long few hours, but we make it to nine a.m.

Bonnie and I can go home to Los Angeles for a bit after that twenty-four-hour because this year I already have a training Team set up in Key West before I get there. Dee Brady has her boat *Voyager* there and ready, and Bartlett will visit for navigation scoutings. And my new stalwarts 2012 are the Berrys, owners of a fabulous English pub on the Gulf Coast of Florida, famous for its three-story-high former ice house brick walls and raucous twelve-board dart tournaments. Pauline and John—or Johnberry, as we call him—become dear friends of mine through our dedicated months in Key West. Pauline is a nurse, and so many of her skills and instincts come immediately into play. Johnberry is flat out the most even-keeled, unflappable person I've ever met. He's a big guy, shaved head, never far from his phone to check on the Orioles, which makes for fun as New Yorkers and Yankee fans, Dee and I get into it with him all summer. Mark and Angie will come over at red alert.

Back in Los Angeles, we get wind that the fantastic Australian champion ocean swimmer Penny Palfrey is in Havana, ready to give the crossing a try. Bonnie and I huddle together at the computer and are in hourly touch with our Key West crew, as well as with Mark in St. Maarten.

Penny has a lengthy and impressive résumé. She has done most of the recognized swims around the world and is known for her ability to endure the long hours of the ultraswims as well. I am anxious. Maybe even miffed. There is no logic to my thinking it isn't right for someone else to pursue my Dream. After all, it isn't my ocean. Nevertheless, it's only natural that our Team, wishing of course no harm to Penny, hopes she will fall short in the end.

On Penny's site, a GPS tracker follows her progress with a ping every twenty minutes. She starts at night. Seems to us she's going strong, a good north track off the Cuban shore. She doesn't appear to have been stopped by the dusk jellyfish brigade. Bonnie and I go to bed around midnight, Penny moving north to northeast very steadily. The next morning we get on a plane to Key West, unable to check the swimmer's progress all day long.

By nine p.m., we're at the Team house, all of us glued to the computer. Now she's way beyond the halfway point and CNN is running continuous reports: "Australian champ nearing the Florida coast." Bonnie and I go back to our condo and to bed around eleven p.m. and, unbeknownst to us, just a couple of hours later, Penny is pulled from the water. Her navigators were dumbfounded to see their compasses swirling in circles and then pointing southeast, Penny being tugged away from Florida. Our Team knew she had been turned around by one of the counterclockwise eddies, the kiss of defeat. And then she was stung. The Team had still been up and knew what had happened but thought better of making me miss a night's sleep. When Bonnie and I wake up around six a.m., we immediately turn on CNN, without considering their news crawl hasn't been updated. The "Australian champ nearing Florida coast" blurb still crawls across the screen. We think she must be very close. Our hearts pounding, we get down to Team Central in a hurry to watch with the others. And we learn the news.

The Palfrey navigation team has reported they were utterly perplexed by the circular currents and their inability to turn back around from a southeast heading. Bartlett is elated. He wants his chance out there. We never did find out if it was box or other jellies but she was evidently stung all over the face. Penny was rushed by speedboat to the closest hospital for the sting symptoms, and for that I felt empathy. But I admit I was relieved. As a matter of fact, that is a gross understatement. I had steeled myself, once Penny started off from Cuba, to write the Team and post on social media a message of sportsmanship. If Penny made it across, I would congratulate her, sincerely. This is indeed the Mount Everest of the oceans. The few of us in the ultra end of the sport know only too well what it would take to finally make it all the way. How could I not respect the first person to cross? I would have had to work through disappointment at her beating me to the punch, but that would have been a temporary blow, and it certainly wouldn't have made me quit. I believed too much in the honor of the quest to quit, first or not. Yes, my stomach was in knots, following her tracker pinging steadily northeast, but I was prepared to rise above all that and give Penny her due. I send Penny my regards for her heroic effort.

Now it's my turn.

TWENTY-SIX

In Medias Res

The pressure is higher this year, the fourth attempt. And the whole world is watching now. This is the first day in three years I've totally broken down. Patience is a virtue, and mine is running threadbare.

It's August, two months since Penny Palfrey's attempt, and today I am in full-blown meltdown. My Key West crew gets it. They just let me cry. Bonnie, Dee, Pauline, Johnberry, and I have patiently carried out the summer routine, but on this day I just can't take it anymore. Pauline lets me sob on her shoulder and then makes me a hot cocoa.

I've been strong and steady these two months. We've had all the gear and provisions prepped for weeks, ready any day for amber alert. We trudge faithfully to the marina for our endless short swims. Nobody talks. Dee warms the engines. Johnberry lowers the boom for the streamer. Bonnie and Pauline get my cooler organized, grease me up. I stretch on the bow as we trawl out and check the weather radar for our best route for the day.

One day, our Fleet Captain Vanessa comes down to the dock to give us the day's forecast. Late summer means sudden afternoon squalls. We swim through just about everything unless the lightning is cracking directly above. V tells us there's been a great white shark sighted right out front of the marina. He's been lurking without moving on for about twenty-four hours now. Not a hard decision for us this day. We'll scoot around under the bridge and train in the shallows on the other side.

We're not in Key West to party. We don't dine. We're on a mission, and even our meals are utilitarian. It's our professional meteorologists who will dictate our go day, yet the five us can't help ourselves. We are completely neurotic about the weather and cluster around the computer in our non-training hours every day, going from site to site, looking at the patterns down in the Caribbean, over in the Gulf of Mexico. Bartlett is equally vigilant in his weather and stream reconnaissance from his home up on the Gulf Coast and he calls in to us daily.

I hate to admit it, but I have let the pressure get the best of me. Come mid-August my nerves are frazzled and I start second-guessing every forecast. I'm not acting the consummate professional. Signs of an early fall are being reported up and down the eastern seaboard. Input from our three trusty meteorologists are split. One wants us to grit it out and wait. The other two seduce me into worrying that time is running out on us. They are concerned all indicators point to several weeks of strong winds deep into September.

A short, not-so-perfect mid-August window might be the only one for this year. And it's a tight window, for sure, very little wiggle room on the back end. There might be three decent, not ideal days, but the fourth shows big winds picking back up. My emotions overshadow my brain. I project to the end of September and can't sustain the anxiety. I panic.

We don't bother with amber alert; we sound the red alert alarm. The exodus to Havana, the crew via boats, Bonnie and I via plane, comes together in twenty-four hours.

This is where Vanessa's prowess is invaluable. *Voyager* and core crew have been on immediate standby all summer. But the four mother ships and crew have to be put together on a moment's notice. Most boat captains and crew are working fishing trips and tour excursions. They simply can't put making their living on permanent hold while we wait for weather. Vanessa has been scrambling all the way up and down the Florida coast with every amber alert false alarm through the summer to get the right fleet, the right personnel, a constant wrangling of boats and crews on rotating lists of availability. On top of that, there are the rigorous U.S. customs and U.S. Coast Guard clearances when it comes to traveling to Cuba, and those officials can't be pushed just because we have a sudden window and need to zip over to Havana in a hurry. We have the big licenses from D.C. and Havana, but these local government clearances can't be filed until we have the precise boats and list of personnel passports. Red alert now, Vanessa rocks it to pull our fleet together and on their way to Cuba.

The usual rituals at Marina Hemingway are hurried; the press conference and Team meeting, cursory.

Mark reminds us this is not our first rodeo. Do your own job and do it to perfection. We are professionals. Don't do other people's jobs.

Bonnie urges everyone to stay grounded and not be naïve at any point, as to how far we've gone. We may be ecstatic about our position at one particular GPS point, but there will be a mountain of Mother Nature still to climb. Let's keep our heads straight. No celebrating until Bartlett gives us our cue.

I address my Team: "We are ready. I am proud of you. And I am depending on you. We have not stopped short on one training outing. We have researched every possible obstacle out there and brought in all of you, the best in your fields, to probe for solutions to all of them. I stand here to thank you for your loyalty. Many of you have given up time from your work, your families, your own dreams, to make this historic crossing. I promise you I will not let you down. It will not be because of lack of will or lack of physical preparation on my part that we don't make it all the way. I'm here to give you, give the Team, everything I've got. Over the next two to three days, I ask the same from you. Every single one of you is crucial to our mission. As Mark asks it of you, be smart, stay focused. Take care of yourselves. I need you to be rested, hydrated, fed, and ready to tackle your shifts with one hundred percent of your best selves. ONWARD!"

The response is rousing: "ONWARD!"

What I don't know is that on the way to Cuba with the flotilla, Bartlett has not at all been happy about the current readings. The Gulf Stream itself is not cooperating. It is blazing hard to the east, sometimes even southeast, horrible positioning for us. In addition to that, he doesn't at all like the countercurrent running due west, about four to five miles wide just off the Cuban shore. So, evidently, we are looking at a hard west current right off shore for a while; then we'll run into a hard east current for the majority of the trip. Swimming north doesn't look good. He has a private meeting with Bonnie, Mark, and Dee at the Havana docks. Back in the Acuario room, I have no way of being aware of this but their tense body language as they hunch together on *Voyager*'s deck speaks volumes to the rest of the Team. All is not well in Xtreme Dreamville.

Bartlett feels stuck between the proverbial rock and hard place. He knows I don't want to risk waiting for a better weather window. We're all in Havana now, ready to go. To retreat to Florida would require further applications for U.S. permits. I am not apprised of his concerns, and we set the start time for sunrise the next day. But he's plenty worried.

Adding to stress over the currents, the already short weather window gets shorter by the hour. I am told the new forecast: Strong winds are to pick up on the back end during the third day, not the fourth. We quickly powwow and throw the entire operation into urgent overdrive. We won't wait for tomorrow daylight. We'll leave at four p.m. today. Everybody scrambles. August 17, 2012, 3:43 p.m. I leap off those rocks again.

Sure enough, that countercurrent along the Cuban shore takes me due west. It's so strong and so wide that I travel over fifteen hours to the west, barely any northing at all. I am confused, and disheartened, to look backward at every single ninety-minute feeding and never see the Havana skyline recede at all. Into the first night hours, those damn lights are right there, as if I haven't made an iota of progress.

At dusk I pull on all the jellyfish clothing. The suit, the gloves, the booties, the panty hose hoodie, the duct-tape wrappings. Angel also instructs Bonnie to smear a glob of her green gel all around my mouth, my only exposed area. It's not ideal, as it is inevitable that my hands occasionally touch my mouth, and then my hands touch my goggles. As soon as the gel clouds my goggles, my sight faculty is even more useless than usual. Then when I tug my cap down below my ears, as I do after every feeding and often in quick pulls between strokes, the goo from my hands makes the cap greasy and slippery and it starts to ride up above my ears, leaving that skin area exposed and leaving my head partially unprotected and subject to heat loss. The goo is, literally, a mess.

Just a few hours in, I feel a sharp sting at the back of the right ankle.

WOW! It's numbing. It's a big rip. It's painful. I stop to hyperventilate, clench my teeth and fists, deal with it. Bonnie calls Angel down to the Handler's platform. I lift the right leg in the air, and they notice the duct tape has loosened there. Sure enough, there is a little strip of exposed skin. Angel calls me near, asks me to try to hold my leg up above the surface for just a minute. It's tiring, feathering hard with my hands to keep my leg aloft. I am breathing hard with the effort. She rubs her substance on the affected area, and Bonnie rewraps with duct tape.

It is clear to me that having Angel on our Team has saved me from anaphylactic shock, paralysis, dire pulmonary distress, even death. This ankle sting is a box, and it's painful. But because we are better prepared, I consider it a relatively minor event. During this episode, Angel is remarking in awe at the minefield of jellies—species in addition to the box—that I'm swimming through. She tells me, in all her years of night diving around the world, she's never witnessed a crowded field of jellies such as this. She says they are so thick, so voluminous, that I am literally swiping hundreds of them back and away with every stroke. I can't see them or feel them, so my coat of armor has clearly been the right tactic. And her gel has been the right solution for the box in the areas we just couldn't cover with material.

The night is still young when the chorus of thunderclaps begins. Lightning is crackling from every point on the horizon. I make a 360 turn and can't find any direction where storms are not firing. The wind is escalating. *Voyager* is rising and dipping in huge arcs now, and I am stopped, treading, listening to all of them talking on their radios. Mark, Ops Chief, is calling loud and clear: "Storm protocol."

The storm protocol we have practiced is for all boats to position downwind of me, so that none would be blown toward me and possibly run me over. Next, the Shark Divers would quickly get their storm safety bag, with flares, water, and supplies to last us in case we're separated from the flotilla for a while. The Kayakers are to untie a Shark Shield from the bottom of one of their boats and make sure the Divers have it with us. We would also have a compass and get a final point-setting direction from Bartlett before we go off into the night and get separated from the boats. But in heavy winds, the goal of our little band of me and the Shark Divers out there on our own isn't really to make forward progress. It is to stay safe until the storm passes and we're able to regroup with the flotilla again. If the gear malfunctioned, if we were stranded without functioning flares, with no direct radio capability, there is a real chance that we would never be found by the flotilla again. Our small training crew has rehearsed this storm protocol, but the entire crew never has. With the winds whipping up suddenly and violently now, conditions are different than we expected. Chaos threatens.

Voyager is taking on water. Fast. One of the hulls of the catamaran is filling quickly. Bartlett goes into crisis mode. His piano-playing fingers are dancing fast in front of him when he says: "Mark, we have a situation here."

Two Kayakers, Shark Shields attached, and two Shark Divers are assigned to stay in the water close as they can to me. I can't discern just what's going on, but there are many commands from Mark to the rest of the boats. Everybody is shuttled fast as possible off *Voyager.* Official observer Steve Munatones declares the situation a "life-or-death emergency" and orders the swim to stop temporarily. The lightning is now startling, it's so close. Steve says it will not be called a staged swim. Safety dictates my being pulled from the water onto one of the mother ships.

This is a nightmare. The good news is Bartlett and Mark solve the *Voyager* leak issue and safety is restored there. The drag is that the usual summer storms in the Straits, the ones we have encountered dozens of times in training, the ones for which our storm protocol was designed, pounce with little warning and swoop out just as quickly. But this is a huge system of many connected gales, ripping winds and lightning from all directions. They continue to crack and whip heavy seas for hours, not just minutes. I am on Steve and Candace's mother ship, and I hear them talking about the fear of being in dire trouble way out here, nature's whims raging in a 360-degree circle, no hope for rescue if a crew member were swept overboard or if one of our vessels capsizes. The focus of the mission is entirely on the swimmer, but we are duty-bound to take responsibility for all the people way out here with us. Steve, for all his time out on the open waters of the world, is sincerely afraid this night. No Coast Guard vessel, no helicopter, could make it out to us on this night.

My mother Lucy,
classy and shy

My father Aris,
charismatic scoundrel

TOP Me, circa 1952, with my mom and brother
ABOVE Mom, my brother Bill, my little sister Liza, and me
LEFT Me, age seven, always at the pool

Me, age thirteen. The discipline of the sport spoke to me.

TOP High school yearbook, Pine Crest School

MIDDLE My sister Liza and I had eight wonderful years with Mom at the end of her life.

BOTTOM At the end, Mom in the throes of Alzheimer's, we found many tender moments together.

OPPOSITE, TOP Liza and I discover our Greek roots on a trip to the Aegean.

OPPOSITE, MIDDLE LEFT My nephew Tim has rocked my world with joy from the moment he was born.

OPPOSITE, MIDDLE RIGHT Tim is still my favorite boy, although now he's a man. His documentary film about my journey, *The Other Shore*, has earned professional and public acclaim.

OPPOSITE, BOTTOM My nephew Tim; his wife KJ, my sister Liza, my brother Sharif (he changed his name from Bill), and me

TOP The 1970s, my first era of champion open-water swimming
BOTTOM Broke the forty-eight-year-old record for circling Manhattan Island. 1975: 7 hours, 57 minutes

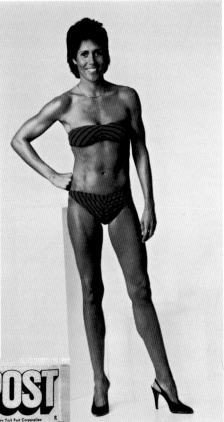

NEW YORK POST

THURSDAY, APRIL 14, 1977 25 CENTS © 1977 The New York Post Corporation R

An assist for athletes

Marathon swimmer Diana Nyad and Jackie Onassis were at a party here yesterday to advance plans for a Carnegie Hall concert to benefit Lenox Hill Hospital and the Institute of Sports Medicine. The April 27 gala will star Frank Sinatra and Robert Merrill, with Walter Cronkite as MC.

TOP Age thirty. Ah, thirty is a distant memory!

BOTTOM My twenties were a high-octane time in New York City, spending time with the likes of Jackie Onassis.

TOP LEFT I met Candace Lyle Hogan when we were both twenty-six. My first love.

TOP RIGHT Billie Jean King, always my hero, supported me every stroke of the Cuba journey.

BOTTOM Candace and I have been lifelong friends, here riding with giraffes in Kenya.

TOP In my first attempt at Cuba to Florida, 1978, Candace is my Handler.

BOTTOM My other Head Handler in 1978, Margie Carroll, anguishes over our 41 hours, 49 minutes of extreme effort, denied the final destination.

TOP 1979: I walk up onto the beach in Jupiter, Florida, having swum 102 miles from the island of Bimini in the Bahamas. My Handler Jon Hennessey (red shirt, yellow shorts) holds back the crowd.

TOP Bonnie Stoll was top five in the world on the women's pro racquetball tour in the 1980s, when we met. We couldn't have imagined Bonnie becoming my Head Handler thirty years later. **BOTTOM** Bonnie and I have been special friends since the day we met, 1980.

TOP LEFT Nina Lederman and I met in New York City, 1984. A deep love. Now a deep friendship.

TOP RIGHT Six weeks after the Cuba success, I swam forty-eight hours in New York City to raise funds for Hurricane Sandy victims. These charity swims will be my swimming legacy in the future.

MIDDLE LEFT AND BOTTOM LEFT I spent thirty years as a sports broadcaster.

MIDDLE RIGHT Team photo 2011, Havana

OPPOSITE, TOP LEFT Bonnie and Candace embrace with emotion, just an hour from the final stroke.

OPPOSITE, TOP RIGHT My Navigator John Bartlett and I grab each other with pride and love. We lost John just three months after the swim. Rest in peace, our intrepid Navigator.

OPPOSITE, MIDDLE Team photo 2013, Key West

OPPOSITE, BOTTOM Bonnie and I return to the swim start point, Havana, on the year anniversary, Labor Day, 2014. The journey of a lifetime.

THIS PAGE My dear friends John and Pauline Berry took a snapshot of me every day of training off Key West, leaping into another long day in the ocean.

OPPOSITE The leaps from the shore in Havana, five leaps over thirty-five years (not pictured here is 1978), were both metaphoric leaps of belief and real leaps of bold action, believing we would find a way toward that elusive Florida shore. The whole world declared the event impossible. I never lost faith.

ABOVE I am the first American to be honored with the Cuban Sports Medal of Honor.

RIGHT I have been a public speaker for forty years. The opportunity to inspire is a privilege.

BELOW It was my honor to meet President Obama in the Oval Office.

ABOVE The epic Cuba Swim touched my soul. There is no other ocean crossing that would move me to dream again, to train like that again. Now it's my challenge to live that same fierce way out of the water.

I admit I'm not of a mind-set to worry about the safety of the crew right now. I am anxious and need to resume swimming immediately. Bonnie holds my goggles and gear, both of us concerned at how much time is passing. I sit there on deck, dazed, floating in and out of consciousness, and recall the Latin phrase "in medias res," meaning "in the middle of things," picturing Othello in that dramatic opening scene in the middle of a ferocious storm. On the boat I'm loopy. It grips me, this concept that we are in the middle of these savage storms, that I am in the middle of my fierce journey. Finally, after almost five long hours out of the water, it is deemed safe enough to get back in. The worst is over. Bartlett directs the flotilla back to the precise GPS point where we stopped.

On deck, I pull the jellyfish gear on. I hop off the stern of this mother ship, *Voyager* quickly swings into place, and we are back to our normal formation, *Voyager* out front, setting the course.

We make it through the rest of the night without incident, but each hour past daylight gets bumpier and bumpier. The east winds are building up again, long before our forecast data indicated they would. This isn't a chop. These are big, long rollers. The swimming is tough. I'm dipping way down into deep troughs where Bonnie doesn't see me for long periods and I don't see her. I strain for literally hours at a time for a glimpse of her wraparound glasses and never succeed. The Kayakers are having a heck of a time not lifting, catching two to three feet of air, and slamming down on top of me. The Shark Divers, working on top of *Voyager,* have their work cut out for them. When it's flat as glass, the visibility is tremendous in the pure blue Gulf Stream. But with these huge rollers, the surface is messy, the crests lined with dark edges. It's difficult to discern shapes below or fins above.

I'm doing okay, all in all. But I can't stop thinking of how long we were out of the water for the storms. This is undoubtedly going to be categorized a staged swim—hell, if no one else does, then I will. We're too far into it now to be worried about that, so I just keep doing my best. With the sun going down in a couple of hours, we make a plan to get the jellyfish gear on at about seven p.m. The Handlers are very careful to cover that skin gap on the right ankle this time. But, like clockwork, only a few minutes after dusk, as I start to settle in for the night with the panty hose hoodie over my head, I sense what feels like a wisp of human hair pass over my lips, vertically. I take my hand, although not easy for me to articulate the fingers with the latex surgeon's gloves, and try to tug at the hair. It's still there. I stop and tread, again trying to pull that hair off my lips. Then the symptoms start. Not extreme, as they were in 2011, but not open to interpretation. This is box. I get a rush of shivers all over, along with shortness of breath and a slight paralysis sensation center of my ribs in the back, at the lungs. I call to Bonnie, who calls for Angel. She confirms that the box tentacles are delicate and indeed feel just like a single strand of human hair.

Angel instructs Bonnie through the post-sting care again. And again we seem to get past the worst of the stings without too much distress to my body.

Bonnie reinforces my mouth and nose area with even more duct tape, now a warrior visage, but paranoia and fear of these animals in the dark prompts me to roll over and do backstroke. I can't see the streamer underneath this way, and the waves are constantly rolling me toward the hull of Voyager. Bonnie and my Handlers are yelling, just about every stroke, for me to stroke away from the boat. The waves are frothing and coming over my head, so I'm taking in quite a bit of salt water, and am worried about swallowing a box. We had heard the gruesome tale of an Australian swimmer swallowing a box, being stung on the interior wall of the esophagus, and dying. Even being stung on the lips again is a distinct possibility, with the waves continually washing over my face.

Hours of the backstroke go by. It's not easy. I have to stop to vomit at least twice an hour. And replenishing those liquids isn't trouble-free in those waves. The stomach is terribly unhappy. But, somehow, we are making our way through these unfavorable conditions.

Then we hear the first boom. It's like a cannon, as sound travels efficiently over water. Then another. Now the lightning show of last night fires up again, and again from all points on the compass. The wind whips up in an instant. It was already at about fifteen miles per hour, way above comfortable swimming winds, but it quickly reaches forty-five to fifty-five. And Mark is again calling for storm protocol.

This time it's Luke Tipple, our Shark Captain, who doesn't like the situation. Bonnie goes to Voyager's upper deck to confer with Luke, Mark, and Bartlett. Meanwhile, weaker and more tired than when all of this went on last night, I'm confused. Why aren't we simply rolling into shark protocol, me going to sea with the Divers and their safety bag for a while?

My Handler Allison Milgard is with me, down low at the Handler's platform. She decides it's best to get my attention off the chaos. She calls to me. It's pitch-black, but I come as close as I can, with the wind and waves, and I see Allison's face.

"Diana, let's do some breathing together, shall we?"

"Okay."

"Good. Here we go. Let's breathe slowly and count together. Take big strides with your legs, the way the doctors have taught you, to keep your body as warm as possible. Ready. Now. One."

It's true that I had never known, until the University of Miami docs told me, that the best way to generate body heat in the water is to kick your legs in big movements, getting those large muscles to fire your metabolism and raise your pulse slightly.

Allison, a tall blonde to start with, looms above me. She appears to be a Norse goddess, and I am under her spell. I totally forget about the storms and what the Team is busy organizing. There are a lot of radio commands and chatter, people moving boat to boat, Kayakers getting their shells up out of the water and tied down. But Allison and I are in our own private world. Breathing, counting, together. She is rising and falling in huge sweeps with the enormous swells under the transom, but I am fixated on her.

Deep inhale and exhale. Then the count. Sixty-five. We go to 120. I ask if we should continue. She says we should. We go to four hundred.

I'm not afraid in the water in forty-five-mile-per-hour winds. But only three swimmers in history have ever swum nonstop more than fifty hours in the open sea, two of those along a coastline, so near safety all the time, and one in a confined bay, again near rescue. For some of our crew, there is a literal fear of never seeing their children again, should calamity occur, with gale-force winds blowing this hard in the pitch black of night.

Luke's apprehensions prevail. He cannot allow his Dive Team, including himself, to be out in this kind of huge wind and possibly get separated from the boats. He is firm. It's out of the question. The swim is once again halted. This time, though, I am hauled onto *Voyager* instead of one of the bigger mother ships. Bonnie, Dee, Allison, and I squeeze into the catamaran's small cabin, pressed together as the boat tosses violently in the storm. Lightning strikes immediately to our left and right, front and back. Thunder follows each strike instantly, meaning the storms are on top of us.

There is a tool belt on the cabin floor. I hadn't noticed it, but Bonnie is asking Dee about the little bearded men. I'm out of it, rocking uncontrollably, cold, nauseous, not sure whether this conversation is real or not. It is a circular leather strap that has hammers and screwdrivers and the like hanging at intervals all the way around it. Bonnie asks Dee if those are little bearded men. Dee asks what bearded men she's talking about. Bonnie points to the belt, and Dee realizes she is hallucinating and thinks the tools are the little men. That is the first time I realize Bonnie is just about as sleep-deprived as I am.

Bonnie and I also discover that we had the same nighttime hallucination on several of the various Cuba attempts. We both thought we saw giant pine trees in the sky. Pines that stretched from one horizon point all the way above and over to the horizon point on the opposite side. I saw them so clearly. Gargantuan trunks and branches that covered the entire night sky, that obscured the stars. Bonnie saw them, too.

So now we're out of the water again on this attempt. Bonnie is seeing little bearded men and I'm doubled over, rocking, trying to stay sane and warm until the next decision—which for some reason is for the first time in my swimming career out of my hands—is made. The swim is now in the staged category. I'm not even in the water, dictating my own fate. This is an unmitigated disaster. Bartlett and Mark come to us with the reality check.

I've been in the water fifty-one hours, five minutes, not counting the first storm break. But we've only covered a mere 55.4 miles. Because we spent the first fifteen hours basically traveling west, then the next more than fifteen hours heading east, occasionally southeast, we've only been able to move north toward our target at an overall slow speed of just over one mile per hour. Bartlett estimates, especially in these rising seas, now huge eight-footers pitching us forcefully from high to low, we would be a minimum of fifty hours more in trying to make Florida. The currents were not our friend on this crossing. And now the weather has turned against us.

Bonnie and I both scan the seas in every direction. Whitecaps are foaming. The surf is enormous. It's not a verdict that requires any pondering. Our attempt 2012 is a bust.

On that too-familiar boat ride back to Key West, I don't sleep. Not really. I do pass out a few times and one of our escort boat drivers, Nancy Jordan, tries to comfort me by laying her hands on my shoulders. She says my muscles are extremely warm, almost hot, and I am swinging my shoulders forward and back, as if I'm still swimming. And I bolt awake a few times, thinking those fifty-one hours a dream, that we hadn't yet embarked on attempt number four. It's too much. Four tries, four failures. Angel's goo got us through the jellies. We had a victory there. The only minor saving grace about leaving this one behind is that this trip would have been a staged swim, not what I would have settled for. I wouldn't accept another swimmer doing this crossing as a nonstop, being out of the water five hours at one time, then out again the next night. No way. I have to live by the standards I expect of myself.

In the monstrous seas, we bang and slam our way toward shore for nine long hours. The arrival at the Key West docks breaks my heart. I am sick and tired of facing my friends and the media in crushing disappointment, stepping off a boat crestfallen, instead of walking up onto a beach, finally victorious.

The joy and appreciation of the journey is harder to root out this time. We realize our effort was the stuff of a herculean echelon. We are a smart, researched, trained, devoted Team. Yet to fail again flattens us. We're beyond sad this time. We're mad.

I'm especially mad at myself for pushing us into this nasty weather. It was just plain wrong, and I was responsible. The cumulative years of training and waiting got to me. I cracked, lost my professional cool, and jumped the gun.

I don't even go home to Los Angeles this time. My heart is heavy, and desperation comes creeping in. Once again, I start rationalizing that the season isn't truly over yet. I start gaining back the weight I lost over the fifty-one hours, about eighteen pounds. The Team is lukewarm about going again, and my three mainstays, Bonnie, Mark, and Bartlett, are pretty much fed up. Bartlett and Steve Munatones have a heart-to-heart with me. They've put their heads together and come up with some empirical calculations. They put the likelihood of all the variables—each of them alone an imposing obstacle—cooperating all at once, for a minimum of a three-day spell, at slim to zero. To be a bit more positive, they set the odds of any swimmer's chance of ever crossing all the way at 2 percent. What was once high-minded inspiration to Bartlett now seems doomed impossibility. It was a short ten weeks ago, on the heels of the Palfrey navigation mishaps, that Bartlett licked his chops at solving the myriad mysteries of this crossing. Now it's a Melville-type saga, as if the mighty sea has beaten him down.

I myself at this point wouldn't send any friend to Vegas to bet on me. I'm either a stubborn fool, obsessed with an irrational, quixotic Dream, or I'm a valiant warrior who will not let my faith be broken.

I go about my daily business in Key West. Bonnie is back in Los Angeles and we speak as many as six times a day. Mark is back in St. Maarten. We are in constant touch. He'll come back for me, but he's wary. Bartlett wishes I would give it up, though he's standing by, reluctantly.

Dee, Pauline, Johnberry, and I continue with a few short swims, as we watch summer fade to fall. On October 17, we pack it in. We barely speak. My hopes are shattered. This is the e-mail I write that day to John Bartlett, back by now at his home on Florida's Gulf Coast:

October 17, 2012

Dear John,

So much to say to you. So deep.

It's over.

Big winds coming early Sunday, 18 knots at sunrise, 25 knots by end of day. Will last a week. Water temps dropping.

Such a beautiful Dream, Cuba. Frankly, don't want to train another long, difficult year. I'm ready for the Big Game, right now, but there is no game to play.

Thank you for all the knowledge, all the spirit, all the wisdom you brought to the Xtreme Dream experience, John. I'll never forget you in it.

It's over for 2012, but I daresay it's not over for me.

As always, Onward!

Diana

TWENTY-SEVEN

Will: No Limits

I find myself more alone this time. What is still burning in my heart has lost luster for many of the others.

Back in Los Angeles, Tim needs to wrap his film. He has spent three years on it and simply can't put any more time and resources into my Dream. He needs a final interview. I'm still a believer, though, and he can't help but step beyond the bounds of documentary filmmaker and into his role as my nephew. He presses me, clearly frustrated: "How many years of your life are you going to give to this?"

Bartlett: "It breaks my heart to leave you on your own because I know you will not stop, but the odds are just too great. It has been a thrill, but I need to get back to my life."

My sister, Liza: "This has become selfish. We all want to move on."

Nina: "It's just simple math. We spend a full day on the friends boat, going four to five times your speed, in trying to join up with you and your flotilla way out there. When you're pulled out, you're only about halfway across, and each time it takes the boats some nine to twelve hours to make it back to the Florida shore. The math doesn't add up."

Bonnie. And this is the one that hurts. The others I can shrug off and accept, that they don't share my conviction. Why should they? And

I'm not mad at them. I don't feel defiant or extra motivation to prove them wrong. I simply and calmly don't understand their doubts. Their letting go makes me a bit sad that we've lost the communal excitement together, but it doesn't affect my commitment. But Bonnie knows what I'm made of. I can't and don't want to do it without her. And yet from Bonnie comes: "Diana, listen, if anybody could have made this swim, you would have been the one. I believe that with all my heart. But it just cannot be done. Not by you. Not by any swimmer."

Ironically, the one who was resistant in the very beginning, Candace, now has no quarrel with where I am in not wanting to let it go. It's not so much that she has become a believer in the ultimate success; it's that she has thrilled to the elevated experience of the odyssey itself. She appreciates my radical tenacity. Candace gives me a license plate she picked up in Havana. The letters FAR appear at the bottom of the green metal. It's really an acronym for the Cuban police, but Candace tells me I made the distance seem "not so far" this past time. I will keep that license plate forever. An emblem of unyielding faith.

Candace wrote me this note when she gave me that license plate:

Well, no one can say you're not consistent. When we met 40 years ago your motto was "May your reach exceed your grasp." Every indication is that the swim itself is impossible for a human being. Yet you still believe in yourself, and that's enough for you. You believe it's possible, so that's enough for me. How could I not be there with you? I love you. Besides, I don't want to miss anything.

CNN is out. So is all the media who for three years found ours such an inspiring story. They tell me if I ever make it, they'll be on the other shore, waiting for me.

I heard from sports scientists, nutritionists, marine biologists, other marathon swimmers, other endurance athletes, plenty of fans. The whole world had now stamped this quest impossible. Our friend from South Africa, Dr. Tim Noakes, wrote me. (Bonnie learned from Tim to feed me real food, not so many compressed goos and gels, and we found tremendous improvement over nausea with my Handlers dropping handfuls of plain cooked pasta into my mouth. There is surely a job waiting for me at Sea World.) Tim sent an empirical chart of the severity of glycogen deprivation, the difficulty of digesting in the supine position, all the factors that render the crossing nonviable.

Well, professionals and lay observers, core Teammates, close friends, and strangers can assess the long list of obstacles out there and deem them impossible to overcome, but they're all forgetting the one key factor that surpasses all the rest. That's the power of the human spirit.

I drag out an old Teddy Roosevelt quote I used to have on my office wall. He basically addresses the spectator with disdain. He goads him to sit back in a comfortable chair and watch as the guy in the ring gets dirty and bloody and falls and fails over and over again. Roosevelt says he'd rather be the guy in the ring who "spends himself in a worthy cause." And the quote continues: "if he fails, at least [he] fails while daring greatly, so that his place shall never be with those cold and timid souls who know neither victory nor defeat."

When Bonnie hears me say I'm not so fixated on making it anymore, that what it's truly about now is not giving up, that the cause is that worthy to me, we have come full circle to the journey-versus-destination debate. This Swim was about my reawakening to a bold life, a calling to fill my days with acute passion, goals more noble than actually making it from Cuba to Florida. I refuse to take a place among timid souls.

I also tell Bonnie I am more a consummate professional than a fool. This is not blind ambition. I wouldn't come at it a fifth time if I didn't intend to bring more to it this time. There is more jellyfish protection to innovate. There is more knowledge of those swirling eddies to fully discover. Nobody could criticize me for calling it quits after four valiant tries, but I weigh sitting at home wondering the rest of my life if I could in fact have brought new layers of expertise to the mission, as opposed to trying again, maybe not making it a fifth time, entirely at peace that I did bring better protocols to the effort. At peace that I didn't give up.

I realize Bonnie and Candace have truly feared for my life out there. I know it doesn't seem remotely likely that all of nature's powers we've met up with will cooperate at once. But I am convinced that the person gutsy enough to go out there five times has a much better chance of getting it all going her way than the ones who pack it up at the first defeat. I can see it. I can envision that other shore.

Bonnie falls silent. I know better than to push her. She promises to help me through training and asks me to leave the Cuba issue alone. The cause has been worthy to her so far, and I can only hope it will rise as such to her again in the coming months.

Right or wrong, I am not deterred. Perhaps I am stubborn to a fault. I just don't pay much attention to parameters and restrictions and limiting definitions. My particular brand of "outsider" mentality started young. I remember observing my outlandishly dramatic father and my lovely but meek mother, at a very young age, and deciding that I was going to carve my own unique path, devise my own rules.

When Steve Jobs died, Bonnie and I watched the 60 *Minutes* episode dedicated to him. Somebody said, in effect, "Steve just didn't think rules pertained to him. He saw himself operating under some other standards." His colleagues were continually flabbergasted when Jobs would demand that certain programming or new design platforms be completed on some wildly unrealistic timetable, yet they seemed to somehow produce what he envisioned, on his irrational deadlines.

When Bonnie and I heard the bit about Jobs being oblivious to laws, she slowly turned toward me and stared. It's true. Starting with the rules laid down in my house when I was a child, I have never much respected society's expected standards. A woman asked me after a speech during the Cuba prep how I could train at this level, with the normal aches and pains that come at my age. I answered, "Don't put your assumptions of what one is supposed to feel at my age on me. I defy those suppositions of limitations. If you feel aches and pains, say so. But I don't, and I refuse to follow your or anybody else's controlling and denigrating parameters of mediocrity." Antiestablishment to the quick, and not always gently so, I admit—perhaps not even sensibly so. If I come to a red light at four a.m., have stopped and looked carefully in all directions, I can't find the logic of sitting there for a couple of minutes, waiting for the light to turn green. I proceed. When some television executive tells me the story I'm working on has to have a linear structure and start at the beginning, I revolt and take my case to the highest command, arguing that to embark on this particular story in the middle and work the early part in later hits the sublime emotion of it. Ask Shakespeare about in medias res. And when people from right and left and everywhere in between declared Cuba impossible, I ignored them and turned to my own analysis and instincts for the answer that rang true for me.

In seeking medical counsel on my torn biceps tendon during heavy training in 2011, when I got news I couldn't bear, I booked another doctor, to hear a different diagnosis. And I made it, my shoulder made it, in part because I refused to buy into these particular doctors' definitions of limitations.

It's not that I don't thrill to working with bright and knowledgeable people. Collaboration can be the ultimate joy of a journey. My highest times during this Cuba quest, the most meaningful moments, had so far been working with Bonnie. And Candace. And Tim. And Mark. And Dee. And Johnberry. And Pauline. And Kathy Loretta. John Bartlett's knowledge of moving across the sea was impressive to the core. Angel Yanagihara's grasp of jellyfish and all things pertaining to the ocean blows one's mind. I am respectful to the point of smitten when in the company of masters of their expertise and extraordinary personalities and heroic individuals.

I am simply unwilling to accept blanket limits about the ceiling of performance. Not any one of us knows the power of the human spirit.

There are scientists who believe will has a genetic, chemical component. Dr. Martin Paulus, a psychiatrist at University of California, San Diego, along with a neuroscientist out of Harvard, have been conducting a study for several years now. They start with the premise that, in dire physical circumstances, the mind gets signals from the body that time is running out, that breathing or heart function or something vital to immediate survival is about to shut down. The hypothesis for these two scientists is that certain individuals, due to a brain chemistry different from the norm, can override these warnings and direct their bodies to function beyond the limits that mean danger or even death to most people.

Dr. Paulus's study involves doing an MRI of the brain. If you've had an MRI, you know the freakishly loud electronic banging, in uneven intervals, the variety of odd sounds from minute to minute. Well, during this particular MRI, you take a simple visual test by pressing buttons with the first two fingers of both hands. For instance, you are quickly shown an image of two men with beards. That image, shown in just a flash, fades away, and a third image of a different man appears. You're supposed to use your finger buttons to indicate which of the first two beards is closest to this third man's beard. While you're taking these visual tests, and of course you're competitive, so you want to score higher than anyone who's ever had the MRI, your oxygen is restricted now and then.

In the MRI capsule, you are breathing through a mouthpiece similar to that of a snorkel. You are not told when the restriction will come, how long it will last, or how tight your air hose will be squeezed, but at various times the hose is clamped from the outside to the diameter of a pea. You are suddenly straining, sipping air through a tiny tube.

You of course know that you can press the alarm bell at any time and stop the test. But even though you've been assured that there's no risk to your health, you don't like the oxygen restriction. It makes you feel claustrophobic, even more than already being enclosed in the MRI chamber. And the air restriction, along with the anticipation of the restriction, make you less adept at the testing. That's the point. They are testing for performance under stress and ability to withstand discomfort.

So they test my brain. Dr. Paulus shows us the results afterward. First, he indicates, very far down on the graph, the dots that represent the control group, thousands of anonymous volunteers randomly recruited from the campuses and towns of the two scientists. Most are clumped near the bottom of the chart, indicating these people have done very poorly on the test during the periods of oxygen restriction and when they were anticipating the upcoming oxygen restriction. Next, a group significantly above the control group, has done much better; these are the marines. The next grouping is a big bump up from that: Navy SEALS.

Then Dr. Paulus points high up to the right, almost off the computer screen. This, he says, is me. I am, according to this particular test, superior at remaining calm under stress and performing under physically stressful conditions.

Well, maybe. I have no doubt that genetics govern a great deal of who we are. Back in my youth, a New Jersey doctor tested my lung capacity and found it greater than that of every player on the New York Jets football team. Even compared to these giants with huge chest cavities and, thus, much bigger lungs in term of cubic inches, I had certain assets: the high-level training of distance swimming, which had increased my lung functions, such as VO_2 max, as well as a number of genetic factors that allowed my heart and lungs to perform at a superior level. Then or now, I test at very high performance levels of aerobic functions.

But our will? Now we're back to Nature vs. Nurture. I'm not sure there's a genetic component for will. I don't believe, for instance that I have a blanket gift for resisting pain. When Bonnie and I got our tattoos, teenage girls giggled as they were inked, guys were chatting up the World Series, while I bit down on a towel, a sheet of tears drenching my entire body.

I don't have a gene for fearlessness, either. Descending the steep, slippery, thickly jungled slopes of the Rwandan mountains while gorilla trekking, my legs trembled uncontrollably, not from exertion but from fear.

I don't believe I was genetically equipped to override the heinous pain of those box jellyfish stings. I was shocked when they hit. But I had set my will ahead of time. It was deliberate, conscious resolve that allowed me to withstand that monstrous pain, or any pain I would encounter. Same deal with the MRI. I clenched that mouthpiece and commanded my pulse to stay low. I pretended I was hiding in a closet while a dangerous intruder robbed my home. I stilled my heart and my breath. And I focused on the test images as if my life depended on getting those answers right.

It seems to me it's not genetic gifts for tolerating stress or resisting pain that takes individuals through extraordinary feats of endurance.

When it comes to the most daring of Earth's expeditions, success always seems to come down to four factors:

One: Physical preparation. Training. *You* are truly the only thing you have complete control over. No stone unturned.

Two: Know everything possible about the elements, the obstacles. Knowledge is power.

Three: Surround yourself with brilliant and honorable people.

Four: Unshakable faith. Go so far as defiance. Refuse to accept limitations and mediocrity. I won't let anybody tell me I can't touch the stars, because I just might get there. And I will surely never get there if I don't keep trying.

It's as Thomas Edison said it:

"Our greatest weakness is giving up. The most certain way to success is to try one more time."

Attempt number five is inevitable.

TWENTY-EIGHT

Impasse: 2013

Fall 2012, back home in Los Angeles, there is no soul-searching this time. I am committed. There is no need for deep inner grappling. But the Team is dismantling, and that is majorly disturbing.

I am truly at a loss as to who is going to navigate. In terms of success across, the navigation comes close in importance to the actual swimming. John Bartlett is point-blank the One when it comes to this singular endeavor. It wasn't so long ago that Bartlett found thrilling the challenge of plotting a swimmer's course across the raging Gulf Stream and its unpredictable swirling eddies. Yet now he walks away post 2012's failure because he has lost faith in ever getting lucky and starting off from Havana with three days of both favorable winds and cooperative currents. He is game to help me by phone, offer any ocean or personal guidance he can, but he must bow out of the Swim itself.

Mark is in the same place as Bonnie. We can come down and go through our SXM training camp paces again, but he's not going to Cuba. Really? Am I going to have a snowball's chance in hell of making it across without my core Team? Right now, I just need to put the blinders on and forge ahead with getting myself ready and have faith that it will all somehow come together by summer.

Bonnie, Bartlett, and others suggest I try this one-hundred-mile-plus distance in some other waters. We lay out the nautical charts of equatorial oceans, areas warm enough to last a swim of this length, just as I had back in my twenties in first coming upon the Cuba Dream, and I try to get excited about other crossings. The Maldives are intriguing. This will be one of the first nations to literally submerge entirely, due to global warming. I spend three hours on the phone with Lewis Pugh, he in South Africa in the middle of the night in his pajamas. Lewis is our planet's "environmental swimmer." He's done outrageous swims in Antarctica, halfway up the Himalayas, and in the Maldives to bring attention to such issues as the illegal slaughter of sea animals and global warming. At the end of our conversation Lewis says he can see it's pointless talking about the Maldives. Cuba is my heart place. We look at Guam. And the Gulf of Thailand. But Lewis is right. My heart doesn't pound for any of these places. It's always been Cuba for me. Cuba, 2013. One more time.

Through November and December 2012, it surprises the heck out of me not to find pool training a bear. Ten hours of laps at the Rose Bowl Aquatics Center aren't all that grueling. By this fourth year, I would have thought counting these monotonous laps would have become near torture, but those last few minutes driving up to the pool, I actually enjoy the challenge of deciding what progressions of numbers will keep me occupied for ten hours. Today will be ninety laps in English, then ninety in the other three languages. Then sixty in all four. Then forty, then thirty, and so on. I'm motivated from the first count. Ten straight hours in a pool just doesn't seem outrageous to me any longer.

Actually, anthropologists tell us that we humans are built for long, slow endurance. We are one of the few species that can continue indefinitely at a moderate pace—say, walking from Africa to Asia, as we did all those eons ago. My pulse for these long hours hovers at around 130 per minute. That level of exertion became reasonable to my body for more than two continuous days. We can perhaps explain why the human body is suited to LSD, long slow distance, but not many modern minds can sustain the solitude, the repetition. At this juncture, the fourth year in, I am frankly proud of my freakish ability to persist on, hour after hour, year after year. Proud to be a veritable badass.

All the while training is under way, I am determined to get to 100 percent on the jellyfish solution. I can't solve the weather, or the eddies, or the currents. That's going to take sheer luck, with a degree of educated planning. Maybe I'll be the one who, by virtue of having the chutzpah to go back out there a fifth time, will finally deserve some luck. But as for those treacherous box jellies, surely there's better science than a hoodie fashioned out of panty hose. Angel's gel is genius, and it definitely helped, but I can't settle for not being able to cover the entire face, including the mouth, where I was stung the last time. Why put myself through even a minor episode of those stings? And what if something unexpected were to happen, if massive swarms, hunting for animal protein, attacked my mouth area, not just a single wisp of a tentacle?

In the fall of 2012, I started meeting with an inventive dentist named Chris Nagel, who fabricates mouthguards for athletes. He made several molds for me, but none of them worked. We tried silicone and a number of materials, but all rubbed the inside of the mouth too much. Then he introduced me to Dr. Stefan Knauss, a prosthetics specialist. Stefan makes beautiful, lifelike hands and feet and masks for medical purposes and was intrigued by my dilemma. He worked tirelessly for nine months, prototype after prototype, until we got it right.

I became fond of my silicone mask. I would hold it tenderly, my odd, alien-looking protector. At first we couldn't get the eyes right. Stefan kept making the mold to fit under the goggles, but then the goggles wouldn't seal when I swam. When he had me sit with the goggles on and shaped the mold around them, that issue was finally solved. The nose wasn't right for a while, either. When swimming normally, you inhale and exhale through your nose, as well as your mouth. But with the mask, I couldn't breathe through the nose at all. Worse, water was funneling up into my nose and down into my sinuses, throat, and mouth—a disaster in salt water. We wound up making separate molds for my nostrils, and I plugged them while wearing the mask. It's so unnatural to swim without breath running through the nose. I did it, but I never liked it. My oxygen intake was most definitely restricted. And a slipstream of salt water always found its way into my sinuses, making for nausea.

The mouth confounded us. How could we cover my mouth entirely and still allow me to breathe? I had seen photos of Penny Palfrey on her Cayman Islands swim wearing something akin to a big bee bonnet. Her entire head was swathed in a huge netting, leaving some space between her mouth and the bonnet for breathing. But of course it dragged her down. Absurd to try turning the head quickly hundreds of thousands of times with such a structure. Penny had dropped the bee bonnet for her Cuba 2012 attempt, and she'd been stung all over the face.

Once the eyes and nose were perfect, and the shape of the mask across the cheekbones was right, and the thinner cloth material down the back of the head covered the nape of the neck, we worked tirelessly on the mouth.

In January, when I was away from home, training in warm oceans, Stefan pursued multiple other mouth configurations; we'd try them out when I was back on my respites for pool swims in California. The issue was always that I couldn't latch onto the silicone that furled into the interior of the mouth with my teeth and open the mouth space wide enough to control breathing. Then one day Stefan had his brilliant aha moment. He sent me back to Dr. Nagel, the original dentist, to have retainer molds made for both my upper and lower teeth. Then he used those molds to make his own retainers on the inside of the mask, hot-sealing to the silicone itself. We went through several versions of those retainers, several materials. They had to be firm enough for me to lock into them, to control opening and closing them. One material was too hard and stiff; it caused cuts even in fresh water. Salt friction would be a nightmare. Another material was too flaccid and fell off the teeth with the constant movement of the jaw. Then he found it. A special dental acrylic. It took a few more weeks to constantly trim and heat-melt the tiny protrusions and edges so they weren't jabbing the soft edges of my mouth, but we had it. My striking, eccentric mask was done.

It wasn't easy to swim in. I would first do just a couple of laps at the Rose Bowl and couldn't quite get enough oxygen. But with patience and persistence, I could go longer and longer. The ocean was another challenge, times fifty. The first swim with the mask in St. Maarten was on a choppy day. The pool required only a slightly higher lift of the face, but with the wave action I was having to press hard with the right hand and almost lurch up to get the mouth completely clear of the water. I also discovered that I couldn't feel the water on my face and thus couldn't judge when to skip a breath if a wave surged at a particular moment. Without the mask, even on a very rough day, I would rarely take in any seawater, maybe a couple of rude gulps. But with the mask on a windy day, I was quickly seasick with all the saltwater intake.

My rationalization was that we wouldn't be out in rough seas on the Cuba Swim, if we chose the right weather window. Bonnie was impressed that so much tenacity had gone into the mask innovation, but she saw how difficult it was to maintain good forward progress in a chop. She just couldn't fathom it working all through the night, much less two or maybe three nights.

If I'd been up front about it, I had the same concerns about the mask. But I was also proud of the pluck Stefan and I showed in crafting it. And it was all I had.

But I am heartened in other ways coming into the New Year, 2013. The body is at its peak this year. The shoulders are powerful. I am strutting around, a very strong, well-built swimmer.

Same for the mind. I'm impressed with my continued fortitude when it comes to the long, lonely hours at sea. The analogy is perhaps when you think a bad flu is coming on but you're in the middle of some important project and you just can't afford to be sick. Then, wham, as soon as your obligations are over and you can relax, the fever spikes, because you are not holding it at bay anymore. There was an internal governor working for me, starting with the first long swims winter of 2010 and still working four years later, winter 2012–13. Whether for ten continuous hours in a fifty-meter pool or fifteen hours in the ocean, it's a triumph of the will to put your head down and somehow, some way, engage your mind, hour after hour, day after day, and now year after year. In the beginning, I'd envisioned only one year of such single-mindedness, and now it amazes me that I can keep my mind interested in counting so many different progressions of numbers, so many series of songs, not once counting or singing the same series twice.

During one fourteen-hour swim, the plan is to count to one hundred strokes in each of my four languages and sing a series of the same songs in between each hundred. "Country Road," "Suwannee River," "Carolina in My Mind," and the Beatles' "Mean Mr. Mustard." Then count from one hundred backward with a new set of songs between each. The Fine Young Cannibals' "She Drives Me Crazy," Grace Slick's "White Rabbit," Elton John's "Daniel," and the Bangles' "Manic Monday."

I am often asked if I meditate. Well, if the basic definition of meditation is to clear the mind of ego and useless daily monkey chatter, to free the mind with a goal of peaceful well-being, I guess there's no more focused meditation than swimming for many, many hours. The metronomic rhythm of the arm stroke, the six-beat kick, quickly takes you away from daily mind-traps. Even people who swim short times, under an hour in a pool, sense getting away from normal patterns of worrying and planning. So imagine being in an ocean, with no turns, no concerns of running into a wall or another person, the brain and body both on automatic pilot after doing this so many years.

As with classic meditation, without consciously thinking about everyday issues, you wind up sorting out the deeper aspects of your life after continuous hours swimming in the sea. The added factor of sensory deprivation, eyes and ears barely functioning out there, pushes the conscious under and brings the unconscious up. Without ever realizing I've been thinking about, say, a particular individual or situation about which I've been feeling some stress, I exit the water, as if I had been under hypnosis the whole day, having reached some clarity about whatever it was that was bothering me.

And the nights are particularly hypnotic—not on the Cuba crossing itself where the focus is intense and the jellyfish are a clear and present danger, but on training swims. The silence takes on an eerie, otherworldly tone. My breath seems exaggerated, akin to the whooshing sounds of a baby's ultrasound. Each hand entry makes a light, tickly slap. With the left-arm push comes the inhale, like a creature slowly gasping. Then the right-arm push brings a stronger life force of air, a deeper whooshing basso.

The night swimming transports me far from ego. The experience is transformative. I'd go so far as to call it life-changing.

And so the training went. Days into nights. Nights into days. And so on. And so on. Just like the person coming onto the flu, I can't afford to be fed up with the mind-numbing solitude. I must find a way to tolerate the monotony until it's finally over, until I finally reach that other shore. It's not easy, when you truly have no idea when that day might come. By this time, winter 2013, I have learned not to assume this will be the last year. I've cried each of the previous three years, on the last stroke of what I thought was the last tough training day. This year I won't make that naïve assumption again.

The body and mind are in the best shape ever, but the spirit is lonely in 2013. Bonnie and I are locked in a difficult but admirable impasse. I can't give up on the Dream, but my confidence of making it without Bonnie is tenuous. Bonnie doesn't want to keep me from my clear path, but she is black-and-white about not putting herself through either the danger to me or what she sees as inevitable failure again. My beef there is that I am bringing new ammunition to the mission, not just beating my head against the same brick wall. But at least she will still accompany me to St. Maarten and Mexico. Still advise me on training and resting and new nutritional ideas and yet another level of jellyfish protection. We go through the entire training year, neither trying to convince the other, both of us assuming she will not stand sentry on her perch. It's constantly on my mind, imagining, not being able to imagine, lifting my eyes hundreds of thousands of times, and not see Bonnie there—to feel the emptiness of pursuing the golden destination without my buddy, my ultimate lifeguard. We aren't mad at each other. We are mutually respectful. It's a friendship straight out of legendary lore, where the heroics are traditionally reserved for men. Two devoted equals. Each one true to herself. Each one true to the other.

Pauline Berry will be my Handler. I trust Pauline. She's the next best to Bonnie. She has been Bonnie's protégée, has rolled up her shirtsleeves and wound up sterling in all ways large and small, and I have utter trust in Pauline to take care of me. It's just that we all know that nobody can command my attention and make the critical decisions as Bonnie can. Also, she is my voice when I'm in the water. She is the only one who knows precisely what I'm thinking and feeling. I have no reason to believe Bonnie will come around. But I do believe it.

Meanwhile, things come to a head with Mark in St. Maarten. Nobody comprehends the sacrifice of the training in this sport except those wrapped tight into it. The Sollingers are on their third year of those sacrifices now. They've also taken a heavy hit this year with losses to their water-sports business at the hands of Hurricane Sandy. While they're working overtime to rebuild their company, they're also slaving to organize and execute these long days out on the water for me. At some point, Mark has no more to give. I should have seen it coming. Maybe I did but, self-obsessed, I pressed on in SXM, the routine there so fluid by now. I hadn't given a moment's thought to any immediate alternatives, because they would be tough to dig up in short order. On his side, Mark is bleary-eyed tired but doesn't want to let me down. Mid-April, he breaks, and down comes the collapse of Camp SXM.

Mark and I have been through too much to let any temporary strain diminish our friendship. But as far as the Cuba Swim goes, Mark is done.

The relationships on these types of expeditions tend to be fragile, at least as far as the core group goes. Emotions run deep. Many of the jobs, although important, don't come in until we actually go to Cuba. But for Mark at this point there has been a whole lot of guts and zero glory. It's not the issue of no pay for such hard work, either. Nobody gets paid. I have raised, by this fourth year $1 million, just the bare cash expenses of the Expedition. Salaries for the crew would have jacked up that number. Yet everyone involved was attracted to the historic, unique, multifaceted challenge of the quest. I asked our Kayaker Buco after the 2012 attempt if he was interested in giving it another go. He told me, "Diana, I repair air conditioners. To be out in that wilderness ocean with you, witnessing your incredible tenacity, being part of something so extreme, so thrilling, yes, I want to go again. This journey with you has been the most exciting adventure of my life."

Money was never an issue with Mark. He even refused reimbursement for all the expenses of training. Midway through that 2013 spring, he is just plain whipped, exhausted, fed up. We barely get through what turns out to be our last swim together, and I know he has nothing left. When I come in for feedings, his usual good-natured stories turn to silent stares. I don't speak all day out there, which is miserable. It's hard enough, fourteen hours of pushing forth, but to also feel the wrath of your Teammate, well, it breaks my heart.

That next morning was rugged, when I packed up the SXM training camp. Mark and I hugged without words. There was love, but you could have cut the tension with a knife. Angie was distraught. She understood both sides. Even little Sam was disturbed. And I was torn. Four years into this, I had learned that Teammates reach breaking points or their schedules just won't allow further involvement. Or I have realized they're not appropriate for the position and I've had to let them go. Each case causes emotional upheaval on both sides.

After Mark has worked so hard for so long for our shared Dream, walking out of his house and moving on without him was one of the hardest moments of the entire endeavor. I knew he would be in my heart when I reached that beach. I hoped I would be in his.

Every single person who serves the mission is forever part of the Team. Not every individual can hang in for the long haul—in this case, a haul much longer than any of us anticipated—but everyone shares the entire experience and earns a piece of the victory in the end.

I was deeply sad to lose Mark from the Team, but the minute I left his house, I admit, my thoughts turned to my own pragmatic concerns. I was shell-shocked and worried. I needed three more long swims in April, before getting down to Puerto Morelos in Mexico in May. And I had to get those swims organized in a hurry. Where in the world was I going to go?

TWENTY-NINE

Atheist in Awe

A life lesson. When your well-oiled routine is flipped upside down, have faith something good is lurking around the corner; be willing to imagine it and orchestrate it. On the plane from St. Maarten to Los Angeles, just hours after that wrenching good-bye to Mark, I tell myself I will get a three-swim April locale organized within twenty-four hours. Minutes after landing in Los Angeles, the phone rings with an offer of a corporate speech in St. Thomas, the Virgin Islands. I had basically quit television, radio, and even public speaking—all income avenues—when earnest training started in 2009. But, serendipitously, a lecture booker thought I was training in St. Maarten and figured I might be interested in a quick jaunt over to St. Thomas for one day. I could pick up a welcome bit of cash and not interrupt my focus.

I know who to call: Dee Brady. Dee's a professional organizer. Her job for thirty years was logistics manager for an international freight company. She starts to research and map out this St. Thomas trip. We need boats, captains, knowledge of the local waters, licenses, all kinds of stuff, pronto. We know that Bonnie won't be able to go due to schedule. Dee lines up Pauline and Johnberry. They make sure the pub is covered. Dee also reaches out to Vanessa in Key West, who knows boaters on every island of the Caribbean. I line up a house for the four of us.

It is a huge lift to be in a new environment. While St. Maarten is open, the aquamarine vistas expanding for many miles in every direction, St. Thomas is nestled in a cluster of the U.S. and British Virgin Islands. It's entertaining to buzz from this one to that one, with all kinds of ferries and sailboats trafficking to and fro. I circle St. John counterclockwise so that, as I breathe to the left, I can check out the hillside homes and moored boats.

The house is wonderful. After all our time in Key West together, the four of us fit like a glove at this point. Johnberry is constantly tuned into the Orioles; Dee has her crossword puzzles neatly folded; Pauline works to get my swim food measured out and into the coolers; and my schedule takes on its usual pattern during sets of long swims. I'm either stretching and meditating and getting my gear squared away before going out or I'm stunned useless with fatigue, barely able to eat, crashing once we're back in. In all our time together—especially considering that much of it has been mired in stress—not one moment of friction has ever even faintly come up among us.

The refreshing new milieu buoys my spirits, and I cruise on a natural high throughout our three swims in St. Thomas.

Dee hears on Facebook that a paddle boarder knows we're training in her backyard and asks if she can come out and join us for a while. They go back and forth, Dee trying to give her a general vicinity of where we'll be heading the next day. On a feeding, Johnberry has sighted this paddler, but he says it's a strange shape out there. The person appears to be wearing an oversized Sunday bonnet contraption. He signals her. It takes another couple of hours for us to rendezvous, and we learn first off that this woman has suffered through a bad cancer the past two years. As a matter of fact, she is still undergoing chemotherapy—hence the reason for the headgear and the long, bulky clothing. She cannot endure any sun exposure. We chat a bit, and she stays with us all afternoon, She's a fan of mine and tells us I have inspired her to be the first person to stand-up paddle around the entire island of Puerto Rico; she even asks the Team to accompany her once she's healthy.

On our last chat before she paddles away, I ask her what gave her the strength to beat this cancer. She says it was God. Then she tells me she knows it was God who gave me the strength to live such a bold life. And her parting words to me are: "It's amazing to be out here with God, isn't it? Can't you feel his grace everywhere?"

I don't usually shy away from a debate about God, at least not when I am pushed by presumption, but I refrain in this case. I give her a smile and quietly go back to swimming.

Many people have assumed that I am feeling God, thanking God, while I'm out in the vast, beatific ocean. For me, for sure, emotions of grandeur and awe are elevated far out at sea, a feeling expanded even further by the fact that I am there on my own steam, propelled by my own strength of character. I sometimes have a giddy sensation of swimming over the curvature of the Earth. I feel the tidal pull and, thus, the magnetism of the moon. A playful sea lion followed me all day in Argentina once, letting me slap his face. He would duck under, surface right next to me, and shake his whiskers, asking for a slap and a tickle again and again. Whereas it's true that I don't have much visual or aural acuity when actually stroking, my time to take in the ocean and the planet and the universe is on the short feeding breaks. But sometimes while actually swimming I get a treat, such as is happening to me here in St. Thomas, thousands of pretty little blue fish encircling me, honoring me as dead center of their perfect, shimmering school. I am in rapture in the sea, but for me that rapture isn't God. It's awe.

I have no quarrel with anybody's worldview, religious views, or practices. More likely than not, the human race will have come and gone without our ever knowing why we are here and whether we're watched over by a higher power. Perhaps it is part of the very definition of human life, that we will never know the answer to these existential questions.

For me, piecing together my personal worldview started early. My father, paradoxically, shattered his own doctrine of destiny—which was what he prescribed to me by pointing out my name defined as "champion swimmer" in bold black and white in the dictionary—when he violated me. That was the moment I began the turn away from what today has become the slogan du jour "It was meant to be." I learned through my own life's journey that one makes oneself a champion and all the other things one becomes. With the philosophy that we are all exactly where we should be, learning the lessons we were put on Earth to learn at exactly the time we were meant to learn them, that everything that happens to us happens for a reason, that every moment of our lives was meant to be just as it is—well, then, where is hope? Where does will come in? Where is the inspiration to change and better oneself?

I don't sense a master plan. Chaos and random events that were clearly not meant to be occur all around us, every day. What I came to, starting in childhood, is an intention to embrace the chaos and try my best to create a meaningful and joyful life within the maelstrom.

And I came to discover that life unfolds as a plethora of coincidence and serendipity and even delightful whimsy, woven into the fabric of the chaos. On a trip to the Amazon years ago, I found my hosts distraught because it was the fifth day their puppy was missing. By then, they had forsaken him as taken by the surrounding wilds. I had a dog at home, one I shared with Bonnie and her partner; he'd had a seizure just before I left, and I had almost canceled my trip. I was driven to an outpost hours away from my host's hacienda and waited more hours to get a satellite call through to Bonnie. When she finally came through, she could barely speak. "He's dead. Moses is dead," she wailed. I was helpless. I wasn't there to console her. I couldn't hold our dog in his final minutes.

Back at the hacienda, everybody went to bed, but I sat out in the field under the stars. I was writing about Moses in my journal when the puppy, skinny and bedraggled, came out of nowhere and jumped into my lap. I woke everybody up, and a tearful celebration ensued in the middle of the night. I'm quite sure the interpretation could easily be made that this little puppy was some kind of sign from the universe, Moses's spirit reincarnated for me to hold close. To me, it was a sad passing followed by a happy coincidence, a cue to embrace the chaos, in itself a paradox of joy and sorrow, life and death existing in the same moment, neither canceling the other out. Just part of the wondrous, random world, not something meant to be.

It was also early on that atheism started brewing for me, age eight or so. My father, who was Greek Orthodox, left me off at a Christian Sunday school one day. When he came to pick me up afterward, I was moping around in the parking lot. He asked me what was wrong. I told him I didn't want to go again. When he asked why, I told him I didn't like being told lies.

"They told us this ridiculous story. God created all the oceans and rivers one day, then all the forests the next, and he was busy all week creating the rest of Earth. Then he was tired, so he rested on Sunday, so that's why we all rest and pray on Sundays. Dad, I just can't sit there and pretend I believe those lies."

"Okay," he said in his thick accent. "You don't everr have to go again. But iz not rrespectful for you to call zose storries lies. Zose arre beautiful fables zat cerrtain people rrely on az basis of zeir faith. Faith iz perrsonal. Don't judge zem. Make yourr way toward yourr own beliefs."

Precepts of organized religion are no longer lies to me. Through my reading and searching and observing, my belief system as an atheist has solidified deeper and deeper through the years, but I never question a Christian, a Jew, a Muslim, a Buddhist, or a paddler still grappling with cancer about their beliefs.

During those three months of bed rest with the heart disease in high school, when Liza would bring me library books, I was hard hit by a story of a young man on a summer internship at an archaeological dig in Jordan. While these digs rarely uncover anything exciting, this one happened to come upon an entire lost city. This young man was relegated to menial work, but he sat on a hill one day on a break and watched as the senior workers dug and carefully brushed away large sections. They had revealed a length of wheel tracks and footprints that had traveled the road of this city. And this young man wept. He wept to think that these people had lived, and loved, and cared and had probably perished instantaneously one day during an earthquake or some such catastrophe. He wept to think how many millions of people have lived precious lives, twenty to forty to sixty to eighty years at a time, and how many are now gone and forgotten.

That image of those forgotten souls has stayed with me all these years, although I'm not religious. What brings us all together is that overarching ideology of honoring all of humanity—past, present, future—as it hit that young man on that dig in Jordan that summer.

That's why faith is such a personal domain and why it's dangerous for us to mandate any religious precepts onto our neighbors, in our schools, for the population at large. The regard for all individuals' inalienable rights to freedom, to equality, to compassion, to basic needs and quality of life layers the bedrock of our underlying values. Religion—the overlay—should be left to each person. Religion is a private matter, not a universal truth. Love is the universal truth.

To stand at the edge of the Olduvai Gorge, to feel that prehistoric wind on your face, or to sit in the mist among the gorillas of Rwanda, is to feel the collective history of mankind, to palpably sense our evolution. Global cultural exposure has rendered the Earth to me a small, intimate, enchanting habitat and has led me to sense that we the human race has a collective spirit. My mother died in 2007. I personally don't believe she's above, watching over me. But all she was, all she gave me still lives within me, just as some remnant of DNA and energy from our *Homo erectus* ancestors still lives within me. It's powerful, our collective spirit. We are moved to kindness and harmony by the human spirit.

Swimming across the planet in this new athlete era for me is to bathe in kindness and harmony. It's a joy to be this age, to have relinquished that tight control that governed my younger years. I am free in the acceptance that, even though my will is indeed powerful and I refuse to surrender to definitions of limitation, I cannot control either the universe or others.

Along with perspective and wisdom, we seem to achieve balance as we age. An antique scale in my house reminds me of the particular balance between the drive of will and the grace of acceptance. My thirty-two-year-old friend fought a ravaging cancer. She battled with true grit, traveled every road of science and hope, never a moment of self-pity. But at the end she was even braver in finding the grace to say a peaceful good-bye to her husband and children.

In my sixties, my will is as fierce as it ever was. But I am at the same time infinitely more accepting, this swim laying bare the crux of those two attributes in a harmonious concert.

I have often been asked how I can be an atheist, as someone fully and constantly engaged in life and all its wonders. People often misjudge atheists, think that we are haters lacking reverence, gloomy pessimists absent of hope. We get a bad, misinformed rap. I can stand shoulder to shoulder with any devoutly religious person and gasp at the beauty of our physical universe, feel profound love for animal and humankind, live out gratitude for these treasured lives of ours, remain humble to remind myself that I am only one of seven billion people currently sharing this planet Earth, no better or worse than all the rest.

So when the paddler asks, assumes, that we all feel God's grace out here, she's not wrong. We are very close in what we're feeling, she and I. She paddles off, feeling God, and I swim on, an atheist in awe.

THIRTY

Infinitude

It comes time to settle into the paradise of my home away from home, Key West, but June 2013 paradise is bittersweet for me. Bonnie has stayed home in California this year. She will only come down for the longer swims. Dee, Johnberry, and Pauline are now my small but loyal crew. Needing a cozy sanctuary more than ever, I am offered a friend's charming cottage. There is a small veranda where I read on rainy afternoons. It's a cocoon of safety for me, this cottage, and I am happily sequestered there, even though Bonnie's being in Los Angeles makes for a discomforting absence as the days drag on.

This is not life as normal. I am never free of the weather anxiety. Not only do I check in with our three weather sources at least once a day, but I scour every Florida Straits online wind forecaster many times a day, too. And most of my out-of-town Teammates are checking in nearly every day for the weather reports from me.

Dee, Johnberry, and Pauline meet me at the marina. They have fueled the boat, filled the ice chests. They are never late, not even a minute late. We power through these Key West swims, after the heavy spring training is done, as consummate professionals, like clockwork. I need to start promptly on schedule, get in the hours, get them over with. Once out there, we do have some laughs during the feeding stops. Pauline shows me videos they've taken of dolphins playing along next to us over the last couple of hours. We joke about personalities on the Team, events in the news. Dee and I talk music. She installed a kick-ass stereo and speaker system on *Voyager* before she even considered the engine selection. I might stop mid-stroke and yell up to Dee at the wheel:

"Dee, how does that line go on the Little Anthony song? First it's 'If we could start anew, I wouldn't hesitate . . .' What's that next line? I just can't dredge it up."

Dee knows the line, every time, every song. I have to rib Johnberry about the Orioles, but he is ruthless this year, the Birds romping. We're in our groove, our tight little unit. I just miss Bonnie, that's all.

As happened last June, when Penny Palfrey gave Cuba a go, now another elite Australian swimmer named Chloë McCardel has her sights on being the first to cross without aid. For all Chloë's long list of open-water accomplishments, she is issuing statements about the Cuba Swim being the Mount Everest of ultradistance swimming. She is calling this the pinnacle swim of her career. She knows I am in Key West, prepping, and she knows I prefer to wait for July, when the water temps hit their upper registers. She's going first.

As I did with Penny, I talk myself off a cliff. And when I answer the media, who want to know how I feel about someone making it before me, I do my best to find grace and sportsmanship. I send Chloë wishes for a safe journey through the Commodore at Marina Hemingway.

We gather to watch a CNN interview with Chloë. When asked what she intends to do about the box jellyfish, she is reminded by the interviewer that I had a brush with death from those stings. Chloë is very respectful of me. She says she has followed my attempts with great admiration, and adds that she was truly relieved when I did not die from those savage stings. But she is confident, even cocky, and I quickly recall being twenty-eight—twenty-eight was my age when I first attempted Cuba. She reminds the viewer that she's from Australia, where the box are familiar residents, and says her team knows their science. They have developed and tested a repellent cream, and she will approach the night swimming with full certainty of getting through without incident. When asked just what this cream consists of, she says she will share it with the world after her crossing is successful.

We all look at each other. What? Something Angel Yanagihara doesn't know about? We are highly suspicious.

Then we see the live footage of Chloë at the start in Havana. Sure enough, we see her Team slathering a white creamy substance onto her shoulders, upper arms, and upper legs. A quick smear to each spot, with most of the surface area of skin still exposed. Really? Is the idea that this substance has a chemical repellent so effective that animals anywhere close to her skin will move away? We are further skeptical as Chloë's jellyfish expert is a man who told me using the sheep's lanolin was dangerous because the jellies are drawn to any animal derivative substance. Angel has educated us to the absurdity of that theory. Would a box attack a leather belt? Of course not.

Off she goes, just after daylight. We take the day off training to follow her. We are nervous wrecks. Chloë is a strong, fast swimmer, and her tracker shows her making impressive progress. She has not hit the Gulf Stream yet, over those first eight hours. Her direction is due north. The next four hours, she veers to the northeast. She must have reached the first of the Stream's currents. Then, it's odd, the tracker stops. It has been emitting a ping and a point on the nautical map every twenty minutes so far, but about twelve hours in, there are no more entries. We check constantly. Nothing at the thirteenth hour. Nothing again at the fourteenth. We figure the tracker has died or malfunctioned temporarily. A couple of hours later we learn from Chloë's website that she had been stung badly at dusk. She is okay, breathing normally. Her Aussie medical crew is fully prepared. But she is done and she says she's never coming back. To be taken down only twelve hours in, after all that training, all that buildup—her spirit is crippled. Welcome to my world, Chloë.

That drama over, we are back to waiting for July and warmer waters. It's an intense time, summer in Key West, as it has been every day, in every location, these past four years. Whether it's eating meals or walking my dogs or winding down at night with a book, just under the surface is the Cuba Swim. It never goes away. The only two times I truly escaped the laser focus of the mission these four years were my brother's funeral, July 2010, and my nephew Tim's wedding, May 2013. As much as this Cuba Dream has electrified the spirit, preparing and waiting for it has at the same time knocked my chi into overload.

Every single day when I enter the front door of my cottage after train-ing, I don't even put my heavy swim bag down. I stand and take in the photograph on the left entrance wall. The frame is a huge mahogany door, mounted sideways, with a grainy black-and-white image of a per-son with his back to the camera, facing the sea. He's staring out at the horizon, in contemplation. And a few lines from the Pablo Neruda poem "Ode to Salt" are hand-painted on the wood at the bottom.

To paraphrase, the poem evokes a kiss from the sea, and the notion that one can taste infinitude in that kiss.

This is what's churning in my soul. The grasp of infinitude. This reaching for the stars, toward infinitude, has brought me to a vibrant life. This intimate time in the magic of immersion has carried me to the infinitude of the sea's salty kiss. Lest I dwell on the drudgery of the cruel training hours, standing transfixed before this photograph reminds me that it has been a divine sensual pleasure, coasting across the surface of our Earth, bejeweled by our oceans. To be able to glide with balletic rhythm, to feel the power of my stroke in concert with the majesty of the sea has been exalting. Arriving at this state of superlative swimming conditioning was supposed to be in the name of physical training toward a goal, yet it is enough to revel in the sheer delight of skimming for mile after mile. I have become an ocean traveler, smooth and efficient, on my own steam. And this intimate love affair with the ocean has opened my entire being to all things possible, to infinitude. This piece of art gives me solace all summer long. It gives me hope.

All we need now is for the lips of good fortune to blow a still calm of infinitude across our seas.

And we need Bonnie. When Bonnie was a baby, her father would sing to her the old folk song and now I've taken to singing it at the end of each training swim.

> My Bonnie lies over the ocean
> My Bonnie lies over the sea
> My Bonnie lies over the ocean
> Oh, bring back my Bonnie to me.

THIRTY-ONE

Find a Way

I need to sit with Bonnie. One more heart-to-heart. I not only don't think my chances are good without her, but I am forlorn to contemplate what reaching that elusive beach will mean to me without her. This swim has come to symbolize many things to me, among them the Homeric strength of our friendship.

Bonnie is willing to meet with a mediator; she has opened her mind that far. We mutually agree on Steve Munatones. I fly back to Los Angeles for the mediation. Steve first listens to both our points of view. Why Bonnie doesn't want to go again. Why I must. He understands. Bonnie wants to know, with Steve's vast experience of other ocean swimmers, what else out there could be either dangerous or an unknown obstacle to our success. I don't blame her for doubting that we are finally aware of every potential pitfall. We have been professionally prepared each outing, yet each outing has brought us eye to eye with real and virtual storms we didn't foresee. Steve has been with us as independent observer on three of our attempts, and he doesn't believe there is anything more beyond what we know.

Bonnie also wants to know if I really could die out there. Steve says the box are no joke. Their sting can be, has been, a fatal event for swimmers. If we think we've solved that factor, that's huge. He hasn't witnessed any other swimmer cross the threshold of innovation to somehow survive in that animal's treacherous environment. He's also impressed with our Team's shark protocol; he's sure our diligence would not allow me to go under in the middle of the night.

The last question Bonnie poses to Steve: "Can she do this swim? Hasn't she proven it's indisputably impossible?"

Steve: "Improbable. As I've stated, I put anybody's chances at two percent. But for Diana, 'impossible' does seem to take on a more special interpretation."

We ride home the ninety minutes from Steve's in complete silence. My way is to chatter, spell out every tangent of the subject, but it's not Bonnie's way, and this is Bonnie's decision. I leave her at her house, uncertain and, frankly, afraid of what she's thinking. The next day she asks me to come over. I steel myself. I've gone this whole year, hoping against hope that she's going to have a change of heart. This is the day the final word comes down.

Bonnie isn't a blabber. If it can be said in a few spare words, Bonnie finds them. I come in. We have no exchange of pleasantries. My fanny hasn't even hit the sofa yet when she says, "I'm in."

I am reeling. I cry. "What was it that brought you back, Bonnie?"

She says, "If I don't go and you're not successful, or if you're hurt, I'll regret not being there the rest of my life. If you are successful, I'll have even more regret. I started this journey with you, and I'm going to see the journey through to its end, whatever that end might be. Your Roosevelt story really affected me. I, too, don't want to be the timid soul who stands by. Let's do this thing."

All is right with the world.

I'm not happy that Mark won't be serving as Ops Chief, but Johnberry has stepped up in that role. Johnberry is cool. Measured. He's capable under pressure. I have no doubts about Johnberry.

The navigation, however, without John Bartlett, proves to be an emotional nightmare. We have turned to an experienced sailor on our Team and, loud as the warning bells are from the very beginning, that this is not the right person for the huge strategic job, we don't have the luxury of other choices. The math computations of a swimmer, considering drift and a moving axis against a variable current, take a specific strategist.

Week after week, swim after swim, our sailor makes mistakes, misjudges winds and currents, and, worst of all, does not communicate well with her mates. We run aground. We don't make it back to anywhere close to our training starting point, due to miscalculations. On an eighteen-hour crucial swim, Shark Divers and Kayakers needing their night training, our sailor misjudges the approach to the reef at night. Sitting on the deck for many cold hours on the way back to the marina, Pauline and I are huddled together under a towel, shaking our heads as the sailor argues as to the best direction home. When Johnberry overrides her command and takes common sense into his own hands, our sailor pouts the rest of the trip home, alone on the bow. The Team is close to mutiny. We try to break it all down in a meeting on deck the next day, but it is clear that we desperately need Bartlett. We go so far as to bring in a professional team builder for one last-ditch effort to restore mutual respect. It's a disaster. When I see, from the other side of the room, the team builder teaching Dee and Johnberry, à la kindergarten, to raise their hands in a "stop" signal to our sailor, meaning they refuse to be talked to in rude, demeaning language, Dee flashes me a "we're kidding with this shit, right?" look through her navy blue glasses. I know we're done.

Our sailor and I walk the quiet streets of Key West into the night. She has become a trusted friend to me over these years and has handled another key role for the Team superbly. We both cry. There's anger and disappointment on both sides. There's vulnerability and comradeship. But the path is clear. I simply must get on my knees and beg Bartlett to come back.

Bartlett, like Bonnie, plays his cards very close to the vest. He listens. He has already heard some of the tales of our training-swim blunders from other Teammates. He's pouring heart and soul into the work-of-art boat he's building, and he's on a manic deadline to finish. But he puts it all on hold to come save the day. One, it hurts him to see me so distraught, to have worked so hard and now be left in the lurch. Two, mild-mannered hippie that Bartlett may be, who can resist the role of rescuer? Three, he has never come to peace with the failures of 2011 and

2012. It haunts him, having gloated when Penny didn't make it because her navigators seemed so ignorant of the circular eddies that got them turned around and swimming south. He really did want to rise to the challenge of how to anticipate those eddies and how to get out of them. Like Bonnie, his fire reignites. As Navigator, he agrees to captain the journey right up to that step onto the other shore we've all envisioned for so very long.

Both Bonnie and Bartlett fully understand me. They're cut from the same cloth. I won't be the fearful one who quits, and watches someone else one day make it across this magical ocean. I'd rather fail a fifth time. Maybe a sixth. Maybe the rest of my life, rather than quit. The anxiety over our navigation that had my stomach in knots has lifted.

For the first time, we talk about lessening our standards for low winds. We have always said our threshold is a minimum of three days under 10 knots from the south, southeast, or southwest. Non-swimmers have no idea what even a light surface chop does to forward progress. I can't tell you on how many training swims nice people on their boats or on the docks or the beach would exclaim to us on our way to starting a particularly punishing day: "What a great day for a swim!" This would inevitably come forth on a blustery day when Bonnie, Mark, and I had just finished remarking what hell this day was going to be.

But how can I fault people who don't know our milieu? I try to be gracious for their engagement, no matter how uninformed. I think my favorite question, speaking of uninformed, asked in the early days of the project was whether I'd be having any boats accompany me across from Cuba. I was tempted to turn to full-on sarcasm: "No, no, I'm going to swim with a Bowie knife between my teeth so I can hunt fish and skin them alive for my food. I'll be using the stars for celestial navigation at night. And I'm going to drag a desalinization tank behind me so I can convert seawater to fresh. Yes, I will have boats alongside!" But I was always polite. Why should a stranger to ocean swimming know anything about it? If someone is curious, I am patient, respectful, and flattered that they want to know anything about what we do out there.

But the truth is, a choppy or rolling sea is a whole different animal of a challenge for long, long hours. When it's glass, you are way up on top of the surface. Your drag is minimal. As wind bumps up, you are clearly spending time moving up and down, not just forward. But by mid-August, Bartlett, Bonnie, and I come to an agreement. We will accept a bigger wind speed, as long as the direction remains from some southerly point. Anything from due east means direct force against the Gulf Stream; north wind means right in your face, too much resistance; west wind would get you moving far too fast east with the Stream.

By the third week of August, I'm pretty much a neurotic mess. I can't sleep most nights. At three a.m. I'm in front of the weather maps. Bonnie is back in Los Angeles, and I miss her calm, our unspoken bond. We decide I should take a couple of days off swimming and we'll meet in the middle of the country. We rendezvous in Dallas and spend twenty-four hours playing Scrabble and cribbage, relaxing, talking. It's fun and just what I need.

As soon as I get back to Key West, Dane Clark and our meteorologists are stirring. Dane is lukewarm but does see some factors predicting a lighter wind period across the Straits coming the last week of August. Our other pro, Lee Chesneau, is in Spain but tracking all systems carefully and he's even more upbeat than Dane. August 25: both of them for the first time agree on this window. It's not perfect, by any means. But by midday Friday, August 30, the wind may switch around from east to southeast, with an occasional push from due south. This is not a doldrums period, far from it. Dane warns that he sees six-hour periods, mostly afternoons, bumping up to 10 to 15 knots. That used to be a red-flag amount of gust for us. But we're no longer shooting for perfection. We're looking for doable. I am on the phone six times a day with Bartlett. Same with Bonnie. And Candace. Johnberry, Pauline, Dee, and I meet several times on Monday and Tuesday, August 26 and 27. Vanessa jumps into organizing the fleet, as well as the Coast Guard permits. On Wednesday, August 28, we are at consensus. I issue the red alert. Bonnie's on her way from Los Angeles.

Luke Tipple can't make it, so twenty-five-year-old Niko Gazzale takes charge of the Shark Team. He's green but has shown up all summer for us. He's now our guy. Niko and I have a private meeting. I ask him point-blank if he's ever been in the water with an oceanic whitetip. He says, in his thick New York accent: "I'm not going to lie to you. I never have." Next I ask him if he's ever been in the water with sharks without a speargun in his hand. He says, "I can't lie to you there, either. I never have."

I have four young guys, instead of six. They're speargun fishermen, not shark experts. But Niko says to me: "We won't let you down. We'll make sure you're safe out there." Niko goes over all their plans with me, including showing me the canisters of Shark Repel for emergency measures. I am confident in this young man because I have to be.

Steve Munatones made our swim his priority all summer, but now he is caught last minute heading to Japan and can't quickly get another observer for our trip. He has counseled us on how to keep accurate logs of observation every minute, from my first stroke to my last step. To that end, we have brought two independent observers, Janet Hinkle and Roger McVeigh, with us. Steve says many swims are officiated by even the swimmer's family members, all okay as long as they keep careful logs. Our two observers (neither part of our Team, neither relatives of mine) will tag-team, one on *Voyager* at all times, the other resting on a mother ship for the next shift. The fleet will sail out of Key West just before dusk Thursday, August 29, for the fifteen or so hour trip to Cuba.

Bonnie and I get a ride from a nice guy in a little four-seater private plane in the early-morning dark from Key West to Miami, to catch the charter over to Havana. It's eerie, sweeping up the chain of islands, a simple necklace of red lights in the black below. The familiar adrenaline surge once again takes us to that surreal place we know so well.

We get to Marina Hemingway four hours ahead of our boats. As they start filing down the canals, I can see Candace from afar, her silver hair ablaze in the late-morning sun. We cry. This is it. Candace's job is fanning out the story via social media, but it is understood that Bonnie will call her to *Voyager* at any time, if I need a special dose of Candace serenity. And our plan, dating back to 1978, when we were young and more whimsical, still holds. When we at long last see that Florida shore, Candace will sing, voice up to the heavens: "When you wish upon a star . . ."

Once through immigration, we have a short Team meeting. Then the usual press conference. CNN, Tim's documentary crew, *The New York Times, Good Morning America, The Washington Post,* other national media outlets who reported on our expedition extensively through the years—none of them are sending reporters this time. Only if we make it to the other side will they carry the story. That's okay. After all, at the inception of all this, I was ready to accept only five people greeting me on the other side. Tim was one of those, and I am missing him now. I'm missing Mark, too. But I have to remember what I've read about so many of Earth's great expeditions. They sometimes take years, the forces of nature so great against them. When finally triumphant, the dreamer remembers all those who played important roles along the way, with gratitude.

The believers have thinned out drastically. But the Cubans are still interested. Associated Press Havana, CNN Havana, et al.—we know each other at this point. They ask what I will use to protect against the box jellies, especially having seen Chloë hit by them fairly recently and near their shores. They want to know if the conditions—wind and currents—seem more favorable than last time. There are questions about Cuba-U.S. relations, about the pros and cons of being a sixty-four-year-old athlete. But, mainly, in the end, they want to know if this is the last time.

I talk in Spanish at the press gathering about the fine line that separates the admirable attitude of Never Give Up and the humility we all need summon when the universe looms too large in the face of our dreams. I tell them I am literally standing on that line today. I haven't reached noble surrender. Not yet. I'm still fighting. I'm still a believer.

The Team meeting follows. The energy is high but not fun and raucous, as in years before. Bartlett addresses the Team. He expresses cautious optimism as to the currents and eddies he observed on his way over to Havana from Key West. I stand there observing him: his rich vocabulary, his eyes brimming with care, his fingers playing that virtual piano. John serves as the gatekeeper to our success, and he fills the role with earned gravitas.

We set a nine a.m. swim-out start, hugs all around, and everybody fans out to take care of their individual needs. For me, it's the pool goggle tests. The hundredth check of my gear bags. Angel meets with Bonnie and advises that next morning, along with the greasing of lanolin, to apply our green Sting No More gel under the suit in strategic areas.

Personally, I think any swimmer going out into box jellyfish territory must be a fool to do so without Angel on the boat.

Then the night-before meal of pasta. I am a bit freaked out because I haven't had a cold or any kind of sickness for the entire four years of this pursuit, but tonight I have a sore throat and that odd sensation behind the eyes that signals an infection settling in. While Bonnie is running around with Kathy Loretta, getting the boats settled for a quick morning immigration clearance, Candace gives me a soothing massage. Her healing hands put me to sleep by eight p.m.

Bonnie wakes me at five a.m. to start eating, drinking, stretching. The ghost of a cold is gone. I feel like a million bucks. It's in most ways no different than the previous four attempts. The routine is precisely the same. Neurosis over my gear. Breathing rituals to keep the heart from pounding out of my chest.

But still, the adrenaline surge is through the roof. I know, as nobody else knows, what lies between here and there. The deadly jellyfish, the prowling predator sharks, the unpredictable swirling counterclockwise eddies, the sudden tropical lightning storms with their abrupt fifty-mile-an-hour winds. All the emotion, the anxiety, the hope, the Dream, the potential of history in our grasp, the four failures, the lessons from those failures, the good people who have taken the journey—all of it now pulses through me. This day, Saturday, August 31, 2013, is my day. I admit there is a trace of caution below the skin. But mainly I'm excited.

I am once again perched on the starting-point rocks, at the mouth of the marina. The Cuban journalists ask if I feel some new confidence that this will be the time we make it all the way across. I tell them I have believed all four previous times, with every shred of my being, that we would reach the other shore. I have been thunderstruck each time to have to give it up. But staring out at that distant horizon this time, I do feel a lightness of being, not the unreal weight of the intimidating vastness ahead. I am more grounded, less preoccupied this time.

The Team is pumping fists, calling out cheers from their boats; the cap, goggles, and grease are set. Bonnie grabs my shoulders, looks me square in the eye, and says, "Let's find a way." And I leap.

THIRTY-TWO

The Yellow Brick Road

It's not calm, but the waves are rolling from behind me. I'm pretty happy. I'm into five hundred repetitions of Joe Cocker's "The Letter." I hear his rasp.

> Give me a ticket for an aeroplane
> I ain't got time to take no fast train

The sun is brilliant, Bonnie and Pauline are standing on the Handler's platform, Bartlett is head down into his charts at his nav station, Dee is at the wheel, Johnberry is working the hand radio up on the bow, Niko is way up top, arms crossed, surveying the seascape. Don McCumber and Buco Pantelis, my two main Kayakers, are to the side and behind me. I love when the kayaks come sweeping into formation. The one just to my right, at the end of a three-hour shift, drops to the rear position. The rear kayak heads back to his or her mother ship. And a fresh paddler who is coming off his or her rest rotation slips into position next to me. When I need a quick hit of water, rather than going twenty-one feet toward *Voyager,* the paddler next to me hands me a bottle.

After my Handlers, these are the people closest to me throughout, along with the Shark Divers and Angel, who talk to me during feedings when they are diving. But the paddlers are always there. If I've stopped with a problem, they relay it over to Bonnie. I might just need a quick pee or to pull my cap down around the ears. They know me well, the paddlers. They know when to say something encouraging, when to be silent and bring Bonnie or Pauline into it. My good friend Lois Ann Porter serves as the third Handler on this crossing.

The Shark Divers make a sweep under me every now and then. So does Angel Yanagihara, although their vigilance will dial up a hundredfold come nightfall. They seem to me sleek dark creatures as they glide under me, their long fins undulating with easy fluid motion.

This time, as I glance back during feedings each ninety minutes, the Cuban shore is fading away. Yes, I'd like the sea to be calmer, but all in all it's a good day, Saturday, August 31: what would have been my brother's sixty-first birthday.

It's almost as if I'm glancing through a photo album. I picture little Billy, skinny, his cute curly hair always a bit askew. And I see adult Sharif, his filthy raincoat buttoned wrong, his dreadlocks unwashed for perhaps years, but his smile still that little boy we once knew.

During my heart disease phase in high school, Bill was jealous that Liza was bringing me these stacks of library books, and he'd come in and peruse them. He took special interest in the astrophysics. Flash forward forty years, and sometimes we'd sit on a park bench in Boston, stare up at the night sky, and riff. Does the universe extend to infinity? That's a concept hard to wrap our heads around. Does it have an edge, is it enclosed? For us, that's even harder. When I tell him the way I read it these days is that both time and space curve, so that if you could look out far enough into space, you would eventually be looking at the back of your head. Sharif stands up in hysterics, slapping his thighs. "That's it! Eureka! It doesn't go on forever. It doesn't have an edge. It curves! Wow, where do you get this shit?" I miss my brother.

I actually spend a lot of my ocean time, especially at night, mystified by my readings of the cosmos. My understanding of the physical universe is at the simplest, most rudimentary level, but it's been a lifelong interest and there is no playground more fertile to contemplate it all than out here. Just now, closing in on my first twenty-four hours out of Havana, I'm fixating on the fact that this Earth of ours, in concert with all the other matter that spewed out from the Big Bang, is not actually standing serenely still, as it seems to us. No, we are careening through space at unfathomable speeds, along with all the other objects out there, all of us expanding away and away, to one day not have any view or reference to one another. I'm trying to feel the speed as I touch the Earth's surface with my hands. I'm tripping out. I'm high.

I can go to dinner with like-minded friends who are fascinated with the cosmos, I could take a boat ride out here and look up at the dazzling night sky, but the emotion of swimming all the way out here on my own adds exponentially to the wonderment when musing over it all.

As the sun makes its way down the western half of the sky, I ask Bonnie to discuss with Angel when I'll need to get all the jellyfish gear on. At the next feeding, she says we should target six-thirty p.m., to be safe. Angel considers a number of factors, such as the time of the astronomical twilight, the number of days after the last full moon, and the depth of shelf formations below us in determining the likelihood of the box swarming at dusk. These variables night to night explain why Penny Palfrey was free from stings her first night but then stung on her second night during her attempt. Angel informs us one of those factors is in play this night and we should prepare for full armor. I am dreading the cumbersome clothing, especially the mask. I have not successfully swum with it for a full twelve-hour period. And that's what this night is going to demand. We no longer have the luxury of long summer days.

Bonnie and Pauline blow the whistle at six-thirty p.m. sharp. I reluctantly cruise to the side of *Voyager*. The process of getting all the gear on is certainly faster than it was back in the winter, during SXM training, but it's still frustrating and tiring. Pulling on those latex surgeon's gloves alone takes painstaking patience, to edge the latex over wet skin millimeter by millimeter. There are air bubbles at the tips of the fingers. I am kicking pretty hard to keep my hands above the surface and work each finger at a time. Once they're finally on, I have to lie back to catch my breath for a good minute. I pull on the full-body stinger suit, also an inch-by-inch painstaking proposition. The gloves and booties are taped down, no gaps of skin at the wrists or the ankles. Balancing my legs, one at a time, out of the water for the duct-tape wrap is a big challenge, as always. Now I put the goggles back on. Then the mask. I chomp down on the retainers, make sure the nose pieces are pushed up high into the nostrils. Next I pull on the Lycra hoodie over the mask, both to hold the mask in place and to drape down around the neck for skin coverage there. The final move, putting a bathing cap on over the hoodie, serves to secure it all. I get caught up in being proud of myself for a moment because it took persistence to develop these layers, and now here I am where other swimmers didn't think possible, about to go into a night among deadly animals, and I'll be safe. But as I pull the final item tight, the cap, I get back to the grit it's going to take to make it through the night, encumbered by this unlikely swimmer's costume. To swim is to be free. I am now hamstrung.

The first stroke gets me back in it. Time to bear down. Don't grouse. Work through the night. Work.

The next twelve hours are hell on Earth. The waves are slapping all night long. It's exhausting to press hard with my right hand to push my face high above the surface every breath. Because I can't judge the feel of the waves on my face, I am thwacked by walls of seawater. I gag. I vomit right into the mask. It's very difficult, now that my fingers have lost both dexterity and feel—a normal occurrence after many hours swimming in the ocean but magnified by the latex gloves—to pinch the underside of the mask material, pry my teeth from the retainers, and lift it above my nose to clear the vomit. I swim through the entire night, violently seasick. I'm not even capable of looking for daylight. My vision through the mask is down to zero. I can at least be grateful for the red LED lights on the streamer below. I am in survival mode.

Around seven a.m., the whistle stops me and I drag all the jelly-fish gear off. The relief is overwhelming. I learn that many of the crew were seasick through the night as well. The interior tissues of my mouth—the insides of the cheeks, the sides and underside of the tongue, the roof—are very tender. There is always swelling and even scraping inside the mouth after long hours in salt water. As the tissue becomes distended with salt exposure and the jaw works to open and close almost once per second, the edges of the teeth start to irritate the tissue. But this feels worse than what I've known before. The acrylic of the retainer over the teeth, much as we had worked to shave it down to its smoothest and thinnest layer, overnight had scraped and abraded all that tissue to a point of glaring pain. Salt water washing over those cuts now causes a constant, throbbing torment.

It is daylight. The sun is hot and life-affirming. The canvas of blue sky matching the blue of the Gulf Stream swaddles me in comfort, and I try to focus on the positive. After all, it's the confidence in the absolute protection of that mask that has allowed me to overcome the fear of dying from the box stings out here. But right now such reasoning is no match for the agony raging inside my mouth. Passing anything over those nasty lacerations hurts, so eating and even drinking become an arduous chore. I wince with every attempt to even get a Shot Blok in my mouth. My three Handlers—Bonnie, Pauline, and Lois Ann—coax me all day long to sip down a high-calorie drink, desperate to replace what I've lost from the night's vomiting, as well as trying to get ahead of further depletion when the mask goes back on tonight. Bonnie calls the Med Team over to *Voyager,* but they can't do anything for the cuts while we're still swimming. What they're worried about is further swelling at the back of the throat. I mentioned to Bonnie and Pauline when the mask came off that I thought I was experiencing some mild asthma. After the docs spend a few minutes with me, down at the Handler's station, they're sure I'm feeling constriction in the throat due to the salt exposure swelling, not asthma. I realize I'm in semi-delirium at this point, but I could swear I hear the phrase "emergency tracheotomy" in the midst of their consultation. Bonnie jokes with them: "Forget about whether she can breathe or not. The tragedy will be if she can no longer talk!" They go back to their mother ship, asking to be apprised if I report that throat swelling becoming even tighter. My mouth is painful, but not a deal breaker. We swim on.

Good news is delivered to me by midday. We are some thirty hours in, and I'm on a feeding, taking a bit more time than we usually do, because of the slow intake of food and liquid. I ask Bonnie if we're getting in trouble, dragging east because I'm stopping for maybe ten to twelve minutes now, instead of six to seven, on the ninety-minute cycles. Bartlett pops out of his navigation cabin beaming like he just won the lottery. He says we are in a beautiful position, vis-à-vis the current. He's never seen it so favorable for us out here. He says if I need that extra time on feedings, now is the time to take advantage, in case the current changes direction later and we have to bust hard with very short feeding stops. When John's happy, we're all happy. And John is ecstatic.

This calls for some happy tunes. Israel "Iz" Kamakawiwo'ole's medley of "Somewhere over the Rainbow" mixed with "What a Wonderful World" takes my mind off my mouth. I sing it all the way through the afternoon, over and over again, Iz's heavenly voice soothing my innards and my mouth, as we cruise *onward!*

> Someday I'll wish upon a star
> Wake up where the clouds are far behind me

I imagine from a bird's-eye view, we are a steadily marching flotilla, northing mile by mile, hour by hour. *Voyager* is the epicenter, two arms of a swimmer off to her right by seven yards, two slim kayaks just adjacent and behind, several dolphinlike Divers plunging and darting around and under the swimmer in their reconnaissance scouting, the four mother ships flanking just behind and off to the side, two by two. We are in sync now. This is the teamwork, the dogged yet dependable progress we all worked so hard to achieve. Just as the swimmer's arms lift and glide under the surface in a reliable metronomic cadence, each Teammate cycles through performing his or her job with smooth, professional aplomb. We encounter no crises this day, Sunday, September 1.

Toward the end of the day, I can tell my mind is losing its crisp edge. At one point, I ask if we're going to make it as far as Playa del Carmen, thinking we're in Mexico. And when Bonnie and Pauline call me in to discuss when we're going to put on the jellyfish gear, I'm at first upset. I've lost track of time and was thinking that we had many hours until dark, but in fact it was five p.m. already. They tell me Angel will do some diving, but she is almost 100 percent sure we will be in less danger of the box tonight. I honestly can't imagine how that retainer is going to fit in my swollen mouth.

Sure enough, at six-thirty p.m., they signal me to start suiting up. Angel is zipping around under *Voyager,* popping up and speaking to Bonnie every few seconds. Bonnie gives me the best news I can imagine.

I will need to go full tilt with the suit, the gloves, the booties, the duct tape, but we can forgo the mask; instead, Angel will smear a blob of green Sting No More across my cheeks, lips, nose, neck. I call to Angel. She is still in the water, close to me. I ask her if she is absolutely certain I'll be safe without the mask. Torturous as wearing the mask will be, I have every reason for my fear of those animals, my memory still rife with the trauma of their stings. Angel quickly debriefs me on why, just twenty-four hours after needing full protection last night, we'll be at considerably less risk tonight. I don't like the greasy stuff all over my goggles and cap, but to remain free of the mask is a bountiful windfall, and I roll over onto my back for several deep sighs of relief. Suddenly, all this clothing seems only a minor burden, without having to suffer through the mask another night.

More good news. Heading into darkness, the wind quiets down. It's not glass but pretty darn close. And on each feeding I call up to Bartlett. With the mask, I had been nearly blind. I had no sight of *Voyager,* or Bonnie, or even the Kayakers. Only the red LED lights. Tonight I can see more, even through the gauze haze of the gel that has inevitably smeared over my goggles. And I see Bartlett's head peering out his window, right above the Handler's station. He gives me a big thumbs-up, that grin still beaming ear to ear. I really don't know where we are, but I do have the sense that we're heading in just the right direction.

The body seems to be enduring well, but the mind is losing ground. It seems several hours lumber by after twilight, but I can't dictate to my mind what I want it to focus on. I want to sing some simple marching songs. "When the Saints Go Marching In." But I drift far away, and Grace Slick keeps haunting me with:

> Go ask Alice
> When she's ten feet tall

I can't stop. Alice. Hookah-smoking caterpillars.

I can no longer concentrate. I forget where we are and what we're doing. It was nice and calm for a while, but now it's very bumpy. When I hear the whistle for a feeding, I can't seem to make it to the Handler's platform. I dog-paddle. Hard. But I can't get there. Then I put my head down and swim a few strokes of freestyle toward *Voyager.* Hard. But I'm still not there, and I hear Bonnie and Pauline and Lois Ann, with her southern accent, calling me to get over there. I feel I've entered Kafka's *Castle* world, where K. can never get his bearings, can never arrive at the castle's gate. I see all four of our Shark Divers are in around me. Is there a shark scare? When I do finally get close to my Handlers, there is a big wall of thick etched glass between me and them. I am mesmerized by the etching. I try to reach out and touch the slick glass, feel the contours of the etched design, but my hand slips through thin air. I see shapes that I think are faces, but they're distorted behind this glass structure. I hear them, but it's as if they are calling from a football field away. The chaos is upsetting. We are no longer in the rhythm of swimming with the usual cadence, the usual feeding stops with some welcome banter. I'm confused.

Bonnie yells. Her command voice snaps me back to reality, or semi-reality: "Diana, a storm is sweeping in."

I yell back, "I'm not getting out this time."

Bonnie: "We know. We've got it covered. The winds are picking up quickly. The Divers are all in with you. You guys are going to go off for a while, until we get through the worst of it. Just tread water. Swim some breaststroke if you need to keep warm. Niko has a compass. He'll give you a direction. All the boats are heading downwind of you now. You'll be okay. The guys can't touch you. But they have water if you need it. Hang in there. Do you understand?"

I do.

I am with the four Divers for what I am imagining is about five hours. I learn later it was only ninety minutes. I am hanging on by a thread. At times I start feathering with my hands and thus go under. My mouth is only a half inch above water and I am falling asleep. The Divers circle me and talk to me.

Niko: "Diana. Diana! Come on now. Look over here. Look at me."

It's pitch-black. I hear them around me, but I don't see anything. Not one face, even though they're right there, just a couple of feet to all sides of me. I am shivering now. My teeth are chattering.

Niko: "Diana, do you want to swim a few strokes, try to warm up?"

Me: "Yes."

Niko: "Can you see this green light?"

Niko has a six-inch vertical strand of a neon-green light. He holds it right in front of me and he kicks backward with his big fins, talking to me constantly as I swim my breaststroke–dolphin kick toward the light.

Niko: "That's it. Come on. You're doing great. Right toward the green light. You see the light, Diana? You warming up now?"

It's akin to hypnosis. The light. Niko's New York accent. The sensation of safety with the other three Divers around and behind me. I do warm up with even this minor movement. Several rotations of breaststroke and then stopping, feathering, more breaststroke, more vertical hanging, shivering. I ask where Bonnie is. I want Bonnie. I am childlike now. Then I look to my right and, plain as day, in the ebony dark, I see the Taj Mahal. The real Taj Mahal. It looms high and large and very close by, its columns and arches and domes enthralling. I ask Jason, next to me, if he sees it, too. He says he does. I just can't get back to swimming. I'm so taken with the Taj Mahal. It doesn't occur to me to wonder what it's doing out here in the Florida Straits. This is all the more enigmatic because I've never been to India, never had any fascination with the Taj Mahal. It's like waking up from a dream filled with people or places you've never given a conscious thought to.

Almost as if a stealth airboat slinking through the Everglades, *Voyager* suddenly appears to my left. I have a sensation of being in a bog, steam coming off the lily pads, tall reeds shooting up. There is quiet lapping of small waves onto *Voyager*'s pontoons, but I am thinking *Voyager* is a dock in the marshy mud. I'm worried alligators are on a silent prowl around us. Bonnie's voice snaps me out of it. She's talking to the Divers. The storm is over, and we're about to resume the mission. It takes me a bit to catch on to what we're doing. Bonnie coaxes me. I alternate freestyle with breaststroke for a while. When I lose track and mistakenly swim up behind *Voyager* and disappear under her two pontoons, coming dangerously close to being shredded by the rear engine blades, Bonnie puts a halt to the action. She is sterner than usual.

"Diana! Do you want to blow this? After all the work we've done, do you really want to sabotage it all now?"

She has my rapt attention.

"I don't know how. But you've got to use that strong mind of yours.

NOW. Get with it. Focus. Get a number in your head. Start counting. Don't let your mind wander until you hit that number. DO YOU
HEAR ME?!"

She has extricated some bubble of clarity still inside me. The mind is
a force, beyond what we know. I literally feel my will kick into gear. I
am immediately more awake. I raise both my fists toward her. I do hear
her. I have a number in mind, and I go after it.

We are back to doing what we do well. A couple of feedings go by.
I'm on a forty-five-minute feeding cycle now, needing calories to stay
warm. Bonnie will occasionally call me in even more often, to give me
a mental break. The perpetual bathing of the interior of the mouth
with salt water all these hours since taking the mask off has seemingly
assuaged the pain. I am eating and drinking pretty well, although the
stomach is queasy. I'm amazed to look at my arms on the feedings, and
underwater at my legs. They are swollen and puffy with salt inflation
and sun toxicity. My body is a foreign creature I don't recognize.

I'm not sure, but I keep seeing it. Right below me is the Yellow Brick
Road. Yes, that Yellow Brick Road. I don't say anything. I'm intrigued.
Then I see them. There are people walking the road. I'm squinting, trying to make them out. They're way down there. Finally, I see them. I do
a double take, because it's not Dorothy and the cast of characters that
should be skipping along the Yellow Brick Road. It's the Seven Dwarfs
trudging along with their little knapsacks. I watch them for a while.
Then I yell up to Bonnie: "Bonnie! Do you see the Yellow Brick Road
and the Seven Dwarfs right under me here?" She peers down where I'm
looking and yells back: "Yes, yes, I see them. And you know what's
great about them? They're going exactly where you're going. Just follow
them, okay?"

Well, I can't tell you how helpful they are. I follow them for what
seems like many hours. I try to remember each of their names. Time
flies by, watching them march animatedly down that winding road.
As I turn to the left to breathe, my right ear dips toward the ocean
floor and I can hear them, faintly, singing and whistling: "Heigh-ho,
heigh-ho, it's off to work we go."

Now it seems a distant memory, those dwarfs singing. I'm at a new
low. I am swimming but barely. I'm shivering while the arms are going

through their motions. Usually, I only feel cold while stopped. Even the output of stroking isn't now enough to stop my shivers. My pressure pushing the hands back is weak. I'm floundering. Bonnie calls me over. She tells me to lift my goggles up, to pull my cap off. This has never happened before. You try never to unseal the goggles, once the face tissue is swollen. You may never get them back on again. The only time we remove the goggles is to get on the mask or if they're leaking and I've got to switch them out. Or, gulp, there is one other reason I'm asked to remove my goggles. I am gripped with fear that I'm going to hear the same bad news I've heard four wretched times before: Our only landing point possible is the Bahamas. We have one hundred more hours to make land. It's over. . . .

But it's none of that.

Since I'm not doing well mentally, Bonnie has decided to give me a wake-up jolt of good news, way before she and Bartlett had planned on doing so.

Bonnie: "Diana. Can you hear me? Do you understand me?"

I nod yes. It's still inky black. I see her vague outline. That mirage wall of etched glass is still there. More important, I hear her.

Bonnie: "I have two important things to tell you. One, you are never going to have to put the jellyfish suit on again. Never."

That doesn't register. Does she mean the jellyfish won't be a problem at all our third night?

Bonnie sees I'm puzzled. She says, "We're not going into a third night. You'll never have to put the suit on again."

Whoa, whoa, whoa! Does she mean, if I can just keep these arms lifting and pressing, we are going to get there at some hour during the coming day? I realize my mind is working slowly, but is this what she means?

Yes, that's what she means.

I go onto my back for a cry. It doesn't matter how many hours lie in front of me. Bonnie is telling me it can't be as many as twenty-four now. I am calculating. I don't know what time it is but, at the most conservative estimate, she thinks we will finish before seven p.m. I am overjoyed. My goggles are still up on my forehead, tears are gently rolling down my cheeks.

Bonnie allows me that minute of jubilation but quickly reminds me there's still a long way to go. Much can happen between here and there, so we've got to bear down and get back to swimming with regular cadence, normal forward motion now.

As I start to get my cap and goggles ready, Bonnie says, "But there's something else."

Me: "Something bad?"

Bonnie: "Something very good. Look ahead. Toward the horizon, but just to the right there. Do you see?"

I lurch up a bit. The storm past, the surface is again flat and calm now. Though my vision is majorly impaired, I see a thin white filament where Bonnie is indicating. It's the first hint of the sunrise. I've been cold, and this means I will soon get to take the jellyfish stuff off and my body will feel the warmth of the sun's rays.

Me: "It's the sun!"

Bonnie's choked up. "No. It's better than the sun."

Pause. Long pause. I'm straining, looking. What could be better than the sun?

Bonnie: "Those are the lights of Key West."

Stunned silence. For thirty-five years I've envisioned those lights. For thirty-five years, I have refused to lose faith that one day I would really make it all the way across. Now the tears flow harder.

THIRTY-THREE

Never, Ever Give Up

No more songs. No more counting. No more tripping out on the universe. I want to spend all these last hours in a reverent state of awareness. I want to focus on what this journey has meant.

I start picturing each person who dived into this Dream with me. The list is so darn long. Many who helped with training but never came to Cuba, others who beat the pavement for me to raise funds, friends and strangers alike who found the endeavor inspiring and helped in myriad small and large ways. As I keep stroking, I take each of their faces, one at a time, and think about them. Frontline Teammates who served with great gusto but aren't here this time—they will be with me on that beach, as deeply in my heart as the forty-four who are out here now. Each face appears in front of me as if projected onto the lenses of my goggles. I am loosely counting and realizing there must be a mini-mum two hundred of these good people. It takes a village, indeed.

The dark continues for many more hours than I had imagined were left. I am drifting in and out of hallucinations these early-morning hours of Monday, September 2. The paddlers, each shift of two, are now yelling out at me to go "LEFT, LEFT, LEFT!" I am drifting far out to the right of *Voyager,* sometimes as many as a hundred yards away from the boat. The Handlers, Divers, and Kayakers are frustrated at my being so far from the boat, for safety reasons. But it's also simple logic that I am swimming way over to the east and then struggling to swim way back over to the west, time and time again, instead of staying on top of the streamer and heading north, toward our destination. Buco, usually a mild-mannered guy, has a talk with me on one of the feedings.

"Diana, you're going to wind up swimming a lot less, even a couple of miles less, if you'd just stay over at the streamer, instead of drifting way off to the right."

"I realize that, Buco. If I could stay on the streamer, I would."

Sometimes I just can't understand why the paddlers are so insistent on yelling "LEFT!" What's the urgency? At some moments, I think the Cuba Swim is over and we're out there doing something else. Why are they pushing me so vehemently?

Buco decides to go hard-core. He parks his kayak inches from my body on the right side. I brush his boat with my right hand a couple of times and lift my eyes to give him a glare. When I whap my hand into the blade of his paddle, I'm hopping mad. We have worked diligently in practice to make sure the paddlers never contact my hand with their blades. Buco knows he's incurred my wrath, but he doesn't care. Hours of their yelling "LEFT!" has not kept me from zigzagging far right, back left, far right, back left again. Buco has permission from Bonnie to stop me cold. I was fuming, but that was the end of the zigzagging.

The ultramarathon lesson relearned. Just when you think you're coasting, you sink into yet another valley. It is a very long night. I am in and out of lucidity, mostly out. Those etched-glass walls pop up between me and my Handlers. Eating is revolting now. Bonnie, Pauline, and Lois Ann urge me to take down even tiny bites of banana, protein bar, honey sandwich. I gag at each attempt to swallow solids. We are on to liquids only. They shake a dose of protein powder and electrolytes into water so at least some nutrients are serving to keep up my strength.

The valley is deep, and I am crawling along its underbelly. I am wrestling in my own mind. Where am I? Who am I? Oh, yes. Come on. Dig down. Hold on. And then, honestly not even remembering that night turns to day, dawn announces itself.

Wisps of light glance off the horizon off to my right. An hour later, the sun is gathering its force again. And so am I. My focus sharpens. My mood lightens. I don't dare ask how long. I don't even look forward. The body language of the crew on *Voyager* doesn't signal excitement. I assume we're ready to take off the jellyfish suit, gloves, and booties, but Bonnie says Angel is nervous about the outer reef, which we will hit midmorning. One point of relief is we will be crossing the outer reef in broad daylight. At night, swordfish do their hunting at the reef and that would be a swimmer's potential hell, to understate it. The swordfish dash in, clocking their deadly blades left and right, right and left, through schools of smaller fish. Then they circle back around to feed on the bloody mess. We won't, thankfully, encounter swordfish this morning, yet they want me to continue on with the jellyfish gear. I'm not arguing.

Suddenly, their black wet suits and dark fins bold against the intense blue backdrop, all four Shark Divers and Angel are gliding around me, under me.

"Bonnie, are there sharks?"

Bonnie: "No, we're approaching the outer reef. They're scouting for sharks, swordfish, and jellyfish. Just keep swimming. But keep close to the boat, okay? This is not a gimme yet. We have several hours to go."

"Okay." I'm with that, all the way. Not yet time for jubilation. Head down. Left arm, right arm.

A couple of hours later, I pause and start tugging on the duct tape at my wrists. Bonnie yells: "Wait a minute. WAIT! What are you doing?"

"We must be past the reef now, right? Angel said I could take everything off once we cleared the reef."

Bonnie: "No, she never said that."

I usually follow Bonnie's orders to the letter, but I can't fathom why I need the gear any longer, so I keep yanking at it, stripping down to my suit.

Bonnie calls Angel by radio on her mother ship. Angel's upset. She wants me to put that gear back on right away. It could be a critical mistake, but I just can't take it anymore. I want to swim free. I had in my mind the reward of stripping off the suit right after sunrise. The sun is soaring high now. I defy Angel. And Bonnie. Stupid. Why do I have an expert such as Angel if I'm not going to follow her instructions?

Still no stirring on the boat. I am constantly looking for the scurrying to begin. When I see the crew packing up bags, stowing gear, I'll know we're finally approaching land. This is the scene I long for at the end of every training swim. But they're not even looking forward. Evidently, there are "miles to go before we sleep."

John Bartlett's work is not done, either. He told us many times over the years that we would absolutely have to finish this swim up the Keys somewhere, that the pull of the Gulf Stream would never allow a swimmer to get right into Key West. But, just as I've been in semi-shock to finally be coming into any shore at all, he's been bowled over to be taking us directly toward the southernmost point in the United States, our treasured outpost. But the outgoing tide has been tricky to navigate these last few hours. At one point, he's not happy that we are going to be swept to the north and east, maybe land at Sugarloaf Key. The entire Team hears John working on the radio, getting tide and current information from local marine sources. He also wants to avoid hitting shore up the Keys where I might be forced to wade through the thick, nasty mangrove swamps. It would be tough, after swimming all this time, to find the balance to negotiate through the dense thickets of the tangled mangrove roots. He's determined to figure it out. He brings us out in an arc to get a better angle at the turning of the tide. He's done it. We are going right for Smathers Beach, dead center of the beautiful island of Key West.

I see a cruise ship off to my left and am told they made a special wide circle off their normal route, to save us from their wake. The upwelling, all that deep ocean and sea life that stirs up from way below a large hull, carries jellies and cold water and all kinds of things we don't want to run into at this point. Yet literally one minute after I am told about the kindness of the ship's captain changing his route, *bam!*, I am shocked to feel a whole-body stinging. It's not box, but I get chills head to toe when a rash of small buzzing stings rip all over me. I don't stop, but I emote. "OOOWWWW!"

We are evidently passing through thousands and thousands of moon jellies. One of the Shark Divers, his good intentions being to sweep some of them into his net right in front of me, in fact breaks up their bodies, and their stingers fire in a cloud that engulfs me. Angel quickly instructs him not to sweep any more. She even scoops up a box jelly-fish, in broad daylight! I am slightly freaked out. I'm still not looking ahead. Head still down. Bonnie whistles, and I stop to look up at her. She points behind me. I turn, and there is a big yacht looming almost directly above my head. It's not in our fleet; it's too big. I'm not sure. But then I see. It's Tim, his dreadlocks clear against the blue sky. And it's Nina, her smile as wide as the Grand Canyon. They're crying. And that gets me crying. None of us has words. I blow them kisses. They blow back. I also see a couple of helicopters swarming above. And boats left and right, accompanying us. A drone zooms by.

In a sheer moment of spontaneity, I ask Bonnie to bring our other four boats in close. I want to talk to everybody. The Divers and Angel are in the water with me, *Voyager* is very close by, and now the rest of the flotilla present in a semicircle so they can hear me. I cry like a baby. I want to tell them something, but my throat is clenched with emotion. When I can talk, I'm not sure they can understand me; the cuts inside my mouth are slurring my speech.

"I guess I'm going to stumble up onto that beach sometime soon. And I guess some people are going to take my picture. But never forget that *we* did this *together.* *We* made history *together.* I will never forget how much you all sacrificed, that you guys never stopped believing. I am so proud of you, my Team."

Before we swim toward shore, the flotilla still in semicircle formation, Candace stands tall, arms open wide, a maidenhead on the bow of her ship, and she sings to me, and to the world, just as we had planned it thirty-five long years ago:

> When you wish upon a star
> Your dreams come true.

I lie back and take in the pleasure of Candace's melodic voice, content to my inner core. I reached for the stars, and my dream has come true.

I turn toward the shore and actually see the outline of palm trees now. It won't be long. Maybe two thousand strokes. This all escalates from surreal to überreal. I go back to swimming. Could it be that even more than exuberance at the prospect of really walking up onto that elusive shore, I am savoring these last few strokes, holding dear what will be the end of this magnificent, almost mythical saga?

I notice that Candace is now down on the Handler's platform. She and Bonnie hug. They are crying. Now Pauline and Bonnie hug and cry. And the crew is scurrying around now.

Bonnie leaves the Handler's platform, and I see her up on the deck, talking on the radio. She's telling the various media outlets where we are, how we're doing. Pauline and Johnberry are down on the platform, just the way we had passed countless hours of Key West training, and they are waving me in to the left.

This feels like the magical ending to a lifelong fairy tale. Are we really about to touch the seemingly impossible, unreachable Other Shore?

I have no perspective that there are thousands of people on Smathers Beach. As I swim into shallow waters, the rippled sand less than a yard beneath me, my underwater seascape is pairs of legs everywhere. People have waded out to greet me. My Team has jumped off the boats in advance, and they now form two human walls, to make sure nobody touches me with even an innocent brush of a shoulder or a finger until I am, as the rule states, "where no more sea water lies beyond." The clock won't stop until I stand on true terra firma, not even ankles or toes still below water.

When the water is less than two feet deep, I try to stand. My sea legs wobble and collapse. I try to rise again but again fall to my knees in the shallows. I hear Johnberry yell to me: "Just swim, Diana, keep swimming up!"

I can't really take proper strokes in such shallow surf, but I crab my way another thirty or so pulls. I see the sets of legs on either side, my human barricade. My path between the two walls is clear. Now there are only inches of water, so I try again to stand. I'm unsteady. I'm awkward. I almost topple, but I take a couple of staggered steps and now I'm walking, slowly but surely. I know some of the faces left and right. Teammates and friends, arms locked, legs braced hard, yelling, "DON'T TOUCH HER! STAY BACK! SHE'LL BE DISQUALIFIED IF ANYBODY TOUCHES HER! STAY BACK!"

Bonnie appears seemingly from thin air in front of me. She is walking backward, her arms wide and outstretched, signaling me to make a beeline toward her. I hear the voices. They are screaming. I take a look around. Many of them are crying. I pull off my cap and goggles, to see and hear better. It's a high like none I've ever known.

There's Candace, crying. And Tim. Nina is crying. Pauline, too.

Bonnie is inching backward, looking down to know when we cross the "no more sea water" line. The crowd is pressing in closer now, their collective fervor creating a searing heat. Bonnie and I are inching a victory dance, she backward, me forward. Then she signals me into her arms. We have reached dry land. At long last, my beautiful Dream is realized.

Labor Day, September 2, 2013.

110.86 miles.

Fifty-two hours, fifty-four minutes, eighteen seconds.

THIRTY-FOUR

One Wild and Precious Life

The walk up onto that other shore wasn't so very long ago. I am still charged with the moment. The faces, thousands of them, are coming in and out of view as I take these halting steps up out of the sea and onto dry land. The crowd's passion ignites the scene to a blistering temperature, many of them weeping openly, the heat coming more from their jubilation than the actual afternoon sun. I am transfixed on Bonnie's open arms. She and I are locked, steps and eyes in tandem, just the way we had traversed the entire journey. Candace and Tim are only inches away, on either side of me. I flash on sparks of blue, the many Xtreme Dream T-shirts peppered throughout the chaos, Teammates and strangers alike electrified by the ending we've all wanted for this story. I take in the swirl of voices, cheering wildly. I make eye contact, one by one, with my trusted crew. My pride erupts through my chest and radiates out into the universe.

For thirty-five years, I always had some heroic oration in mind for the beach at the end of this grand quest. I had rehearsed a number of poetic phrases through the years. But that's not the way it's playing out. Swimming in those last few minutes, I am stunned. The moment sweeps me up and folds me into its intensity, and I have no words at all. Just emotions. Exploding emotions. And then, from some unconscious well of truth, words do flow. They speak the messages I authentically carried with me all the way across, all the way through the years of the endeavor:

"One: Never, ever give up.

"Two: You're never too old to chase your dreams.

"Three: It looks a solitary sport, but it's a Team."

For me, that moment on Smathers Beach was not a sports moment. It was a life moment. My feet touching that sand was my version of touching a star. I chased this possibly impossible Dream to demand the fiercest and boldest me to live large, and there I stood, the body ready to drop but the spirit unquestionably fierce and bold.

I faded by that last word, "Team." And the only regret I harbored for a couple of months afterward was not having the strength or the presence of mind to turn around to embrace my entire Team. John Bartlett, Angel, Dee, Pauline, John Berry, Buco, Don McCumber, Niko. I wished I had had the wherewithal to turn back toward them, to celebrate with them in our hour of glory. But they have told me since, all of them, that the "speech" I gave them a couple of hours from shore was our special time. My moment to thank them was as it should be, out at sea.

As Bonnie was celebrating with them all, she found Niko, our young Shark Captain. "Niko, you started this trip a boy and you finished it a man." How will I ever thank those Divers, putting my life ahead of theirs, to be in with me those two long nights, positioning themselves between me and the predators below?

I was dazed, physically, on the beach. There was very little left. Could I have gone another ten hours? Would I have made it through another night, if necessary? We'll never know.

I learned later that the press had set up a finish area down the beach a couple of hundred yards. They had mounted a platform for the video camera tripods, even created a decorative lane of buoys for me to swim up the middle and walk safely untouched to the media center. Our Ops Chief, John Berry, was asked later why I hadn't been guided right to their nicely arranged spot.

"I guess we figured, after she just swam fifty-three continuous hours, she would get to any point on shore the best she could, and the crowd could walk a few yards to get to her."

My heart was bursting with both joy and relief, to stand on solid sand, after not only those fifty-three hours but the hundreds of tough hours it took to arrive at the Dream's destination. In the end, it was the journey that inspired. Had the journey not been extended over thirty-five years, had we not suffered through four failures and risen to cutting-edge solutions, had I not almost died from the box stings, had these special people not traveled this journey with me, this final scene on Smathers Beach wouldn't have presented itself as the Homeric journey's end it became to me, my Team, and the public at large. So for that journey-versus-destination debate, to my mind it's all about the journey. Yes, I remember the end and the feeling of the walk up that beach still sparks euphoria. But the journey lives somewhere even deeper than memory.

I was propped on a stretcher under a palm tree for a little bit, an IV inserted into a vein, to at least share a few minutes with the good people who had waited for our arrival. Several of them told me that it was a visceral moment when they could first get a visual sighting of *Voyager,* out at the horizon. It sounded much the way mankind first discovered the Earth is round, when the tip-top of a mast would appear out at sea, not the entire ship, and as more of the ship would be revealed, top to bottom, we knew the ship was coming up over a curve, instead of appearing whole and very small from across a flat distance, then larger and larger as it came closer. These fans told me they'd been watching like hawks, with binoculars, and when the tiny speck of *Voyager's* top deck came into view, their hearts soared. It made me cry, that image of our boat, still far out at sea, having crossed so many miles of treacherous ocean and then within view, a symbol of hope and the ultimate victory.

I spent the next several hours in the Key West hospital, having routine tests of heart and brain, letting an IV drip restore hydration and calories. The hospital personnel could see how much discomfort the chopped tissue on the inside of my mouth was causing me but couldn't do much about it. The good news, they said, was that interior mouth tissue heals very quickly. It would be ten days before I could eat solid food. Candace, Tim, and Nina came to visit me. The rest of the Team was stuck processing through Customs. Mark sent word from St. Maarten: *"FUCKING AWESOME!"*

Bonnie stayed with me the whole time. Before this last go, we got matching tattoos, which read *"ishin denshin,"* meaning in Japanese "one heart, one mind." The Cuba Swim was an epic endeavor in large part due to our epic friendship. I was willing to ink myself permanently with *"ishin denshin"* because taking this expedition of life with my friend Bonnie made it one, noble journey. We have never been, never will be, Bonnie and I, timid souls. As Roosevelt said it, we "dared greatly," our bond forever sealed by courage and character..

I think it was about midnight when I was released from the hospital. After a few fitful hours of sleep, my mouth in agony, I awoke to hear the local weather report. For the first time in four years, *I didn't give a damn* what the forecast was portending.

There was an empty field across from the cottage, and when I walked outside just after daybreak, it looked like a war zone of correspondents over there. It had rained heavily just before dawn, so they had all pitched tents to cover their cameras; I beheld a semicircle of ABC, NBC, CBS, ESPN, FOX, foreign outlets, et al. Hillary Clinton wrote, "Feels like I swim with sharks, but you actually did it!" Hillary also sent me a handwritten note, signed "Onward!" President Obama tweeted: "Congratulations @DianaNyad. Never give up on your dreams."

The whole Team gathered at a packed press conference around ten a.m. I wore my "Happy" T-shirt. I couldn't express it any more clearly. This was the first moment we shared our triumph all together and our joy pressed back the walls of the room.

The media, representing their viewers and listeners and readers, also understood that this was not a sporting event. The public understood every fiber of the story. They tuned in for the implicit underlying life credos that kept inspiring me to chase this Dream for so very long. They weren't detached from an athlete who did something so foreign and extreme that they could only applaud her, not relate to her; they were drawn toward a human being who demonstrated out loud to them that you can live out your dreams if you refuse to ever, ever give up. And for all this time afterward, I hear the universal response to our journey, that we the human race share the trait of tenacity, that we get knocked down, then we stand up and try again. They are moved to have witnessed an individual who was knocked down over and over again but who endured the defeats and eventually won. If I had bathed in the glorious power of the human spirit way out at sea, I have been awash in it since back on solid ground as well.

I was criticized and questioned for a couple of days by a band of marathon swimmers, their incredulity piqued, I guess, at someone actually achieving this supposedly unachievable feat. They suggested I must have secretly exited the water and slept on the boat for hours at a time. John Bartlett hosted a long conference call with a representative group of them, citing from his computer GPS charts the tracking of literally every quarter mile of the journey, how fast the current was traveling in what direction, plus how fast my swimming speed calculated at each quarter mile. I posted all the data evidence online, along with the minute-by-minute logs from the two independent observers. And then I locked those GPS trackers in a bank vault, to ensure that the history will survive long after I and the forty-four who accompanied me and bore witness to the swim are gone. John's is an impressive mind, and his empirical proof of our course satisfied all but a couple of what they call online "haters." (There are still those who don't believe Neil Armstrong walked on the moon.) There is no keeping a secret among forty-four people. This swim was a noble quest and a matter of indisputable ethics to each one of us. We sleep easily, consciences clear that I swam across fair and square, shore to shore.

Every day since the Cuba Swim, at least one person has asked me, "What's next? What are you going to swim next? The Pacific Ocean?" I know what they mean. It was exciting to follow that computer tracker from Cuba to Florida, in real time. Thousands of people wrote to tell me about their experiences of checking the tracker before bed, then waking up and running to the computer, thrilled to see that we were still making progress. Then they'd go to work, come home, sleep another night, check the tracker again, and there I was, still swimming toward land. Left arm. Right arm. Never, ever give up. I share that same thirst to live that drama again. I do.

It's perhaps odd for me to even broach that thinking, given that I am still in the throes of something kindred to minor post-traumatic stress syndrome. I shudder every time I step into a hot shower, and I mutter to myself, "I'll never have to be cold again." I wake up some nights screaming, "I'm on fire! Bonnie, help me!," with the flashback to the box jellyfish terror. I am relieved never again to suffer those eternal hours, yet I am sad to say good-bye forever to feeling so utterly alive, to my literal immersion in that extreme experience. People remark to me all the time that nothing for me will be that tough to endure, which is cause for both solace and longing. In reading explorer Robert Falcon Scott's famous diaries from his fatal excursion in Antarctica, where his entire expedition perished, I was struck that the day he died, Scott wrote, "How much better has it been than lounging in too great comfort at home."

Post-Cuba, I must find that challenge of the spirit in other arenas. I can't summon another swimming saga that sensational. No other swim could possibly stir my soul as Cuba did. It's done. Like most people, I love a great story. In this case, I got to live one. You could say this was "my time." But it was "my time" throughout the odyssey, not just the final victory steps. It is "our time" for all of us. Our lives in total are "our time" to engage. Our wild and precious time.

I find myself seizing the life force of the Expedition and that was the goal. When I turned sixty, I was stunned silent by the clock's spinning hands because I wasn't engaged. I was wasting time on futile regrets from the past and vapid fantasies for the future. The Cuba Swim was to be a path toward passion. Time whisking by doesn't freak me out anymore. People are always saying they blink and can't fathom it's already July, or Thanksgiving, or Monday. Well, I can believe it. Now that I'm back to every day "not a fingernail better," well, when you're living with that kind of vigor, there's no time for either regrets or agonizing over the ticking of the clock. I walk around these days on a natural high, still full tilt, every waking moment.

Just six weeks after Cuba, mid-October 2013, I did a forty-eight-hour swim in a pool in Herald Square in New York City, under the shadow of the Empire State Building. Frankly, I wasn't fully recovered from Cuba, but it was a fund-raiser for the victims of Hurricane Sandy, a year after the storm ravaged many New York neighborhoods and thousands were still homeless. Firefighters, rescue workers, Sandy victims, even a dog that survived the storm swam in the lane next to me, fifteen minutes at a time. This is the only extreme swimming I will do in the

future, charity fund-raisers, although I won't forgo the body-mind vir-
tues of regular swimming as I did after retiring the first time around.
I'll always swim. I'll always be a swimmer.

Bonnie and I are planning a walk across America, Pacific to Atlantic,
and we're going to get a million people to walk with us. The point isn't
a record of any kind. Many people have walked farther. The Walk is a
mission of social change, a movement to reverse the epidemic of obesity
and sedentary lifestyles in our country, and the egregious cases of childhood diabetes and rampant heart disease that lack of movement causes.
On the personal end, we can't wait to walk all the way across this magnificent nation of ours. Much of the Xtreme Dream Team will join us.

I sit here in my Los Angeles office, writing this memoir, the photograph of the man staring at the sea with the Neruda poem "Ode to
Salt" etched at the bottom now moved from Key West to my home.
A sensory connection to the infinitude of the sea flows through my
veins. That's forever. A muralist has painted scenes of Cuba, the Havana
streets, the ocean, replete with my very own *Voyager,* crew silhouetted
aboard, on the walls of one of my rooms. And the Cuban and American
flags fly side by side on my front lawn. An iconic photograph of Moham-
med Ali in a boxing pose underwater hangs on my office wall, a gift
from Mark Sollinger, because he saw in me a fighter who never gives in.
On my desk is a book made for me by my dear Teammates John and
Pauline Berry, called "The Leap." They took a snapshot of me leaping
off *Voyager*'s platform every time we headed out for a training swim, in
different bathing suits, different seas. Dozens of leaps. Real leaps. Leaps
of faith. The book, and my friendship with John and Pauline, runs deep.
The Berrys and Dee also gave me a beautiful painting of *Voyager* at sunset, the artist a Cuban, which hangs right above my computer and has
served as muse throughout this writing.

On that same wall is Candace's Cuban FAR license plate, her phrase
of faith, *"not so far,"* reminding me every day of the power of the human
spirit.

Tim's "little bit of home video" turned into an award-winning Show-
time documentary, *The Other Shore.* How proud I am of my Tim. I wear
a necklace from Nina, an antique map of Cuba hand-painted on the
face.

My life has been a rocket ship ever since that stumble up onto

Smathers Beach. I am humbled by all the honors that have come my way, but the highlight may have come on the one-year anniversary, on Labor Day weekend 2014. Our Team was invited to Havana but I didn't in my wildest imagination expect what was bestowed upon us. Our Team entered a grand official government building, the white marble floor the expanse of half a football field. We stood side by side, shoulder to shoulder. Facing us, about thirty feet away, was a line of Cuban dignitaries. The vice president of cultural affairs, the minister of sport, our great friend Commodore Escrich, and a general who was high in command during the revolution with Castro, Camilo, and Che. The great Cuban sports champions formed another line. I had admired them—the heavyweight champion of the world Félix Savón and the others—for decades. A military squad marched down the middle, presenting the Cuban and American flags side by side, the first time they had flown together in an official building in Cuba for thirty years. They played the Cuban national anthem. We stood still and respectful. Then they played "The Star-Spangled Banner"—again the first time our anthem had been played there in thirty years. I don't usually cry when I hear our national anthem. But this day I wept. I glanced at Bonnie to my right, Candace next to her, then Dee, and Angel and Johnberry and Pauline and Kathy Loretta and Maya Marchant and down our line. Every single one of us, hands over hearts, was weeping openly. The emotions escalated yet higher when we saw the Cubans crying, too. They saw how deeply honored we were. The politicians' speeches were warm and sincere, not dry protocol. And none of them used the words "woman" or "sixty-four-year-old" or even "athlete." Their recognition was, as they put it, for the "potential of all humankind." They understood that my life message was global: Whatever your Other Shore is, whatever you must do, whatever inspires you, you will find a way to get there.

And, of course, there was the human connection between our two countries. They rendered me that afternoon the first American since the embargo to receive the Cuban Sports Medal of Honor. I accepted on behalf of the Team, and we were all overjoyed. I slept as would a ten-year-old that night, with the beautiful medal pinned to my pajamas, waking Bonnie up several times, "Look! It's the Cuban Sports Medal of Honor!"

It was surreal to be at the Hotel Acuario again, to go with the Team to the starting rocks at Marina Hemingway. I wasn't wound up with fear and adrenaline this time, and that was bizarre. I'm of course not going to go my whole life fixated every day on the memories of the Cuba Swim, but that weekend in Havana, a precise year later, took me back, hour by hour, to just where we were the year before. I'd glance at my watch while we were dancing salsa in the picturesque, cobblestoned Plaza Vieja and, seeing that it was one a.m. on Sunday morning, I would flash back to one a.m. the Sunday morning of 2013, September 1. I would remember the heavy waves of that night, the difficulty of the mask. I stood for a long time with Bonnie and stared out at the northern horizon, our hearts teeming with contentment. Thank you, my dear friend. I never could have made it without you. *Ishin denshin.*

Candace and I also embraced a long time there on the Havana shore, where we had stood together before all five crossings, each time true to the hope of one day making it all the way. What a special journey this has been for me and Candace. A veritable lifetime of shared adventure and fulfillment.

Dee came to me in a private moment. Our resident hippie succinctly summed the entire experience up: "So cool." So Dee.

Maybe the same way Martina Navratilova now walks onto the grass at Wimbledon, the way she knelt and plucked a tuft of that grass when she left her champion playing days behind, I gazed out at my version of Wimbledon's Centre Court, the ocean wilderness between Cuba and Florida. I was unutterably happy to be a champion ocean swimmer, for this particular, magnificent ocean to be my place of garnering wisdom, of friendship, the humility of failure, and the majesty of triumph.

The sea has been the magical and dramatic subject of literature and art throughout history. To be part of that history brings me nothing short of sublime honor.

We returned to Key West the next day for our Labor Day celebration. Again, I was intensely aware of the time, day and night, each hour taking me back, right up to two p.m. on Labor Day, the time I emerged from the sea. The good citizens and officials of the city celebrated us at the exact finish point at Smathers Beach. They had made a handsome and regal bronze plaque that is now installed in the concrete at that spot, commemorating our achievement. The plaque reads:

DIANA NYAD COMPLETES HISTORIC SWIM

Diana Nyad came ashore at this point on Smathers Beach on September 2, 2013, having swum 110.86 miles nonstop from Havana to Key West, the first to achieve this epic crossing without a shark cage. Successful on her fifth try (52 hours, 54 minutes), Diana first attempted the feat in 1978. Thousands on this spot and millions worldwide took inspiration from the 64-year-old's first words upon realizing her lifelong dream: "Never, Ever, Give Up."

It was a heady time, being with the Team where we all stood, exhausted and elated, only a year before. I walked alone down to the water's edge and took a moment to stare out at the horizon and talk to my mom. "Remember all those years ago when you pointed toward Cuba, Mom, and told me 'It's so close you could almost swim there'? Oh, how I wish I could tell you today, 'Somebody actually has.' "

Emotions flowed hard when I later heard the news of the Cuban-U.S. rapprochement from President Obama and Raúl Castro. I am thrilled for the Cuban people and hopeful for a bright future for them. I'm happy for both our countries, true neighbors after all. And I am proud to think our Cuba Swim was even a small gesture toward that long-awaited reconciliation.

The one heartbreak suffered since the swim has been the loss of our genius, John Bartlett. Only sixty-six, John died of heart failure three months later. He had told me that the challenge and the victory were highlights of his life. Knowing John has certainly been a highlight of mine. I will forever keep the note John wrote me just a few weeks before he died. I've stowed it in the bank vault with his GPS trackers. That's how much it means to me.

Dear Diana,

Still thinking of you constantly.

People I know are asking me what it was like to be part of such an historic event.

This is my answer: It was simply the observance of someone's depth of character, applied dedication, perseverance in the actual field, applied skill, and dogged willpower to achieve one's stated goal, out-matching all the press releases, preparation talks, expectations.

There's that cliché, something about walking and talking. Isn't it the walk that it's all about? It is having seen, and to have been part of an incredible "Walk" by an incredible person, that is the source of my emotion.

Standing by to serve any mission you lead.

John

Rest in peace, our intrepid Navigator.

John and I going over navigation charts.

What I've truly been living, above and beyond these wonderful occasions and shared acclaim with my Team, is my inner voice, deeply satisfied for not giving up. I am reminded every single day of the training, of the failures, of the unrelenting perseverance. Every time I blink and see the clock read three a.m., I sigh with the pride that I never once chose to sleep in. I got up for those twelve-hour swims. I never once let a twelve-hour swim be enough at eleven hours, fifty-nine minutes. I came home from those dashed attempts and quietly went about putting it all together again. I've been living out loud the Henry David Thoreau saying: "What you get by achieving your goals is not as important as what you become by achieving your goals."

The quest of the Cuba Swim squared up my value system. It ushered me down a grueling path toward becoming a person I can truly admire. I am not defined by transient fame, or by childhood sexual abuse, or by world records. I don't wake up each morning a woman, a senior citizen, a lesbian, a Democrat, a human rights advocate, an atheist, a pacifist, an animal lover, an environmentalist. I may be all of these things, although above all I'm just a person who cherishes a bold journey. A person who refuses to let this one wild and precious life slip quietly by.

Credit Due

I usually glaze over when I read an author's thanks to their editors, the same way I tune out when an actor thanks their team of agents at the Oscars. But now that I've spent two years working with talented, dedicated, caring editors and agents on this book, it is abundantly clear to me that these acknowledgments are not rote obligations. These thanks derive from utter and profound sincerity.

Just as the marathon swimmer appears the solitary figure, suffering and striving and arriving at the shore all alone, yet could never have achieved her destination without her team, my name appears alone on the jacket of this memoir, yet a brilliant team dived in with all their layers of expertise to make this book a labor of love that has come to make all of us gush with pride.

A number of publishers were interested in my life story. But after all the meetings at a swank conference table in a swank office in New York, there was one editor who proved to be above and beyond. The One. Jordan Pavlin, longtime esteemed editor at Knopf, pursued the book with such focus and respect and unbridled enthusiasm that I was instantly charmed. Through the months of the writing, Jordan was at first laissez-faire, giving me free rein, and then with the crucial final draft she rolled up her experienced shirtsleeves and weighed in with such enlightened perspective that I thrilled to our conversations. You gave me the opportunity of a dazzlingly rich experience, Jordan, and then you deftly steered me toward the most powerful storytelling I am capable of. How will I ever properly thank you?

Knopf is pure class. To stand in their lobby, glorious books reaching two stories high in grand display, knowing that my own book would be honored with the Knopf stature, the iconic Borzoi dog imprinted on the spine, made me swoon. From the senior management to the photo and marketing and sales and art departments, they are the cream of the publishing world, in love, all of them, with books, and all of them highly impressive individuals. As we would progress through our stages—master editor Maria Massey at the helm—they would express what a joy it was to work on this particular book. Believe me, the privilege was all mine.

My lifelong special friend Candace Lyle Hogan, a writer and masterly editor in her own right, does not work for Knopf, but came to be called by Jordan "our secret weapon." After I finished the first draft, Candace put her exceptional brain into the critical thinking of what a memoir truly is, what this memoir should be. We had dozens of philosophical conversations. She pored over literally every word. And her indispensable counsel was to make sure all the stories came from a place that "sits low" within. If this book is a tribute to perseverance, an homage to never, ever giving up until we somehow find a way to our respective other shores, it is Candace I can thank for guiding me to pursue that "sit low" facet of my story throughout. The gratitude I harbor for you, Candace, for the commitment of your vast range of capabilities to this book, runs deeper than I can manage to express.

My other best friend Bonnie was my Head Handler on the Cuba Swim, my lifeline. But Bonnie is also a big-time reader. And she read this book, cover to cover, four times over the period of writing. Just as Bonnie had the right instincts for me out on the ocean, her reactions to specific stories, whole chapters, even one word here and there, seemed to always bear out as true. The book is all the better, Bonnie, for your reading and speaking your truth with each draft. Bonnie also delivered crucial reportage from the epicenter of the navigation boat. She never left her station for the fifty-three hours I was swimming so I relied on Bonnie to fill me in on just what was happening from her Handler perch, and from Bartlett the Navigator, Niko the Shark Diver, Angel the jellyfish expert, all the other central posts.

My literary agent and longtime friend Amy Rennert expertly guided me through the business aspects of signing, writing, and publishing. And then Amy gave more. She was constantly available and eager to discuss the big picture of the story arc as well as the minutia of specific phrases. It was a pleasure, Amy. Thank you for your buoying, supportive spirit every step of the way.

Simon Green at Creative Artists Agency, you threw yourself into this project, and I so appreciate your fire in helping me land the best opportunity to tell my story. And while I mention CAA, I must tell you, Peter Jacobs, that I've never been represented in all my career with the respect that you give me. It means the world.

Speaking of respect, my dear friends and colleagues Pam Derderian and Nancy Becker threw their hearts and souls into my endeavor, my life, with integrity and with high-minded inspiration. Ours is a mutual comradeship that I hold in utter regard.

The photos of a memoir are, I daresay, as significant as the written pages themselves. Along with Knopf's skilled photo editors, I had the great fortune of working with a friend, Pam Singleton, on all the wonderful images you see here. It took Pam and me three months to ferret out, select, format, bring to correct resolution the entire series and I am so deeply appreciative to you, Pam, for your willingness to strive for what we both envisioned as the perfect storytelling magic to come alive and jump off the pages and into the reader's imagination. And thanks again to Candace and to her colleague Kathleen Morgan for slaving over the arduous process of photo permissions.

The image on the back of the jacket has been generously donated by talented visionary photographer Andrea Mead Cross and her business/life partner, Kelley Kwiatkowski. Andrea and Kelley, I adore this photo and I admire the spirit with which you conduct your lives.

As is usually the case for authors, it was difficult for me to let go of working on this book. Yet, because of the extraordinary contributions of all these gifted friends and colleagues, I stepped away on the last deadline day the same way I walked off the Key West beach after swimming all the way from Cuba: bursting with pride that I and my team refused to give any less than our best selves to what we all believed to be a noble and worthy journey, the finished book our final destination.

Notes from the Author

I have regretted more than once not keeping a journal over the years. Then I came to writing this memoir in my mid-sixties, and the time spent delving back into those decades of living this charmed life have served to fill in the pages of that lifelong journal.

Naturally, I hope *Find a Way* comes to be a story of inspiration to many of you readers. But even if the writing had been a private exercise, no readers to ever set their eyes on it, I can tell you that it was a privileged and enlightening immersion for me, to sit down and write out just about everything and everyone I could ever remember. The analogy is again similar to the Cuba Swim. I had said all along that, even if the five closest people in my life were the only ones to greet me on that Florida beach, the journey was entirely worth taking.

Eighty percent of what I wrote isn't in the book, but the pursuit of recalling a lifetime of experiences proved to be one of the most illuminating things I've ever done. Perspective of what was in the end important surfaced. Gratitude for this rocket ship of a life I've gotten to live overwhelmed me. I thought, for instance, that I had processed just about everything there was regarding my mother and our relationship. But in writing about Lucy, off and on for months, the layers deepened, the revelations unfolded.

I highly recommend the undertaking of a memoir to anybody my age or thereabouts, publish or not. And it's a privilege of those our age, to call it a memoir. It's not merely a book. It takes on a French lilt of mystique, the *memoir*.

In reading a number of memoirs while I was writing, I at first didn't grasp the perpetual remarks that it was agony for the authors to pick and choose the particular slices of life to recount. But I came to fully understand that it might have been occasionally hard to leave out a story, because my life has been replete with an embarrassment of riches when it comes to both profound and simply delightful occasions, but it was pure agony to leave people out.

I've been lucky to live a fast-paced, widely traveled existence and that means I've come across many, many golden-hearted, unique, and exceptional people. For the Cuba Swim venture alone, I have included a Team list on other pages here in the book. But there are others, people I truly cherish, and it shocked me to not mention some of you, my treasured friends, in this specific narrative. My editor, Jordan Pavlin, from the beginning asked me to keep the narrative on a fairly direct course. She warned me it was going to hurt for me to not even mention many people I hold dear. But she asked me to consider the reader, the integrity of the story flow, and I finally stopped arguing with her. In the early going, Jordan would jot notes, ever so politely, in the margins, telling me I should sincerely consider dropping the mention of this or that person, that they really didn't fit into the storyline of this book. A year later, Jordan's margin notes on the subject, and as we now knew each other much better, became a lot more direct on this subject. She basically said I needed to cut this person out—or she would. And Jordan was right.

I am lucky to have many valued friends. But this book isn't the place for their stories.

Kelley Cornish. Marcia Cross. Cathy Opie. Linda Stoick. Heidi Horner. Pam Derderian. Nancy Becker. Julie and Anita Van Reingold. Maggie Hamilton. Jackie Pennoyer. Cindy de Rocher.

Jean Golden. Jon and Deborah Hennessey. Lila Stoll. Robin, Stu, Jesse, and Jake Morris. Amy Rennert. Louise Kollenbaum. Tory Polone. Alex and Martha Wallau. And there are more. I could fill pages with your names. My love runs true and deep for you, my wondrous friends. You know who you are to me. Alas, the sacrifice of the *memoir*.

The Xtreme Dream Team

THE HANDLERS
Bonnie Stoll
Pauline Berry
Candace Hogan
Allison Milgard
Jon Hennessey
Deborah Hennessey
Jesse Morris
Heidi Horner
Liza Eversole
Lois Ann Porter
Steve Germansky
Wendy Lawrence
Margie Carroll

THE KAYAKERS
Don McCumber
Buco Pantelis
Mike Devlin
Katie Leigh
Stuart Knaggs
Alex Nebe
Elke Thuerling
Brenda Anderson
David Harper
Dave Kaplan
Darlene Meadows
Patrick Marshall
George Knight
Joseph Taboada

THE JELLYFISH EXPERT
Angel Yanagihara

THE SHARK DIVERS
Niko Gazzale
Luke Tipple
Matteo Gazzale
Ben Shepardson
Jason Tiller
Caleb Bucci
Rob MacDonald
Andy Olday
Jon Rose

THE NAVIGATORS
John Bartlett
David Marchant

THE OPS CHIEFS
Mark Sollinger
John Berry
Vanessa Linsley
Kathy Loretta
Cindy de Rocher

THE NAVIGATION DRIVERS
Dee Brady
Maya Marchant
Nancy Jordan
Dave Whidden

Steven Claridge

Bruce Blomgren

Fred Steele

Wayne Lewin

TIMOTHY WHEELER'S
DOCUMENTARY UNIT

Timothy Wheeler

Karen Christensen

Simeon Houtman

Eric Myerson

CNN DOCUMENTARY UNIT

Sanjay Gupta

Jennifer Hyde

Matt Sloane

Orlando Ruiz

Leon Jobe

THE MEDICAL TEAM

Jon Rose

Michael Broder

Bruce Handelman

University of Miami Sports Medicine
    and ER Units

THE INDEPENDENT OBSERVERS

Steve Munatones

Lexie Kelly

Kate Alexander

Janet Hinkle

Roger McVeigh

THE PHOTOGRAPHERS

Christi Barli

Dawn Blomgren

THE SOCIAL MEDIA TEAM

Candace Hogan

Angie Sollinger

Elaine Lafferty

Gunnar Schrade

Alex de Cordoba

Katie Leigh

Jen Baers

THE METEOROLOGISTS
AND CURRENT EXPERTS

Dane Clark

Jenifer Clark

Frank Bohlen

Lee Chesneau

ALL THE DEDICATED BOAT CAPTAINS
AND CREWS

THE SUPPORT TEAM

Wendy Aresty

Carrie Babich

Beth Bass

Wendy Battles

Nancy Becker

Gloria Borrega

Lori Bosco

Heather Carruthers

Geir Gaseidnes

Liz Callahan

Theresa Chiaia

Taylor Cline

Hillary Clinton

Ron Clutter

Jennifer Cornell

Kelley Cornish

Andrea Mead Cross

Marcia Cross

Jeff Davis

Katie Davis

Kal Becker Derderian

Pam Derderian

Judy Dlugacz

Cathy Ebert

Dr. Neil ElAttrache

Lloyd Englert

Jose Miguel Escrich

Conn Fishburn

Tony Ganz

Ginger Garrett

Jean Golden

Bob Gries

Dr. Jo Hannafin

Kelly Herrington

Austin Hopp

Marlin Hopp

Deanna Hopp

Seth Hopp

Chloe Horner

Peter Johnson

Teri Johnston

Karen Joubert

Abbey Kaufman

Peter Kiernan

Mick Kilgos

Billie Jean King

Laura Kirby

Ilana Kloss

Stefan Knauss

Louise Kollenbaum

Kelley Kwiatkowski

Nina Lederman

Steven Lindecke

Sharon Love

Nancy Machinist

Dave and Beverly Magnone

Shelly Mandell

Dr. Gerald Markovitz

Ed and Roseanne Martinet

Diane May and the Worldwide
    TT Community

Peg McCloud

Andrea Metkus

Julie Milligan

John Mix

Stuart Morris

Susan Morrison

Chris Moschini

Aimee Mullins

Gail Mutrux

Chris Nagel

Vic Nagel

Martina Navratilova

Cira Nickerson

Nancy Nielsen

Bob Olin

Catherine Opie

Oliver Opie

Jackie Pennoyer

Tory Polone

Teri Pushek

Karen Ratts

Matthew Ray

Joey Reiman

Amy Rennert

Kevin Rew

Julie Rivera

Robin Roberts

Hilary Rosen
Mike Ruetz
Roni Selig
Lisa Sherman
Launny Stephans
Lydia Stephans
Melvin Stewart
Robert Stiskin
Linda Stoick
Stephanie Tolleson
Alyce Tordsen
Evan Urbana
Anita Van Reingold
Julie Van Reingold
Stephen Whisnant

THE SPONSORS

Spire Sports Institute
La Samanna Hotel
Southernmost on the Beach Hotel
Olivia
Secret
Hammer Nutrition
Camelbak
Elete
TYR
Key West Canvas
Water Water Stock Island
Burt's Bees
Koru Naturals
Neutrogena
FINIS
Kevin Abrams and Maury Gallagher
of Ketchum Labs

Training Logs

Diana Nyad: THE CUBA SWIM   2009–2013

only swims 4 hours and longer noted • personal journal notes excluded
land workouts not included • 1978 Logs lost

Thursday, October 15, 2009
4hrs, 16mins / 50 meter pool
Saturday, October 17, 2009
4hrs / 50 meter pool
Sunday, October 18, 2009
4hrs, 30mins / 50 meter pool
Tuesday, October 20, 2009
4hrs, 42mins / 50 meter pool
Thursday, October 22, 2009
5hrs / 50 meter pool
Saturday, October 24, 2009
5hrs / 50 meter pool
Monday, October 26, 2009
5hrs / 50 meter pool
Wednesday, October 28, 2009
5hrs, 22mins / 50 meter pool
Friday, October 30, 2009
5hrs, 35mins / 50 meter pool
Sunday, November 1, 2009
6hrs / 50 meter pool
Tuesday, November 3, 2009
6hrs / 50 meter pool
Thursday, November 5, 2009
6hrs / 50 meter pool
Saturday, November 7, 2009
6hrs / 50 meter pool
Monday, November 9, 2009
6hrs / 50 meter pool
Wednesday, November 11, 2009
6hrs, 30mins / 50 meter pool
Friday, November 13, 2009
7hrs, 5mins / 50 meter pool
Sunday, November 15, 2009
7hrs, 44mins / 50 meter pool
Tuesday, November 17, 2009
6hrs, 15mins / 50 meter pool
Thursday, November 19, 2009
7hrs, 35mins / 50 meter pool

Saturday, November 21, 2009
7hrs, 6mins / 50 meter pool
Monday, November 23, 2009
7hrs, 33mins / 50 meter pool
Wednesday, November 25, 2009
6hrs / 50 meter pool
Friday, November 27, 2009
5hrs / 50 meter pool
Sunday, November 29, 2009
5hrs, 15mins / 50 meter pool
Monday, November 30, 2009
7hrs / 50 meter pool
Wednesday, December 2, 2009
7hrs, 50mins / 50 meter pool
Friday, December 4, 2009
7hrs, 23mins / 50 meter pool
Sunday, December 6, 2009
6hrs, 30mins / 50 meter pool
Tuesday, December 8, 2009
7hrs, 17mins / 50 meter pool
Thursday, December 10, 2009
7hrs, 3mins / 50 meter pool
Saturday, December 12, 2009
6hrs, 20mins / 50 meter pool
Monday, December 14, 2009
5hrs, 15mins / 50 meter pool
Wednesday, December 16, 2009
7hrs / 50 meter pool
Friday, December 18, 2009
7hrs, 55mins / 50 meter pool
Sunday, December 20, 2009
6hrs / 50 meter pool
Monday, December 21, 2009
6hrs / 50 meter pool
Friday, December 25, 2009
4hrs / Mazatlan, Mexico
First ocean swim in 30 years!

Sunday, December 27, 2009
7hrs, 45mins / 50 meter pool
Tuesday, December 29, 2009
8hrs / 50 meter pool
Thursday, December 31, 2009
6hrs / 50 meter pool
Saturday, January 2, 2010
5hrs, 30mins / 50 meter pool
Tuesday, January 5, 2010
6hrs, 22mins / Todos Santos, Mexico
Friday, January 8, 2010
6hrs / 50 meter pool
Sunday, January 10, 2010
8hrs / 50 meter pool
Tuesday, January 12, 2010
9hrs / 50 meter pool
Friday, January 15, 2010
6hrs, 40mins / Sea of Cortez, Mexico
Sunday, January 17, 2010
8hrs, 14mins / Sea of Cortez, Mexico
Thursday, January 21, 2010
8hrs / 50 meter pool
Monday, January 25, 2010
8hrs / St. Maarten
Wednesday, January 27, 2010
8hrs / St. Maarten
Friday, January 29, 2010
8hrs / St. Maarten
Wednesday, February 3, 2010
4hrs / 50 meter pool
Friday, February 5, 2010
8hrs / 50 meter pool
Sunday, February 7, 2010
9hrs / 50 meter pool
Tuesday, February 9, 2010
9hrs / 50 meter pool
Thursday, February 11, 2010
8hrs, 30mins / 50 meter pool
Saturday, February 13, 2010
6hrs, 35mins / 50 meter pool
Monday, February 15, 2010
9hrs / 50 meter pool
Wednesday, February 17, 2010
8hrs / 50 meter pool
Friday, February 19, 2010
10hrs / 50 meter pool
Sunday, February 21, 2010
6hrs / 50 meter pool
Thursday, February 25, 2010
13hrs / St. Maarten
Saturday, February 27, 2010
11hrs / St. Maarten
Monday, March 1, 2010
10hrs / St. Maarten
Sunday, March 7, 2010
10hrs / 50 meter pool
Tuesday, March 9, 2010
7hrs / 50 meter pool

Thursday, March 11, 2010
9hrs / 50 meter pool
Saturday, March 13, 2010
10hrs / 50 meter pool
Monday, March 15, 2010
8hrs / 50 meter pool
Wednesday, March 17, 2010
6hrs / 50 meter pool
Sunday, March 21, 2010
15hrs / St. Maarten
Tuesday, March 23, 2010
12hrs / St. Maarten
Thursday, March 25, 2010
10hrs / St. Maarten
Monday, March 29, 2010
5hrs / 50 meter pool
Thursday, April 1, 2010
9hrs / 50 meter pool
Saturday, April 3, 2010
10hrs / 50 meter pool
Monday, April 5, 2010
10hrs / 50 meter pool
Wednesday, April 7, 2010
9hrs / 50 meter pool
Friday, April 9, 2010
7hrs / 50 meter pool
Sunday, April 11, 2010
5hrs / 50 meter pool
Thursday, April 15, 2010
14hrs / Puerto Morelos, Mexico
Saturday, April 17, 2010
12hrs / Puerto Morelos, Mexico
Monday, April 19, 2010
10hrs / Puerto Morelos, Mexico
Friday, April 23, 2010
8hrs / 50 meter pool
Sunday, April 25, 2010
7hrs / 50 meter pool
Tuesday, April 27, 2010
6hrs / 50 meter pool
Saturday, May 1, 2010
16hrs / St. Maarten
Monday, May 3, 2010
14hrs / St. Maarten
Wednesday, May 5, 2010
13hrs / St. Maarten
Sunday, May 9, 2010
8hrs / 50 meter pool
Tuesday, May 11, 2010
6hrs / 50 meter pool
Thursday, May 13, 2010
4hrs, 30mins / 50 meter pool
Sunday, May 16, 2010
15hrs / Puerto Morelos, Mexico
Tuesday, May 18, 2010
14hrs / Puerto Morelos, Mexico
Thursday, May 20, 2010
13hrs / Puerto Morelos, Mexico

Tuesday, May 25, 2010
4hrs / 50 meter pool
Thursday, May 27, 2010
9hrs / 50 meter pool
Saturday, May 29, 2010
7hrs / 50 meter pool
Monday, May 31, 2010
5hrs / 50 meter pool
Friday–Saturday, June 4–5, 2010
18hrs / St. Maarten
Last St. Maarten swim of year
Monday, June 14, 2010
4hrs, 30mins / Key West
Wednesday, June 16, 2010
6hrs / Key West
Friday, June 18, 2010
5hrs / Key West
Sunday, June 20, 2010
4hrs / Key West
Tuesday, June 22, 2010
7hrs / Key West
Thursday, June 24, 2010
5hrs / Key West
Saturday, June 26, 2010
4hrs, 55mins / Key West
Saturday–Sunday, July 10–11
24 hours / Key West
Out in Gulf Stream 50 miles
toward Florida shore
Sunday, July 18, 2010
4hrs / Key West
Tuesday, July 20, 2010
5hrs / Key West
Thursday, July 22, 2010
6hrs, 5mins / Key West
Saturday, July 24, 2010
6hrs, 40mins / Key West
Monday, July 26, 2010
8hrs / Key West
Tuesday, August 3, 2010
5hrs / Key West
Thursday, August 5, 2010
6hrs / Key West
Saturday, August 7, 2010
7hrs / Key West
Monday, August 9, 2010
9hrs / Key West
Wednesday, August 11, 2010
7hrs, 30mins / Key West
Friday, August 13, 2010
5hrs, 50mins / Key West
Sunday, August 15, 2010
4hrs, 30mins / Key West
Friday, August 20, 2010
4hrs, 50mins / 25 yard pool
Sunday, August 22, 2010
4hrs / Key West
Tuesday, August 24, 2010
5hrs / 25 yard pool

Thursday, August 26, 2010
4hrs, 30mins / Key West
Saturday, August 28, 2010
6hrs / Key West
Monday, August 30, 2010
4hrs, 45mins / Key West
Wednesday, September 1, 2010
8hrs / Key West
Friday, September 3, 2010
7hrs / Key West
Sunday, September 5, 2010
9hrs / Key West
Tuesday, September 7, 2010
6hrs, 30mins / Key West
Thursday, September 9, 2010
7hrs, 30mins / Key West
Saturday, September 11, 2010
8hrs / Key West
Monday, September 13, 2010
6hrs, 45mins / Key West
Wednesday, September 15, 2010
6hrs / Key West
Friday, September 17, 2010
5hrs / Key West
Sunday, September 19, 2010
8hrs / Key West
Tuesday, September 21, 2010
7hrs, 30mins / Key West
Thursday, September 23, 2010
8hrs / Key West
Saturday, September 25, 2010
7hrs / Key West
Monday, September 27, 2010
6hrs / Key West
Wednesday, September 29, 2010
4hrs, 30mins / Key West
Last swim of 2010
Cuba not to be, water chilling down
Packing up. Heading home
Tough stuff
October 2010
Off, heal, regroup
Saturday, November 6, 2010
4hrs / 50 meter pool
Monday, November 8, 2010
4hrs / 50 meter pool
Wednesday, November 10, 2010
4hrs, 5mins / 50 meter pool
Friday, November 12, 2010
4hrs, 50mins / 50 meter pool
Sunday, November 14, 2010
5hrs, 16mins / 50 meter pool
Tuesday, November 16, 2010
4hrs / 50 meter pool
Thursday, November 18, 2010
4hrs, 30mins / 50 meter pool
Saturday, November 20, 2010
4hrs, 46mins / 50 meter pool

Monday, November 22, 2010
5hrs, 22mins / 50 meter pool
Wednesday, November 24, 2010
5hrs / 50 meter pool
Saturday, November 27, 2010
5hrs / 50 meter pool
Sunday, November 28, 2010
4 hrs / 50 meter pool
Tuesday, November 30, 2010
6 hrs, 30mins / 50 meter pool
Thursday, December 2, 2010
7 hrs, 25mins / 50 meter pool
Saturday, December 4, 2010
8hrs / 50 meter pool
Monday, December 6, 2010
9hrs / 50 meter pool
Wednesday, December 8, 2010
8 hrs / 50 meter pool
Friday, December 10, 2010
10 hrs / 50 meter pool
Sunday, December 12, 2010
10 hrs / 50 meter pool
December 14, 2010–January 11, 2011
Shoulder rehab, out of water
Wednesday, January 12, 2011
4hrs / 50 meter pool
Thursday, January 13, 2011
4hrs / 50 meter pool
Sunday, January 16, 2011
5hrs / 50 meter pool
Tuesday, January 18, 2011
5hrs / 50 meter pool
Thursday, January 20, 2011
5hrs / 50 meter pool
Saturday, January 22, 2011
5hrs, 20mins / 50 meter pool
Tuesday, January 25, 2011
5hrs, 18mins / 50 meter pool
Thursday, January 27, 2011
6 hrs, 10mins / 50 meter pool
Monday, January 31, 2011
10 hrs / 50 meter pool
Wednesday, February 2, 2011
9hrs / 50 meter pool
Friday, February 4, 2011
8hrs / 50 meter pool
Monday, February 7, 2011
10hrs / St. Maarten
First ocean swim of year
Wednesday, February 9, 2011
9hrs / St. Maarten
Friday, February 11, 2011
8hrs / St. Maarten
Monday, February 14, 2011
7hrs, 10mins / 50 meter pool
Wednesday, February 16, 2011
7hrs, 20mins / 50 meter pool
Friday, February 18, 2011
7hrs / 50 meter pool

Sunday, February 20, 2011
7hrs, 3mins / 50 meter pool
Monday, February 21, 2011
4hrs, 5mins / 50 meter pool
Wednesday, February 23, 2011
7hrs, 30mins / 50 meter pool
Friday, February 25, 2011
6hrs, 30mins / 50 meter pool
Sunday, February 27, 2011
8hrs / 50 meter pool
Monday, February 28, 2011
6hrs / 50 meter pool
Wednesday, March 2, 2011
6hrs, 2mins / 50 meter pool
Friday, March 4, 2011
6hrs, 35mins / 50 meter pool
Monday, March 7, 2011
7hrs / 50 meter pool
Tuesday, March 8, 2011
6hrs, 44mins / 50 meter pool
Friday, March 11, 2011
11hrs / St. Maarten
Sunday, March 13, 2011
10hrs / St. Maarten
Tuesday, March 15, 2011
9hrs / St. Maarten
Thursday, March 17, 2011
8hrs / St. Maarten
Monday, March 21, 2011
4hrs / 50 meter pool
Wednesday, March 23, 2011
4hrs, 50mins / 50 meter pool
Friday, March 25, 2011
6hrs, 9mins / 50 meter pool
Sunday, March 27, 2011
7 hours / 50 meter pool
Wednesday, March 30, 2011
11hrs / St. Maarten
Friday, April 1, 2011
10hrs / St. Maarten
Sunday, April 3, 2011
9hrs / St. Maarten
Thursday, April 7, 2011
5hrs, 13mins / 50 meter pool
Friday, April 8, 2011
5hrs / 50 meter pool
Sunday, April 10, 2011
6hrs, 50mins / 50 meter pool
Tuesday, April 12, 2011
6hrs, 12mins / 50 meter pool
Thursday, April 14, 2011
7hrs, 5mins / 50 meter pool
Sunday, April 17, 2011
13hrs / St. Maarten
Tuesday, April 19, 2011
12hrs / St. Maarten
Thursday, April 21, 2011
11hrs / St. Maarten

Sunday, April 24, 2011
8hrs, 35mins / 50 meter pool
Wednesday, April 27, 2011
9hrs / 50 meter pool
Friday, April 29, 2011
10hrs / 50 meter pool
Sunday, May 1, 2011
10hrs, 10mins / 50 meter pool
Thursday, May 5, 2011
15hrs / Puerto Morelos, Mexico
Saturday, May 7, 2011
13hrs / Puerto Morelos, Mexico
Monday, May 9, 2011
12hrs / Puerto Morelos, Mexico
Wednesday, May 11, 2011
6hrs, 7mins / 50 meter pool
Friday, May 13, 2011
10hrs / 50 meter pool
Monday, May 16, 2011
11 hrs / 50 meter pool
Wednesday, May 18, 2011
9hrs, 30mins / 50 meter pool
Friday, May 20, 2011
9hrs / 50 meter pool
Sunday, May 22, 2011
7hrs / 50 meter pool
Tuesday, May 24, 2011
9hrs, 20mins / 50 meter pool
Friday, May 27, 2011
14 hours / St. Maarten
Sunday, May 29, 2011
13hrs / St. Maarten
Tuesday, May 31, 2011
12hrs / St. Maarten
Saturday, June 4, 2011
4hrs, 15mins / 50 meter pool
Monday, June 6, 2011
10hrs / 50 meter pool
Wednesday, June 8, 2011
10hrs, 11mins / 50 meter pool
Sunday, June 12, 2011
17hrs / St. Maarten
Tuesday, June 14, 2011
15 hours / St. Maarten
Friday, June 17, 2011
4hrs / 50 meter pool
Sunday, June 19, 2011
7hrs / 50 meter pool
Tuesday, June 21, 2011
10hrs / 50 meter pool
Saturday, June 25, 2011
18hrs / St. Maarten
Last St. Maarten swim of year
Tuesday, June 28, 2011
7hrs / first swim in Key West
Thursday, July 30, 2011
9hrs / Key West
Saturday, July 2, 2011
8hrs / Key West

Tuesday, July 5, 2011
6hrs / Key West
Thursday, July 7, 2011
4hrs / Key West
Saturday, July 9, 2011
7hrs / Key West
Tuesday, July 12, 2011
8hrs / Key West
Thursday, July 14, 2011
6hrs / Key West
Saturday, July 16, 2011
8hrs / Key West
Wednesday, July 20, 2011
9hrs / Key West
Friday, July 22, 2011
4hrs / Key West lagoon
Sunday, July 24, 2011
6hrs / Key West
Tuesday, July 26, 2011
6hrs / Key West
Thursday, July 28, 2011
6hrs / Key West
Saturday, July 30, 2011
4hrs / Key West lagoon
Monday, August 1, 2011
5hrs / Key West lagoon
Wednesday, August 3, 2011
4hrs / Key West lagoon
Sunday–Tuesday, August 7–9, 2011
Cuba Attempt #2
58 miles / 28hrs, 43mins
Sunday, August 14
4hrs / 50 meter pool
Tuesday, August 16
5hrs / 50 meter pool
Thursday, August 18
6hrs, 20mins / 50 meter pool
Saturday, August 20, 2011
4hrs / Upper Rhoda Pond, upstate NY
Monday, August 22, 2011
4hrs, 28mins / Upper Rhoda Pond, upstate NY
Wednesday, August 24, 2011
4hrs, 5mins / 50 meter pool
Friday, August 26, 2011
4hrs, 25mins / 50 meter pool
Sunday, August 28, 2011
5hrs / 50 meter pool
Tuesday, August 30, 2011
5hrs / 50 meter pool
Friday, September 2, 2011
4hrs, 30mins / 50 meter pool
Sunday, September 4, 2011
6hrs, 4mins / 50 meter pool
Wednesday, September 7, 2011
5hrs, 20mins / Key West
Friday, September 9, 2011
4hrs / Key West lagoon
Tuesday, September 13, 2011
5hrs / Key West lagoon

Wednesday, September 14, 2011
4hrs / Key West
Friday, September 16, 2011
6hrs, 30mins / Key West
Sunday, September 18, 2011
6hrs / Key West
Friday–Sunday, September 23–25, 2011
Cuba Swim Attempt #3
81.7 miles / 44hrs, 30mins
October 2011
Light laps, healing body and spirit
Monday, October 24, 2011
5hrs / 50 meter pool
Tuesday, October 25, 2011
4hrs / 50 meter pool
Friday, October 28, 2011
6hrs, 41mins / 50 meter pool
Sunday, October 30, 2011
7hrs / 50 meter pool
Tuesday, November 1, 2011
6hrs, 58mins / 50 meter pool
Friday, November 4, 2011
8hrs / 50 meter pool
Monday, November 7, 2011
8hrs, 52mins / 50 meter pool
Tuesday, November 8, 2011
9hrs / 50 meter pool
Wednesday, November 9–Wednesday, November 16
Right shoulder flaring … rest
Thursday, November 17, 2011
5hrs / 50 meter pool
Saturday, November 19, 2011
6hrs / 50 meter pool
Monday, November 21, 2011
4hrs, 20mins / 50 meter pool
Tuesday, November 22, 2011
4hrs, 22mins / 50 meter pool
Wednesday, November 23, 2011
5hrs, 30mins / 50 meter pool
Thursday, November 24–Sunday, November 27, 2011
Took Thanksgiving weekend off, rest shoulder
Monday, November 28, 2011
8hrs / 50 meter pool
Wednesday, November 30, 2011
7hrs, 53mins / 50 meter pool
Saturday, December 3, 2011
5hrs / Punta Cana, Dominican Republic
Wednesday, December 7, 2011
7hrs, 13mins / 50 meter pool
Friday, December 9, 2011
8hrs / 50 meter pool
Tuesday, December 13, 2011
8hrs / 50 meter pool
Friday, December 16, 2011
8hrs, 30mins / 50 meter pool
Tuesday, December 20, 2011
9hrs / 50 meter pool

Thursday, December 22, 2011
8hrs, 50mins / 50 meter pool
Monday, January 2, 2012
10hrs / 50 meter pool
Tuesday, January 3, 2012
10hrs / 50 meter pool
Thursday, January 5, 2012
4hrs, 10mins / 50 meter pool
Friday, January 6, 2012
5hrs, 33mins / 50 meter pool
Monday, January 9, 2012
9hrs / 50 meter pool
Wednesday, January 11, 2012
6hrs / 50 meter pool
Friday, January 13, 2012
5hrs / 50 meter pool
Monday, January 16, 2012
6hrs, 49mins / 50 meter pool
Wednesday, January 18, 2012
8hrs / 50 meter pool
Friday, January 20, 2012
7hrs, 15mins / 50 meter pool
Tuesday, January 24, 2012
12hrs / St. Maarten
Thursday, January 26, 2011
11hrs / St. Maarten
Saturday, January 28, 2011
10hrs / St. Maarten
Wednesday, February 1, 2012
4hrs / 50 meter pool
Friday, February 3, 2012
4hrs / 50 meter pool
Monday, February 6, 2012
4hrs, 25mins / 50 meter pool
Wednesday, February 8, 2012
4hrs, 39mins / 50 meter pool
Friday, February 10, 2012
4hrs, 3mins / 50 meter pool
Monday, February 13, 2012
6hrs, 11mins / 50 meter pool
Tuesday, February 14, 2012
5hrs / 50 meter pool
Friday, February 17, 2012
7hrs, 5mins / 50 meter pool
Tuesday, February 21, 2012
8hrs / 50 meter pool
Wednesday, February 22, 2012
6hrs, 22mins / 50 meter pool
Friday, February 24, 2012
7hrs, 4mins / 50 meter pool
Tuesday, February 28, 2012
9hrs, 16mins / 50 meter pool
Wednesday, February 29, 2012
5hrs / 50 meter pool
Friday, March 2, 2012
9hrs, 33mins / 50 meter pool
Thursday, March 8, 2012
13hrs / St. Maarten

Saturday, March 10, 2012
12hrs / St. Maarten
Monday, March 12, 2012
11hrs / St. Maarten
Monday, March 19, 2012
4hrs / 50 meter pool
Tuesday, March 20, 2012
4hrs, 2mins / 50 meter pool
Friday, March 23, 2012
13hrs / St. Maarten
Sunday, March 25, 2012
11hrs / St. Maarten
Tuesday, March 27, 2012
12hrs / St. Maarten lagoon
Thursday, March 29, 2012
10hrs / St. Maarten
Monday, April 2, 2012
5hrs / 50 meter pool
Wednesday, April 4, 2012
8hrs, 24mins / 50 meter pool
Saturday, April 7, 2012
10hrs / 50 meter pool
Monday, April 9, 2012
5hrs, 20mins / 50 meter pool
Wednesday, April 11, 2012
6hrs, 54mins / 50 meter pool
Friday, April 13, 2012
4hrs, 5mins / 50 meter pool
Monday, April 16, 2012
4hrs, 30mins / 50 meter pool
Thursday, April 19, 2012
14hrs / St. Maarten
Saturday, April 21, 2012
13hrs / St. Maarten
Monday, April 23, 2012
12hrs / St. Maarten
Thursday, April 26, 2012
4hrs / 50 meter pool
Friday, April 27, 2012
4hrs, 6mins / 50 meter pool
Tuesday, May 1, 2012
15hrs / Puerto Morelos, Mexico
Thurs, May 3, 2012
13hrs / Puerto Morelos, Mexico
Saturday, May 5, 2012
12hrs / Puerto Morelos, Mexico
Tuesday, May 8, 2012
4hrs / Cancun, Mexico
Friday, May 11, 2012
5hrs / 50 meter pool
Monday, May 14, 2012
7hrs, 17mins / 50 meter pool
Wednesday, May 16, 2012
6hrs / 50 meter pool
Friday, May 18, 2012
6hrs, 40mins / 50 meter pool
Tuesday, May 22, 2012
16hrs / Puerto Morelos, Mexico

Thursday, May 24, 2012
14hrs / Puerto Morelos, Mexico
Saturday, May 26, 2012
12hrs / Puerto Morelos, Mexico
Friday, June 1, 2012
5hrs, 52mins / 50 meter pool
Sunday, June 3, 2012
6hrs, 35mins / 50 meter pool
Tuesday, June 5, 2012
7hrs, 4mins / 50 meter pool
Thursday, June 7, 2012
8hrs / 50 meter pool
Saturday, June 9, 2012
5hrs, 55mins / 50 meter pool
Wednesday & Thursday, June 13 & 14, 2012
24 hours / St. Maarten
Last St. Maarten training of year!
Monday, June 18, 2012
5hrs, 7mins / 50 meter pool
Wednesday, June 20, 2012
5hrs, 24mins / 25 yard pool
Friday, June 22, 2012
6hrs / 50 meter pool
Monday, June 25, 2012
4hrs / Key West
Wednesday, June 27, 2012
5hrs, 30mins / Key West
Friday, June 29, 2012
6hrs / Key West
Monday, July 2, 2012
5hrs / Key West lagoon
2012-07-03 10:44pm UTC
Tuesday, July 3, 2012
4hrs / 25 yard pool
Thursday, July 5, 2012
4hrs, 45mins / Key West
Saturday, July 7, 2012
6hrs / Key West
Monday, July 9, 2012
5hrs / Night Swim Key West
Wednesday, July 11, 2012
9hrs / Key West
Friday, July 13, 2012
6hrs / Key West lagoon
Saturday, July 14, 2012
5hrs / 25 yard pool
Sunday, July 15, 2012
5hrs, 20mins / Key West lagoon
Tuesday, July 17, 2012
9hrs / Key West
Thursday, July 19, 2012
6hrs / Key West
Saturday, July 21, 2012
7hrs / Key West
Monday, July 23, 2012
6hrs / Key West
Wednesday, July 25, 2012
5hrs / Key West lagoon

Friday, July 27, 2012
6hrs / Key West lagoon
Sunday, July 29, 2012
9hrs / Key West
Tuesday, July 31, 2012
6hrs / Key West
Thursday, August 2, 2012
6hrs, 30mins / Key West
Saturday, August 4, 2012
7hrs, 30mins / Key West
Tuesday, August 7, 2012
9hrs / Key West
Thursday, August 9, 2012
6hrs / 25 yard pool
Saturday, August 11, 2012
10hrs / Key West
Monday, August 13, 2012
4hrs / 25 yard pool
Friday–Sunday, August 17-19, 2012
Cuba Swim Attempt #4
55.4 miles / 51hrs, 5mins
Wednesday, August 29, 2012
5hrs / 50 meter pool
Friday, August 31, 2012
4hrs, 15mins / 50 meter pool
Sunday, September 2, 2012
6hrs / 50 meter pool
Tuesday, September 4, 2012
4hrs / 50 meter pool
Wednesday, September 12, 2012
4hrs / 50 meter pool
Saturday, September 15, 2012
4hrs / Key West
Sunday, September 16, 2012
4hrs / Key West
Tuesday, September 18, 2012
5hrs / Key West
Thursday, September 20, 2012
5hrs, 30mins / Key West
Sunday, September 23, 2012
6hrs / Key West
Tuesday, September 25, 2012
5hrs, 40mins / Key West lagoon
Thursday, September 27, 2012
4hrs / 25 yard pool
Friday, September 28, 2012
6hrs, 18mins / Key West lagoon
Monday, October 2, 2012
5hrs, 50mins / Key West
Saturday, October 6, 2012
6 hours / Key West
Monday, October 8, 2012
5hrs, 5mins / Key West lagoon
Wednesday, October 10, 2012
5hrs / Bay Sugar Loaf Key
Friday, October 12, 2012
5hrs / Key West lagoon
Monday, October 15, 2012
5hrs, 30mins / Ft. Zachary, Key West

Tuesday, October 16, 2012
Water Temps drop. It's over
Wednesday, October 17-Thursday, November 15
Off. Recuperate. Refresh the spirit
Friday, November 16, 2012
4hrs / 50 meter pool
Saturday, November 17–Monday, December 3, 2012
Land workouts only, the mind not ready to dig
back in
Tuesday, December 4, 2012
4hrs, 16mins / 50 meter pool
Friday, December 7, 2012
4hrs, 45mins / 50 meter pool
Sunday, December 9, 2012
5hrs, 5mins / 50 meter pool
Tuesday, December 11, 2012
6hrs / 50 meter pool
Thursday, December 13, 2012
7hrs, 15mins / 50 meter pool
Saturday, December 15, 2012
5hrs, 32mins / 50 meter pool
Tuesday, December 18, 2012
5hrs / 50 meter pool
Thursday, December 20, 2012
7hrs, 22mins / 50 meter pool
Saturday, December 22, 2012
10hrs / 50 meter pool
Wednesday, December 26, 2012
8hrs / 50 meter pool
Monday, January 7, 2013
6hrs / 50 meter pool
Wednesday, January 9, 2013
6hrs, 40mins / 50 meter pool
Friday, January 11, 2013
8hrs / 50 meter pool
Monday, January 14, 2013
4hrs, 40mins / 50 meter pool, NYC
Thursday, January 17, 2013
5hrs / 50 meter pool
Saturday, January 19, 2013
8hrs / 50 meter pool
Monday, January 21, 2013
9hrs / 50 meter pool
Wednesday, January 23, 2013
4hrs / Endless Pool
Friday, January 25, 2013
6hrs, 33mins / 50 meter pool
Sunday, January 27, 2013
6hrs / 50 meter pool
Saturday, February 2, 2013
10hrs / St. Maarten
Monday, February 4, 2013
10hrs / St. Maarten
Wednesday, February 6, 2013
10hrs / St. Maarten
Saturday, February 9, 2013
4hrs / 50 meter pool
Wednesday, February 13, 2013
6hrs / 50 meter pool

Friday, February 15, 2013
5hrs / Endless Pool
Monday, February 17, 2013
6hrs, 48mins / 50 meter pool
Tuesday, February 19, 2013
9hrs / 50 meter pool
Friday, February 22, 2013
6hrs, 50mins / 50 meter pool
Monday, February 25, 2013
7hrs / 50 meter pool
Tuesday, February 26, 2013
7hrs / 50 meter pool
Thursday, February 28, 2013
8hrs / 50 meter pool
Monday, March 4, 2013
14hrs / St. Maarten
Wednesday, March 6, 2013
13hrs / St. Maarten
Friday, March 8, 2013
12hrs / St. Maarten lagoon
Wednesday, March 13, 2013
4hrs, 40mins / 50 meter pool
Friday, March 15, 2013
8hrs / 50 meter pool
Saturday, March 17, 2013
4hrs / 25 yard pool
Tuesday, March 19, 2013
8hrs / 50 meter pool
Thursday, March 21, 2013
8hrs / 50 meter pool
Friday, March 22, 2013
6hrs / 50 meter pool
Wednesday, March 27, 2013
6hrs, 8mins / 50 meter pool
Friday, March 29, 2013
8hrs / 50 meter pool
Sunday, March 31, 2013
6hrs, 5mins / 50 meter pool
Tuesday, April 2, 2013
8hrs, 8mins / 50 meter pool
Sunday, April 7–Monday, April 8, 2013
15hrs, 24mins / St. Maarten
Wednesday, April 10, 2013
12hrs / St. Maarten
Friday, April 12, 2013
11hrs / St. Maarten
Monday, April 15, 2013
8hrs / 50 meter pool
Wednesday, April 17, 2013
4hrs / 50 meter pool
Saturday, April 20–Sunday, April 21, 2013
24 hours / 50 meter pool, Palm Springs
Sunday, April 28, 2013
4hrs, 45mins / 50 meter pool
Wednesday, May 1, 2013
14hrs / St. Thomas, Virgin Islands
Friday, May 3, 2013
13hrs / St. John, Virgin Islands

Sunday, May 5, 2013
12hrs / St. Thomas, Virgin Islands
Thursday, May 9, 2013
4hrs / 50 meter pool
Saturday, May 11, 2013
4hrs / 50 meter pool
Monday, May 13, 2013
5hrs / 50 meter pool
Thursday, May 16, 2013
4hrs / 25 yard pool, Cincinnati
Monday, May 20, 2013
15hrs / Puerto Morelos, Mexico
Wednesday, May 22, 2013
14hrs / Puerto Morelos, Mexico
Friday, May 24, 2013
13hrs / Puerto Morelos, Mexico
Sunday, May 26, 2013
9hrs / 50 meter pool
Monday, May 27, 2013
5hrs / 50 meter pool
Wednesday, May 29, 2013
8hrs, 38mins / 50 meter pool
Friday, May 31, 2013
9hrs, 12mins / 50 meter pool
Sunday, June 2, 2013
10hrs / 50 meter pool
Saturday, June 8, 2013
8hrs, 20mins / Key West
Wednesday, June 12, 2013
7hrs / 50 meter pool
Friday, June 14, 2014
5hrs / 50 meter pool
Monday, June 17, 2013
10hrs / 50 meter pool
Wednesday, June 19, 2013
7hrs, 30mins / 25 yard pool
Friday, June 21, 2013
7hrs, 17mins / 50 meter pool
Monday, June 24, 2013
8hrs / 50 meter pool
Last long pool workout ever?
Saturday, June 29, 2013
9hrs / Key West
Monday, July 1, 2013
9hrs / Key West
Wednesday, July 3, 2013
5hrs / Key West
Friday, July 5, 2013
12hrs / Key West
Monday, July 8, 2013
4hrs, 25mins / Key West
Tuesday, July 9, 2013
5hrs, 5mins / Key West
Thursday, July 11, 2013
5hrs, 30mins / 25 yard pool
Saturday, July 13, 2013
9hrs / Key West
Monday, July 15, 2013
6hrs / Key West

Friday, July 19, 2013
9hrs / Key West
Monday, July 22, 2013
5hrs / Key West
Wednesday, July 24, 2013
5hrs / Key West
Friday, July 26, 2013
5hrs / Key West
Monday, July 29, 2013
4hrs / Key West
Thursday, August 1, 2013
4hrs / 25 yard pool
Saturday, August 3, 2013
9hrs / Key West
Monday, August 5, 2013
5hrs / Key West
Wednesday, August 7, 2013
4hrs, 20mins / 25 yard pool

Sunday, August 11, 2013
9hrs / Key West
Tuesday, August 13, 2013
5hrs / Key West
Thursday, August 15, 2013
5hrs / Key West
Saturday, August 17, 2013
4hrs / 25 yard pool
Monday, August 19, 2013
5hrs / 25 yard pool
Wednesday, August 21, 2013
6hrs / 25 yard pool
Friday, August 23, 2013
11hrs / Key West
Sunday, August 25, 2013
6hrs / Key West

Saturday, August 31–Monday September 2, 2013
Cuba Swim 5th Attempt
At Long Last—SUCCESS!!!!!!
110.86 miles / 52hrs, 54mins

Illustration Credits

INSERT TWO

Page 1: Courtesy of the author

Page 2: Courtesy of the author

Page 3: Courtesy of the author

Page 4: Courtesy of Pine Crest School (top); courtesy of the author (middle and bottom)

Page 5: Courtesy of the author

Page 6: John Marmaras, courtesy of the author (top); Nancy Moran (bottom)

Page 7: Courtesy of the author (top); photograph by Mary Hernandez, from *New York Post* (page 1), April 14 ©1977 New York Post. All rights reserved. Used by permission and protected by the Copyright Laws of the United States. The printing, copying, redistribution, or retransmission of this content without express written permission is prohibited. (bottom)

Page 8: Courtesy of Candace Lyle Hogan (top left and top right); courtesy of the author (bottom)

Page 9: Courtesy of the author

Page 10: Courtesy of the author (top); photograph by Mary Hernandez, from *New York Post* (page 1), April 14 ©1979 New York Post. All rights reserved. Used by permission and protected by the Copyright Laws of the United States. The printing, copying, redistribution, or retransmission of this content without express written permission is prohibited. (bottom)

Page 11: Courtesy of Bonnie Stoll (top); courtesy of the author (bottom)

Page 12: Courtesy of the author (top left); Slaven Vlasic/Getty Images (top right); © American Broadcasting Companies, Inc. (middle left and bottom left); Christi Barli, courtesy of the author, all rights reserved (middle right)

Page 13: Dawn L. Blomgren, courtesy of the author, all rights reserved (top left and right, middle); Janet Hinkle (bottom)

Page 14: John and Pauline Berry

Page 15: Christi Barli, courtesy of the author, all rights reserved (top left, top right, bottom left); Dawn L. Blomgren, courtesy of the author, all rights reserved (bottom right)

Page 16: Janet Hinkle (top); courtesy of the White House (bottom left); courtesy of the author (middle right); Christi Barli, courtesy of the author, all rights reserved (bottom right)

Page 284: Courtesy of the author